Empire from the Margins

McMaster Divinity College Press
McMaster General Series 11

Empire from the Margins

*Religious Minorities in Canada and
the South African War*

edited by
Gordon L. Heath

PICKWICK *Publications* • Eugene, Oregon

EMPIRE FROM THE MARGINS
Religious Minorities in Canada and the South African War

McMaster Divinity College Press General Series 11

Copyright © 2017 Wipf and Stock Publishers. All rights reserved. Except for brief quotations in critical publications or reviews, no part of this book may be reproduced in any manner without prior written permission from the publisher. Write: Permissions, Wipf and Stock Publishers, 199 W. 8th Ave., Suite 3, Eugene, OR 97401.

Pickwick Publications
An Imprint of Wipf and Stock Publishers
199 W. 8th Ave., Suite 3
Eugene, OR 97401

McMaster Divinity College Press
1280 Main Street West
Hamilton, ON, Canada L8S 4K1

www.wipfandstock.com

PAPERBACK ISBN: 978-1-4982-2320-1
HARDCOVER ISBN: 978-1-4982-2322-5
EBOOK ISBN: 978-1-4982-2321-8

Cataloguing-in-Publication data:

Names: Heath, Gordon L., editor.

Title: Empire from the margins : religious minorities in Canada and the South African War / edited by Gordon L. Heath.

Description: Eugene, OR: Pickwick Publications, 2017 | McMaster Divinity College Press General Series 11 | Includes bibliographical references and index.

Identifiers: ISBN 978-1-4982-2320-1 (paperback) | ISBN 978-1-4982-2322-5 (hardcover) | ISBN 978-1-4982-2321-8 (ebook)

Subjects: LCSH: South African War, 1899–1902—Canada | Religious minorities—Canada | Religious and politics—Canada | Canada—Religion.

Classification: BL2530.C3 E49 2017 (print) | BL2530.C3 (ebook)

Manufactured in the U.S.A.   11/27/17

This book is dedicated to my wife, Virginia,
and children, Joshua and Natasha.

Contents

Acknowledgements | ix

List of Contributors | xi

1 Empire from the Margins: An Introduction
   —*Gordon L. Heath* | 1

2 Writing Religious Minorities into Canada's South African
   War, 1899–1902—*Carman Miller* | 16

3 Canada's Non-Francophone Catholics and the South African
   War, 1899–1902—*Mark G. McGowan* | 36

4 "This South African war does not affect all citizens in the
   [same] manner": French Protestants in Quebec during the
   South African War—*Gordon L. Heath and Sid D. Sudiacal* | 69

5 Canada's Salvation Army and War: The *War Cry*, Soul Saving,
   and the South African War—*Eric Crouse* | 85

6 "A Daughter in Her Mother's House": Congregationalists
   Responses to the South African War, 1899–1902
   —*James Tyler Robertson* | 100

7 Canadian Quakers and the South African War
   —*Robynne Rogers Healey* | 120

8 Canada's First Nations in the Anglo-Boer War
   —*Evan J. Habkirk* | 135

Contents

9   "The Boers standing in the way of progress in Africa must be swept aside": Patriotism and Imperialism in the Canadian *Jewish Times* during the South African War—*Gordon L. Heath* | 155

Index of Subjects | 173

Index of Persons | 177

Acknowledgements

Over fifteen years ago I began researching Canadian churches and the South African War. The end product was a dissertation, and then book, on Anglicans, Baptists, Methodists, and Presbyterians and the war. I knew then that there were many religious groups that I never even came close to understanding, but time and human limitations meant that they remained unexplored. A few years ago, I decided to revisit the subject and deal with some of those denominations that I had ignored. This book is the result of that initiative. It is not the final word on the matter, but it is a move in the right direction towards deepening our awareness of how religion shaped, and was shaped by, Canada's first foreign military venture. From the book's inception a few years ago, many people have helped bring about its fruition. A few thanks are in order.

McMaster Divinity College is a place where scholarship is encouraged. Thank you to President Stanley Porter and Academic Dean Phil Zylla for fostering such an environment.

Carman Miller has been an excellent example of scholarly collegiality since my very first foray into the war. His expertise on Canadian participation in the war is unmatched, and his early encouragement and kindness to me was very much appreciated. I am not sure if I would have continued in this area of research if he had been otherwise.

Thank you to all the contributors who made this book a unique contribution to Canadian religious history in general, as well as to the history of the war in particular.

The work of Hughson Ong as copy editor was professional, and thank you as well to my TA Don Springer whose editing was deeply appreciated.

Acknowledgements

Thank you to the Canadian Society of Church History for allowing various authors to share their findings in a panel at the recent annual meeting at Ryerson University, Toronto.

Finally, thank you to my wife Virginia, and two children Joshua and Natasha. Your never-ending support is deeply appreciated.

Contributors

EDITOR AND CONTRIBUTOR

Gordon L. Heath (PhD, St. Michael's College) is professor of Christian history as well as Centenary Chair in World Christianity at McMaster Divinity College, Hamilton, Ontario. He also serves as Director of the Canadian Baptist Archives. His publications include *The British Nation Is Our Nation: The BACSANZ Baptist Press and the South African War, 1899–1902* (Paternoster, 2017), *A War with a Silver Lining: Canadian Protestant Churches and the South African War, 1899–1902* (MQUP, 2009), and *Doing Church History: A User-friendly Introduction to Researching the History of Christianity* (Clements, 2008). He has also edited a number of volumes, such as *American Churches and the First World War* (Pickwick, 2016), and *Canadian Churches and the First World War* (Pickwick, 2014).

CONTRIBUTORS

Eric R. Crouse (PhD, Queen's University) is professor of history and global studies, Tyndale University College, Toronto. He is the author of five books, including *American Christian Support for Israel: Standing with the Chosen People, 1948–1975* (Lexington Books, 2015), *The Cross and Reaganomics: Conservative Christians Defending Ronald Reagan* (Lexington Books, 2013), and *Revival in the City: The Impact of American Evangelists in Canada, 1884–1914* (MQUP, 2005).

Evan J. Habkirk is a PhD candidate in history and a lecturer in the First Nations Studies Program at Western University, London, Ontario. He completed his MA in Canadian and Indigenous Studies at Trent University exploring the response of the Six Nations of the Grand River Territory, outside Brantford Ontario, to the First World War, and is now exploring the Six Nations military from the end of the War of 1812 to the First World War. He served as a consultant researcher for the Truth and Reconciliation Commission on Residential Schools and is a founding board member of the Great War Centenary Association Brantford, Brant County, and Six Nations. His research interests include indigenous militaries, British imperialism, Canadian residential schools, and indigenous and newcomer relations. His latest article, co-authored with Dr. Janice Forsyth, is entitled, "Truth, Reconciliation, and the Politics of the Body in Indian Residential School History" (Activehistory.ca, 2016).

Robynne Rogers Healey (PhD, University of Alberta) is professor of history and co-director of the Gender Studies Institute at Trinity Western University in Langley, British Columbia. She convenes the Conference of Quaker Historians and Archivists and is publications chair for the Canadian Friends Historical Association. Her publications include chapters in *The Quakers, 1656–1723: The Evolution of an Alternative Community* (Penn State UP, forthcoming), *Early Quakers and Their Theology* (CUP, 2015), *The Oxford Handbook of Quaker Studies* (OUP, 2013), *American Churches and the First World War* (Pickwick, 2016), *Canadian Churches and the First World War* (Pickwick, 2014), and the book *From Quaker to Upper Canadian: Faith and Community among Yonge Street Friends, 1801–1850* (MQUP, 2006).

Mark G. McGowan is professor of history at the University of Toronto and Principal Emeritus at St. Michael's College. He has many award-winning publications, including *The Waning of the Green: Catholics, the Irish, and Identity in Toronto, 1887–1922* (MQUP, 1999), *Michael Power: The Challenge to Build the Catholic Church on the Canadian Frontier* (MQUP, 2005), and *Death or Canada: The Irish Famine Migration to Toronto, 1847* (Novalis, 2009). His latest book, *The Imperial Irish: Canada's Irish Catholics Fight the Great War, 1914–1918,* will be published by MQUP in 2017. He is the author of numerous articles on religion, immigration, and media in Canada.

Carman Miller was educated at Acadia, Dalhousie and the University of London. He began teaching at McGill in 1967, where he served two terms as Chair and eight years as Dean of Arts. He is currently an emeritus professor. He is author of four books, including *Painting the Map Red: Canada and the South African War, 1899–1902* (MQUP, 1993, 1998), thirty articles or book chapters, and thirty *Dictionary of Canadian Biography* entries. His

A Knight in Politics: A Biography of Sir Fredrick Borden (MQUP, 2010) won the C. P. Stacey Prize. He was awarded the Queen's Golden Jubilee Medal (2002) and the Queen's Diamond Jubilee Medal (2012).

James Tyler Robertson (PhD, McMaster Divinity College) is the Creative Director of Advanced Education and adjunct professor of Christian history at Tyndale Seminary in Toronto, Canada. He has published numerous book chapters and articles focused on denominational reaction to international conflicts. In addition, he has also published articles on the crusades, Irish religious history, church and culture, peace studies, and Canadian history. His first book *A Good Fight: The Religious War of 1812* is forthcoming.

Sid D. Sudiacal is a PhD candidate at McMaster Divinity College, Hamilton, Ontario. He has previously served as the editor in history for the Asian American Theological Forum (AATF) journal and as a Teaching Fellow for the Pappas Patristic Institute's Summer Study Program in Patristic Studies. He is a graduate of University of Ottawa/ l'Université d'Ottawa (BA) and McMaster University (MTS). His research interests include Roman North African Christianity, religious violence, and the intersection between psychology and theology.

1

Empire from the Margins

An Introduction

GORDON L. HEATH

THROUGHOUT THE SUMMER OF 1899, Canadian newspapers reported on rising tensions between Britain and the Boers, and in October Canadians found themselves embroiled in a bitter and bloody imperial war in distant and exotic South Africa. The causes of war were varied and remain contested.[1] What is beyond dispute is that the Boers invaded British territory on 11 October 1899, and as a result, Britain and its empire became at war.[2] The mighty British Empire was humbled early in the conflict, with the Boers advancing into British territory and besieging the towns of Ladysmith, Mafeking, and Kimberley. However, in the opening months of 1900 the fortunes of war turned, and the British advanced into the two Republics and captured their capitals in March and June. Victory was not immediately forthcoming, for the Boers shifted their strategy to a guerrilla war that prolonged the conflict for two more years. The British were ultimately victorious, but not before experiencing widespread international condemnation over their methods of combating the Boer's guerrilla campaign. The war ended on 31 May 1902 with the signing of the Treaty of

1. For summaries on the events leading up to the hostilities of 1899, see Porter, *The Origins*; Smith, *The Origins*.

2. For accounts of the conflict in general, see Farwell, *The Great Anglo-Boer War*; Judd and Surridge, *The Boer War*; Warwick, *The South African War*; Nasson, *The South African War*; Cuthbertson, et al., *Writing a Wider War*.

Vereeniging. The two Republics were absorbed into the British Empire, and the Union of South Africa was eventually formed in 1910.

The war cost Britain over 220 million pounds, and it took up to 440,000 troops to subdue the two Republics. The human cost of the war was appalling: 22,000 British soldiers (7,800 of them killed in battle, the others died mainly of disease) and between 6,000 and 7,000 Boer soldiers died (the concentration camps were comprised almost solely of Boer women and children); the grim total was somewhere around 28,000, along with 20,000 black Africans.[3] As for the colonial contribution, approximately 30,000 overseas colonial troops participated in the conflict (7,368 Canadians, 16,632 Australians, and 6,343 New Zealanders), while 52,000 came from Natal and Cape Colony (although a number came from the two conquered republics).[4] Canadian casualties were 267.

CANADA, RELIGION, AND THE WAR

The focus of this book is on Canadian religious minorities and the war, a hitherto neglected subject.[5] Carman Miller's chapter on writing religious minorities into the war explores why that has been the case and why the focus of historians has been changing, so there is no need for further elaboration here on those matters. What will be stated is that a formative work in the area of Canadian imperialism is Carl Berger's *The Sense of Power*. Berger explores many facets of imperialism in Canadian culture at the turn of the century, with brief attention paid to religion. He understands the imperial impulse in Canada during the war to be one form of Canadian nationalism, and it was that type of nationalism that explains Canada's enthusiastic participation in an imperial war.[6] Phillip Buckner's work on Canadian imperial identity explores themes such as gender, economics, and

---

3. Omissi and Thompson, "Introduction," 7–8.

4. Pakenham, "The Contribution," 59.

5. Religion's role in Canada's public life is increasingly being recognized for what was an integral shaper of identity, discourse, and action, and the past few decades has seen significant publications on religion and public life. However, focus on religion and war is far more limited. For works on religion and public life in general, see Die, *Religion and Public Life*; Lyon and Die, *Rethinking Church*; Miedema, *For Canada's Sake*; Heath and Wilson, eds., *Baptists and Public*.

6. Berger, *The Sense of Power*. Other important authors in this category are Penlington, *Canada and Imperialism*; Page, "Canada and the Imperial Idea"; Page, *The Boer War*; Page, "Carl Berger," 39–43; Cole, "Canada's 'Nationalistic' Imperialists," 44–45; Cook, "George R. Parkin"; Buckner, "Whatever Happened"; Buckner, "Canada."

technology, but not religion.[7] The standard work on Canada's involvement in the war is Carman Miller's *Painting the Map Red*.[8] While it acknowledges the important role of the churches in forming attitudes towards the war, and claims that they were generally supportive of the war, Miller's work focuses primarily on the experiences of the Canadian troops who went overseas to South Africa. He pays relatively little attention to the reasons for the churches' support for the war. The most focused attention to the churches and the war is *A War with a Silver Lining*, a work that examines the response of Canadian Anglicans, Baptists, Methodists, and Presbyterians to the war.[9] Central to the ministry of the churches was a concern for justice, nation, empire, and missions, and many in the churches believed a British victory in South Africa would help to accomplish all four of those at once. Underlying such support for the imperial cause was the belief in the providential establishing of the empire for the spreading of civilization and Christianity. Consequently, concomitant with those four aims was the idea that a British victory would benefit all involved; it would be good for Canadians, good for Britons, good for the empire, good for the entire world, and even good for the Boers. It was a war with a "silver lining," and how could one not support the imperial effort with the interests of church and missions, nation and empire, the secular and the sacred, so intertwined? However, the book leaves a great deal unexamined, for it deals with the churches that collectively dominated the Protestant religious landscape and pays relatively no attention to religious minorities, Roman Catholics, and various dissenting voices. Roman Catholics in Quebec can hardly be considered a religious minority, and their experience of the war needs to be taken up by someone in the future. The focus of this book is more modest, for it examines religious minorities on the margins.

RELIGION ON THE MARGINS

At the end of the nineteenth century, both new and well-established religious minorities were situated in a nation dominated by the two founding western-European peoples, the French and the British. The churches associated with those two peoples wielded a significant amount of influence in

---

7. Buckner, *Canada and the British Empire*; Buckner, *Canada and the End*.
8. Miller, *Painting the Map*; Reid, *Our Little Army*.
9. Heath, *A War*. Other articles by Heath that deal with the churches and imperialism are as follows: Heath, "'Habit of Deifying Monarchs'"; Heath, "'Citizens of that Mighty Empire'"; Heath, "Sin in the Camp"; Heath, "Passion for Empire."

the formation of public morals, religious beliefs, and political sentiments. In French (along with parts of English) Canada, it was the Roman Catholic Church that held sway with 2,229,600 members, comprising 41.5 percent of Canadians. In English Canada, four Protestant denominations dominated the religious landscape, and by the end of the nineteenth century, there was a broadly-based Protestant consensus to forge ahead with making the new Dominion a Christian nation.[10] In 1901, Methodists were 17.1 percent of the population, Presbyterians 15.7 percent, Anglicans 12.7 percent, and Baptists 5.9 percent. Together, those four denominations comprised 51.4 percent of Canadians. The remaining less than 10 percent was comprised of a wider variety of smaller, mainly, though not exclusively, Christian, groups.[11] Those smaller religious bodies are the focus of this book.

When referring to the demographically smaller religious bodies, the term "sect" has been avoided, and preference is given to referring to the churches outside of the dominant Protestant denominations or the Catholic Church in Quebec as those "on the margins." S. D. Clark's well-known usage of sect was a reference to those that were dissatisfied with mainstream Christianity and subsequently splintered off and formed new denominations.[12] Some of the movements in this study fit his category of sect (such as the Salvation Army), but most others do not (such as Lutherans, Jews, and First Nations). Consequently, in the case of this research, the expression "on the margins" will be used to acknowledge the unique social location of religious groups in relationship to the dominant religious bodies. Its usage refers to groups that for a variety of reasons—religion, ethnicity, demographics, and convictions—were on the margins of Canadian religious and cultural life, and faced the possibility or reality of discrimination due to their relative powerlessness.

The wartime plight of those religious groups on the margins can be illustrated by some brief commentary in a local Manitoba newspaper. The

10. Airhart, "Ordering a New Nation."

11. In 1901, Ontario's Anglican, Baptist, Methodist, and Presbyterian membership made up almost 75 percent of the population. Roman Catholic comprised 18 percent of Ontario's population. The Anglicans, Baptists, Methodists, and Presbyterians dominated the Protestant religious landscape in Ontario, comprising over 95 percent of all Protestants in Ontario. See Semple, *The Lord's Dominion*, 181–82. As for religious minorities, census data in 1901 indicated the following: 28,293 Congregationalists; 15,630 Greek (and Catholic) Orthodox; 101 Jehovah's Witnesses; 16,401 Jews; 92,524 Lutherans; 31,797 Mennonites; 6,891 Mormons; 10,308 Salvation Army. The population of indigenous peoples was 127,941. See http://www.statcan.gc.ca/pub/11-516-x/pdf/5500092-eng.pdf.

12. Clark, *Church and Sect*.

issue at stake in this instance was the loyalty of new "Galician" immigrants from eastern Europe and their response to the outbreak of war. The report read as follows:

> The statement has been frequently made, both on the platform and in the press that the foreign element that was being brought into Canada, would not assimilate with the people or become familiar with the genius of our institutions. That in the case of war the country could not count on their services. But a most effectual answer to the latter statement was made on Monday when L. Cohen, on behalf of twenty able-bodied Galicians, came to the Press office to state that these men were anxious to serve the Queen in the Transvaal war, and were ready for enlistment at any time. It is facts like these that reveal the true character of the foreign settler and the material he is composed of.[13]

The paper's editor felt compelled to add a few brief words to express his pleasure with those signs of Galician patriotism: "The spectacle of twenty able-bodied Galicians manfully offering their services this week to the Queen to fight the Boers is a refutation which speaks louder than words to the charges that these people are not loyal to their adopted country."[14] There had been concerns expressed about the arrival of non-British immigrants before the war, but the conflict heightened suspicions and concerns. In that brief exchange, assumptions regarding the suspect loyalties of minorities were evident, as well as the pressures placed upon minorities to be patriotic and to support the war effort. What exacerbated the situation for those on the margins was the ardent imperialism surging in the dominant four Protestant denominations. That ardent imperialism was brought to a "feverish pitch" by the war, and such excessive displays of imperial passion would not be seen again in Canada until the First World War.[15] And that imperial zeal could make it very uncomfortable—and potentially unsafe— for those on the margins during imperial victory celebrations, as commentary in the *Canadian Baptist* indicated: "[if] there was a Boer sympathizer in the land that was a day for him to keep indoors, and be indoors, and be quiet as a spy in the enemy's camp or the traitor at home, for loyalty ruled in every British home and hearth in the land."[16]

13. As noted in Kaye, *Ukrainian Canadians*, 9.
14. As noted in ibid.
15. Page, *Imperialism and Canada*, 12.
16. *Canadian Baptist*, 8 March 1900, 160.

The focus of this book is on religious minorities, with specific attention paid to the role of religion in the development of constructions of national and imperial identity, discourse for and against war, and attitudes and actions towards enlistment. Of course, those religious minorities with a British background (Congregationalists or Salvation Army) were not as suspect as those who had no British or western European background (such as the Galicians noted above). That being the case, even those with British backgrounds were not immune from criticism, if their professed religious views led them to question the war or condemn the cause. Finding safety on the margins was especially difficult when confronted with zealous visions of a Christian Anglo-Saxon imperial Canada. However, that same imperial discourse that often ostracized those on the margins could also provide an opportunity to move from the margins into mainstream Canadian life. Supportive religious imperial discourse provided a way for those on the margins to participate immediately in the national discourse on the war, thus demonstrating one's loyalty to suspicious and hostile skeptics.

Living on the margins required constant negotiation, and identity was often marked by plurality and fluidity. Identity within the empire was often marked by diversity: "One person might have a number of concurrent identities. Just as in Britain one could be a Liverpudlian, Lancastrian, Englishman, and Briton, so in New Zealand one might be an Aucklander, North Islander, New Zealander, and Briton."[17] As for those on the margins in Canada, ties of blood and land could be resilient leading to a plurality of loyalties. That plurality of identities was evident in instances such as the exhortation in a synagogue that one could love both the Motherland (England and empire) and the Fatherland (Palestine) and at the same time be loyal to both.[18] Loyalties to the homeland were also not static, as Mark McGowan's research on non-Francophone Catholics and Ireland indicates. The problem for those on the margins was that what one calls plurality of loyalty, another may label divided loyalty; thus the need for fluidity and negotiation. Identities on the margins were often "a concocted fictive construct and . . . a negotiated, improvised way of being in the world of nations."[19] The reading of religious imperial discourse on the margins must take into account how groups—whether consciously or not—strategically positioned themselves in relationship to national and imperial expectations, especially when they

17. Bridge and Fedorowich, "Mapping the British World," 6.
18. "Zionism," *Jewish Times*, 27 April 1900, 164–66.
19. Yelin, *From the Margins*, 171.

appeared to be disloyal. That is not to say that discourse was necessarily disingenuous, for, as Evan Habkirk notes, the First Nations took seriously their obligations to a treaty partner. Nevertheless, an examination of those on the margins needs to include a recognition of the fluidity of identity and the negotiation of a safe place on the margins.

"GLIMPSES" AND AVENUES FOR FURTHER RESEARCH

The problem for historians studying Canadian religious groups on the margins is that sometimes little exists by way of necessary archival material. The following are a number of denominations that were on the margins and fit within the parameters of this project. However, limited resources—at this time—make a thorough study not possible. Nevertheless, there are some "glimpses" of wartime attitudes that are enticing, and hopefully, such glimpses will inspire others to further sifting and searching of records so that a fuller treatment of those on the margins can eventually be pursued.

Demographically and ethnically, Lutherans were on the margins, a position reinforced by Lutheranism's distinctly German history and liturgy. Reflecting their relatively small numbers and limited resources was the fact that Canadian Lutheran churches belonged to an American synod. Not having the resources to publish their own religious paper like the dominant Protestant denominations,[20] Canadian Lutherans relied on American papers for their religious news and political commentary. For instance, *The Lutheran* was a weekly paper published in Pennsylvania, but circulated across the border. An anti-British slant was fairly common in wartime U.S. papers; however, the pro-Boer tenor of the paper was distressing for some Lutherans in Lunenburg, Nova Scotia. Early in 1900, a Nova Scotian Lutheran pastor wrote to the editor to express his dismay with the paper's coverage. The editor printed the following summary:

> A letter has been received from one of our Nova Scotia pastors, Rev. F. A. Bowers, of Lunenburg, in which exception is taken to the pro-Boer tenor of some of the articles that have appeared in the Lutheran. As there are loyal British laymen in his congregations, he informs us that the articles referred to are not taken kindly, and hence are not conducive to the spiritual prosperity of the Canadian Lutheran congregations where THE LUTHERAN circulates. He also expresses his conviction that it is foreign to the purpose of

---

20. For a summary of the late nineteenth-century Protestant press, see Heath, "'Forming Sound Public Opinion."

a Church paper to comment on questions of State where an honest difference of opinion is likely to exist.[21]

It is difficult to determine Canadian Lutheran attitudes in general to the war, for church records for this period reveal little of such things.[22] As a result, determining how many "loyal British laymen" were in the Lutheran churches is problematic; but, in that specific instance, there were enough in Rev. Bowers's congregation, who were distressed to compel the pastor to write the editor, to urge him to take Canadian sensibilities into account when commenting on the war.[23] This evidence of pro-British loyalties among Lutherans must be considered alongside of isolated reports in newspapers of pro-Boer sentiments among Canadian Germans (Lutherans).[24] Lutheran attitudes to the empire and war are fairly clear during the First World War,[25] as for the war in South Africa that is not yet the case.

Mennonite's German language, culture, and small numbers kept them on the margins. Further distancing them from mainstream Canadian culture was their theological commitment to pacifism and an intentional detachment from civil affairs. Canadian Mennonites also shared a similar cross-border relationship with their American co-religionists. For instance, their religious papers, *Herald of Truth* (English), *The Mennonite* (English), *Mennonitische Rundschua* (German), and *Herold der Wahrheit* (German), were published in America but circulated among Mennonites in Canada. Commentary on the war in the papers varied; the *Herald of Truth* had very limited coverage of the war, whereas the *Mennonitische Rundschua* had almost weekly reports. In all cases, those papers were read by Canadian Mennonites, and, similar to the Lutheran experience, it is difficult to determine in what ways, if any, Canadian Mennonites agreed with such coverage. There is a well-developed corpus of material on Canadian Mennonites and the First World War,[26] but due to limited primary sources,

---

21. "Rays of Light on South African Affairs: An Objection to Pro-Boer Articles from Nova Scotia," *Lutheran*, 22 March 1900, 2.

22. The German-language secular paper the *Berliner Journal* reported extensively on the war, and a thorough study of the paper may provide evidence of Lutheran attitudes to the war.

23. The editor apologized for his bias and changed the tenor of the paper's reporting on the war.

24. Miller, "English-Canadian Opposition."

25. Threinen, "Canadian Lutherans."

26. Healey, "Quakers and Mennonites." There is a significant amount of literature on Canadian Mennonites and the Great War. For a summary, see Heath, "Canadian

the task of historians is made much more difficult for the period of the war in South Africa.[27]

Eastern Europeans began arriving in Canada in noticeable numbers by the 1890s.[28] What is difficult to determine is how religion informed their understanding of Canada's national and imperial identity. The comments above related to Galician enlistment in a Canadian contingent provide a glimpse of support for the war effort, but there is no identifiable material to illuminate how their clergy or church body spoke of the war, or how war-related issues worked their way into the liturgy and local parish life. What is known for certain is that, during the war, nativist fears of "alien" immigrants from eastern Europe were frequently expressed. As Lubomyr Luciuk has noted, government officials, as well as newspaper editors, columnists, and letter writers, frequently expressed alarm at the influx of non-British immigrants who undermined Canada's imperial identity and loyalty.[29] As one critic claimed "you cannot make Anglo-Saxondom of Doukhobors, Galicians, and Finns" and that their arrival undermined attempts to "build up a race which shall hold and develop Canada for the Empire."[30] The grim reality was that, for some, the ethnic and religious identity of eastern Europeans simply did not fit within nationalistic visions of an Anglo-Saxon Canada firmly situated within the empire,[31] a view expressed after the war by those like prominent socially-conscious churchman, J. S. Woodsworth.[32] Sadly, a trajectory had been established that would lead to the mistreatment of "enemy aliens" in the Great War—despite ample displays of patriotism for the imperial cause.[33]

Churches."

27. Making the historian's task even more difficult was that conference minutes of Mennonite meetings in Ontario made no mention of the war.

28. In 1900, there were roughly 27,000 Galician immigrants in Canada (most were Ukrainians, some Polish, and others ethnic Germans from eastern Europe). They were primarily located in the Prairie Provinces. See Kaye, *Early Ukrainian*, 361.

29. Luciuk, *Searching for Place*, ch. 2. See also Swyripa, *Ukrainian Canadians*.

30. Luciuk, *Searching for Place*, 13.

31. Ferguson, "British-Canadian Intellectuals"; Martynowych, *Ukrainians in Canada*.

32. Woodsworth, *Strangers*.

33. For works on Ukrainian's and the First World War, as well as their treatment in internment camps, see Kaye, *Ukrainian Canadians*; Swyripa and Thompson, *Loyalties in Conflict*; Minenko, "Without Just Cause." For an examination of Canadian Ukrainians and the Second World War, see Prymak, *Maple Leaf and Trident*.

Canadian Dutch communities faced unique pressures, for they naturally had affinity with the Dutch Boers but also sought to be loyal to their new home Canada. The resolutions and actions of American Dutch Reformed bodies were distinctly pro-Boer, but how the Dutch in Canada resonated with their American brothers and sisters on those matters is not entirely clear. It has been argued that the intense pro-British zeal of the dominant Protestant denominations kept the Dutch from assimilating into the Anglo-Saxon community, but more research is needed to form a more complete picture of Canadian Dutch communities and how they negotiated their identity in the heyday of Canadian imperialism.[34]

As for smaller religious bodies in Canada, such as Bible Students (eventually known as Jehovah's Witnesses), Mormons, and Doukhobors, there is minimal material available to ascertain how religion informed their conceptions of national and imperial identity and attitudes to the war. Reactions from mainstream groups also varied, with attitudes towards Mormons less harsh than those towards eastern Europeans.[35] Canadian Mormons received the U.S.-published *Improvement Era*, the denomination's official organ that included articles on the war.[36] Canadian Bible students had U.S.-based publications as well. However, as with the Lutherans and Mennonites, what those U.S. publications tell us about Canadian views is uncertain. Looking elsewhere for evidence, it does seem that Mormons appeared to be enthusiastic celebrants of Dominion Day before the war.[37] But what one extrapolates from that is also limited. Perhaps the best clues to how such groups on the margins thought about war, empire, and national identity during the war in South Africa were their responses to the First World War.[38]

One final religious organization worth noting is the Woman's Christian Temperance Union (WCTU), even though it does not technically fit into the paradigm of religions on the margins. The Canadian superintendent of the WCTU was distressed over the difficulty of carrying out peace

34. Nijhof and Bakker, "The Dutch Community," 1–13.
35. Palmer, "Polygamy and Progress."
36. For instance, see Tanner, "South African War."
37. Palmer, "Polygamy and Progress, 124.
38. Canadian Mormons responded positively to enlistment during the First World War. See Palmer, "Polygamy and Progress," 124. Canadian Jehovah's Witnesses refused to support the war effort against Germany, and were brutally mistreated by the government as a result (that mistreatment was experienced again in the Second World War). See Penton, *Jehovah's Witness*, 41–80.

work in a hyper-charged environment of imperialism and jingoism, what she called a "military craze" that made reasonable dissent seem like disloyalty.[39] Although the WCTU encouraged peace and arbitration in the early months of the war,[40] commentary in its semi-monthly paper *Woman's Journal* related the "good effects" of the war, such as rousing "love and duties" owed to "Queen and country" and the "burst[ing] into bright and ardent flames, the blood of loyalty which flows . . . with fresh vigor through our veins."[41] It also described 200 children ardently singing "Rule Britannia" at the national WCTU meeting in Halifax.[42] At least on one occasion, the WCTU participated in the sendoff of troops.[43] When it seemed that the relief of Ladysmith, Mafeking, and Kimberley was ushering in the end of the war, the *Woman's Journal* included commentary that seems far from pacifistic: "We in Canada also rejoice that the Canadian troops on those faraway battlefields have exhibited the heroic spirit of Englishmen. We rejoice that we have proved that in the newer British communities, as well as in the old mother islands, the blood still runs red in the veins of the race."[44] Those limited examples provide a glimpse into the complexity of the WCTU's response to the war, something worth further examination.

CONCLUSION

Fortunately, not all records of religious minorities are incomplete or nonexistent. As this book's chapters indicate, there are rich and varied extant sources that provide helpful windows into the wartime experience of Canada's religious minorities. Those groups on the margins experienced internal struggles and external pressures related to issues of loyalty and identity. How each faith tradition addressed those challenges was shaped by their own dominant personalities, ethnic identity, history, tradition, and theological convictions. Responses were fluid, divided, and rarely unanimous. Those seeking to address such issues not only had to deal with internal expectations and tension, but also construct a public response that would satisfy often hostile and vocal external critics. Some positions evolved over

39. Socknat, *Witness against War*, 23.
40. Miller, *Painting the Map*, 23–24.
41. "God Save the Queen," *Womans Journal*, 1 June 1900, 1.
42. "Halifax, Ho!" *Womans Journal*, December 1899, 1–3.
43. "A Farewell to the Contingent," *Wesleyan*, 17 January 1900, 5; "The Churches and the Contingent," *Wesleyan*, 24 January 1900, 4.
44. *Womans Journal*, 1 June 1900, 2.

time, leading to new identities, loyalties, and trajectories. In all cases, being on the margins meant dealing with either of the two dominant national and imperial narratives—English or French—both bolstered respectively by powerful Anglo-Saxon Protestantism or French Quebec Catholicism. The following chapters examine how those on the margins sought to do just that.

BIBLIOGRAPHY

Primary Sources

Berliner Journal
Canadian Baptist
Jewish Times
Lutheran
Wesleyan
Womans Journal

Other Sources

Basavarajappa K. G., and Bali Ram. "Section A: Population and Migration." Historical Statistics of Canada. *Statistics Canada* (October 22, 2008). No pages. Online: http://www.statcan.gc.ca/pub/11-516-x/pdf/5500092-eng.pdf.

Secondary Sources

Airhart, Phyllis D. "Ordering a New Nation and Reordering Protestantism, 1867–1914." In *The Canadian Protestant Experience, 1760–1990*, edited by George A. Rawlyk, 98–138. Burlington, ON: Welch, 1990.
Berger, Carl. *The Sense of Power: Studies in the Ideas of Canadian Imperialism, 1867–1914*. Toronto: University of Toronto Press, 1970.
Bridge, Carl, and Kent Fedorowich. "Mapping the British World." *Journal of Imperial and Commonwealth History* 31.2 (2003) 1–15.
Buckner, Phillip. "Canada." In *The Impact of the South African War*, edited by David Omissi and Andrew S. Thompson, 233–50. Houndmills, UK: Palgrave: 2002.
———. "Whatever Happened to the British Empire?" *Journal of the Canadian Historical Association* 4 (1993) 3–32.
———, ed. *Canada and the British Empire*. Oxford: Oxford University Press, 2008.
———. *Canada and the End of Empire*. Vancouver: UBC Press, 2005.
Clark, S. D. *Church and Sect in Canada*. Toronto: University of Toronto Press, 1948.
Cole, Douglas. "Canada's 'Nationalistic' Imperialists." *Journal of Canadian Studies* 5 (August 1970) 44–45.
Cook, Terry. "George R. Parkin and the Concept of Britannic Idealism." *Journal of Canadian Studies* 10 (August 1975) 15–31.
Cuthbertson, Greg, et al., eds. *Writing a Wider War: Rethinking Gender, Race, and Identity in the South African War, 1899–1902*. Athens: Ohio University Press, 2002.

Die, Marguerite Van, ed. *Religion and Public Life in Canada: Historical and Comparative Perspectives*. Toronto: University of Toronto Press, 2001.

Farwell, Byron. *The Great Anglo-Boer War*. New York: Harper & Row, 1976.

Ferguson, Barry. "British-Canadian Intellectuals, Ukrainian Immigrants, and Canadian National Identity." In *Canada's Ukrainians: Negotiating and Identity*, edited by Lubomyr Luciuk and Stella Hryniuk, 304–25. Toronto: University of Toronto Press, 1991.

Healey, Robynne Rogers. "Quakers and Mennonites and the Great War." In *Canadian Churches and the First World War*, edited by Gordon L. Heath, 218–40. Eugene, OR: Pickwick, 2014.

Heath, Gordon L. "Canadian Churches and War: An Introductory Essay and Annotated Bibliography." *McMaster Journal of Theology and Ministry* 12 (2010–2011) 61–124.

———. "'Citizens of that Mighty Empire': Imperial Sentiment among Students at Wesley College, 1897–1902." *Manitoba History* (June 2005) 15–25.

———. "'Forming Sound Public Opinion': The Late-Victorian Canadian Protestant Press and Nation-Building." *Journal of the Canadian Church Historical Society* 48 (2006) 109–59.

———. "Passion for Empire: War Poetry Published in the Canadian English Protestant Press during the South African War, 1899–1902." *Literature and Theology* 16 (June 2002) 127–47.

———. "Sin in the Camp: The Day of Humble Supplication in the Anglican Church in Canada in the Early Months of the South African War." *Journal of the Canadian Church Historical Society* 44 (Fall 2002) 207–26.

———. *A War with a Silver Lining: Canadian Protestant Churches and the South African War, 1899–1902*. Montreal: McGill-Queen's University Press, 2009.

———. "'Were We in the Habit of Deifying Monarchs': Canadian English Protestants and the Death of Queen Victoria, 1901." *Canadian Evangelical Review* (Fall 2005–Spring 2006) 72–97.

Heath, Gordon L., and Paul Wilson, eds. *Baptists and Public Life in Canada*. Eugene, OR: Pickwick, 2012.

Judd, Denis, and Keith T. Surridge. *The Boer War: A History*. London: I. B. Tauris, 2013.

Kaye, Vladimir J. *Early Ukrainian Settlements in Canada, 1895–1900*. Toronto: University of Toronto Press, 1964.

———. *Ukrainian Canadians in Canada's Wars: Materials for Ukrainian Canadian History, Volume I*. Toronto: Ukrainian Canadian Research Foundation, 1983.

Luciuk, Lubomyr. *Searching for Place: Ukrainian Displaced Persons, Canada, and the Migration of Memory*. Toronto: University of Toronto Press, 2000.

Lyon, David, and Marguerite Van Die, eds. *Rethinking Church, State, and Modernity: Canada between Europe and America*. Toronto: University of Toronto Press, 2000.

Martynowych, Orest T. *Ukrainians in Canada: The Formative Period, 1891–1924*. Edmonton: Canadian Institute of Ukrainian Studies Press, 1991.

Miedema, Gary. *For Canada's Sake: Public Religion, Centennial Celebrations, and the Remaking of Canada in the 1960s*. Montreal: McGill-Queens University Press, 2005.

Miller, Carman. "English-Canadian Opposition to the South African War as Seen through the Press." *Canadian Historical Review* 55 (1974) 422–38.

———. *Painting the Map Red: Canada and the South African War, 1899–1902*. Montreal: McGill-Queen's University Press, 1998.

Minenko, Mark. "Without Just Cause: Canada's First National Internment Operations." In *Canada's Ukrainians: Negotiating and Identity*, edited by Lubomyr Luciuk and Stella Hryniuk, 288–303. Toronto: University of Toronto Press, 1991.

Nasson, Bill. *The South African War, 1899–1902*. Oxford: Oxford University Press, 1999.

Nijhof, Timothy, and Catharina De Bakker. "The Dutch Community in the Kildonans (1893–1911): The English Churches and the War." *Canadian Journal of Netherlandic Studies* 26 (2005) 1–13.

Omissi, David, and Andrew Thompson. "Introduction: Investigating the Impact of the War." In *The Impact of the South African War*, edited by David Omissi and Andrew Thompson, 1–20. Houndsmill, U.K.: Palgrave, 2002.

Page, Robert. *The Boer War and Canadian Imperialism*. Ottawa: The Canadian Historical Association, 1987.

———. "Canada and the Imperial Idea in the Boer War Years." *Journal of Canadian Studies* 5 (February 1970) 33–49.

———. "Carl Berger and the Intellectual Origins of Canadian Imperialist Thought, 1867–1914." *Journal of Canadian Studies* 5 (August 1970) 39–43.

———. *Imperialism and Canada: 1895–1903*. Toronto: Holt, Rinehart, and Winston, 1972.

Pakenham, Thomas. "The Contribution of the Colonial Forces." In *One Flag, One Queen, One Tongue: New Zealand, the British Empire and the South African War*, edited by John Crawford and Ian McGinnon, 58–72. Auckland: Auckland University Press, 2003.

Palmer, Howard. "Polygamy and Progress: The Reaction to Mormons in Canada, 1887–1923." In *The Mormon Presence in Canada*, edited by Brigham Y. Card, et al., 108–35. Edmonton: University of Alberta Press, 1990.

Penlington, Norman. *Canada and Imperialism, 1896*. Toronto: University of Toronto Press, 1965.

Penton, M. James. *Jehovah's Witnesses in Canada: Champions of Freedom of Speech and Worship*. Toronto: Macmillan, 1976.

Porter, A. N. *The Origins of the South African War: Joseph Chamberlain and the Diplomacy of Imperialism, 1895–99*. Manchester: Manchester University Press, 1980.

Prymak, Thomas M. *Maple Leaf and Trident: The Ukrainian Canadians during the Second World War*. Toronto: Multicultural History Society of Ontario, 1988.

Reid, Brian A. *Our Little Army in the Field: The Canadians in South Africa*. St. Catharines, ON: Vanwell, 1996.

Semple, Neil. *The Lord's Dominion: The History of Canadian Methodism*. Montreal: McGill-Queen's University Press, 1996.

Smith, Iain R. *The Origins of the South African War, 1899–1902*. London: Longman, 1996.

Socknat, Thomas. *Witness against War: Pacifism in Canada, 1900–1945*. Toronto: University of Toronto Press, 1987.

Swyripa, Francis. *Ukrainian Canadians: A Survey of Their Portrayal in English-Language Works*. Edmonton: University of Alberta Press, 1978.

Swyripa, Frances, and John Herd Thompson, eds. *Loyalties in Conflict: Ukrainians in Canada during the Great War*. Edmonton: Canadian Institute of Ukrainian Studies, 1983.

Tanner, J. M. "South African War." *Improvement Era* 3.3 (January 1900) 209–17.

Threinen, Norm. "Canadian Lutherans and the First World War." In *Canadian Churches and the First World War*, edited by Gordon L. Heath, 197–217. Eugene, OR: Pickwick, 2014.

Warwick, Peter, ed. *The South African War: The Anglo-Boer War 1899–1902*. Burnt Mill, U.K.: Longman, 1980.

Woodsworth, J. S. *Strangers within Our Gates: Or Coming Canadians*. Toronto: F. C. Stephenson, 1909.

Yelin, Louise. *From the Margins of Empire: Christina Stead, Doris Lessing, Nadine Gordimer*. Ithaca, NY: Cornell University Press, 1998.

2

Writing Religious Minorities into Canada's South African War, 1899–1902

Carman Miller

THE WORLD'S THREE "PEOPLES of the Book" have maintained an ambiguous stance on religion's relationship to war. Try as they may, they have never quite reconciled their God of War with their God of Peace.[1] Nor have they managed to maintain a consistent doctrine and practice of warfare; their contradictions and equivocations are exposed more blatantly in wartime, as faith and practice are trumped by national, class, ideological and material interests, and a disregard of conscience. The South African War (1899–1902) that began on 11 October 1899 between the British Empire and two South African republics provides a case in point.

Christianity's fractured response to this conflict between two "Christian states" is evident to Canadian historians of this conflict. It was no less striking to contemporary Canadian opponents to their country's military engagement. War opponents' antipathy to and criticisms of the war, however, failed to deter their government from authorizing a consignment of 1,019 men of all ranks to serve under British command (another 6,349 Canadians would follow over the next thirty-one months),[2] a decision taken only days after war had been declared.

---

1. Josh 11–12; Isa 2:4.

2. These figures are based on the sum of the units' establishment, not individuals, as some men volunteered for more than one unit and joined several others.

On Sunday, 29 October 1899, the day before Canada's first contingent sailed from Quebec City for Cape Town, its commanding officer, Lieutenant-Colonel William D. Otter, marched his battalion's Protestants in a dispiriting drizzle to a farewell service and Holy Communion at the city's Anglican Holy Trinity Cathedral.[3] Likewise, the battalion's Major Oscar Pelletier led its Catholics to Quebec City's Notre Dame Basilica Cathedral where Father Peter O'Leary (who was to become the contingent's iconic Canadian chaplain) celebrated a low mass. In both services the soldiers were surrounded by anxious friends, relatives, and curious spectators, many of whom had come to the city to bid farewell to their friends, relatives, and soldier-heroes on this "patriotic," hazardous mission. At each service, attentive press representatives busily took notes from which to compose text to inform and entertain Canadian audiences from across the country.

Although both services were heavily charged with meaning and emotion, Holy Trinity Cathedral's service assumed the role of an official ceremony. To fulfill this self-appointed role, the Cathedral recruited ten Anglican clergy, including its Dean, its Anglo-Catholic rector of St. Mathews Church, Frederick G. Scott, and the Contingent's twenty-seven-year-old Gaspe-born chaplain attached to Holy Trinity, the Reverend John M. Almond. Together they marshaled an impressive arsenal of patriotic music, scripture, prayers, and admonition to bless "the hands that fight" and inspire the "gallant thousand" with religious purpose. Their rousing, martial hymns set a tone: "O God our Help in Ages Past," "Onward Christian Soldiers," "Fight the Good Fight," and "Stand Up, Stand Up for Jesus." The Scripture reading (Deut 33:27) guaranteed the men the support of God's "everlasting arms," and called upon the men to "destroy" their opponents as Moses had done during his conquest of the promised land. Reverend Scott followed the Scripture reading with an equally bellicose sermon, firmly grounded on Moses' and Joshua's example and citing Moses' final charge to the Israelites. He reminded Canada's young citizen soldiers that they were the Christian heirs of that "charter of the world's freedom," once given to the Israelites but now held "in England's keeping"; and that it could only be maintained if Britain, "that democratic monarchy" together with its empire, that confederation "of peoples, nations, tongues, languages and creeds" were prepared to defend that sacred trust. To that end, the khaki-clad young men must destroy the effete "tyranny of Dutch 17th century despotism" and share that

---

3. Known then as the Church of England in Canada.

charter with those being oppressed by Dutch terrorism.[4] Canadian "poets," inspired by Scott's message, took up his refrain, hailing the Canadian recruits as "Missionaries togged in khaki, Bibles at the end of guns," who must be "ready to fight and bleed for the world's great need."[5]

Meanwhile, in South Africa, Paul Kruger, the South African Republic's president, a devoted adherent to the Dutch Reformed Church, implored his God and exhorted his people to defend their Holy Land that they had wrested from its African inhabitants and that was now being assailed by contemporary Canaanites and mercenary infidels. Offended war advocates rebuked President Kruger's audacity: how dare he compare his people to "the children of Israel" and his opponents to Canaanites![6]

Canadian war opponents saw things differently. They too were offended. But they were offended by the cruel spectacle of their country assailing pious Afrikaners (or Boers as they were then normally called) who worshiped "the same God we profess and follow and who are pleading the righteousness of their cause at his feet."[7] Others with more explicit pacifist sympathies with the "Sober, God fearing Boers" wondered what "Jesus might [have] do[ne] if he were still on earth," to which more cynical Canadian war opponents reminded their readers that God was "always on the side that had the most men and the largest number of guns."[8] Others quietly reminded their readers that "God was no respector [sic] and loves [loved] President Kruger as well as Queen Victoria."[9]

These dissenting and dissonant voices, persons who questioned the justness of the war or the necessity of Canada's participation, though few in number, remind us that Canada's response to the South African War was more complex and nuanced than Canadian historians have often suggested. In this oft-told historical tale of ethno-linguistic tension, minorities are erased and the story reduced to a Manichean political contest of wills between French and English speaking Canadians. Historians' narratives, of course, depend upon and reflect their discipline's research and agenda.

---

4. Scott's sermon was printed in *The Mitre*, November 1899. For a full summary of the sermon and for coverage of other Canadian farewell services, see Heath, *War with a Silver Lining*, 18–19, 63–65.

5. Borthwick, *Poems and Songs*, 125.

6. *The (Toronto) Globe*, 14 October, 1899.

7. *Regina Standard*, 1 Nov 1899.

8. Miller, *Painting the Map*, 22–23.

9. *Citizen and Country*, 2 February 1900.

And during those formative decades of the 1960s and 70s, as the historical discipline expanded, replicated itself, re-staffed history departments, and influenced funding agencies, the study of war and of religion were causalities of fashion, subject to a two-pronged confrontation. The first came from a wave of social historians whose agenda was to give power to the powerless by exposing the social structures that constrained the poor and oppressed, structures whose existence and *longue duree* could best be established by statistical analysis rather than by "the froth of history"; their subject, object, and method made them uncomfortable colleagues of historians of war and religion. Indeed, in some quarters, historians of war and religion became the object of suspicion and scorn, and dismissed as war mongers and proselytizers who produced a species of "court history," "PR, puffery and self-promotion," "official but not history."[10] Unfair as these generalizations were, especially to Canada's francophone military historians,[11] the social historians' criticisms contained a grain of truth. Religious and military historians' unfashionable dependence on literary sources and their linear narrative of persons (notably men), governance, doctrine, and liturgy or power, policy, politics, administration, and operations made them appear indifferent to structures and oppression, "scientific" analysis, and quantification, interested largely in the triumphant progress of history. Then, well before the social historians' hegemony had run its course, historians of war and religion were confronted by a rising historical generation of cultural-linguistic historians that still left the historians of war and religion on the wrong page. The new wave had re-discovered agency, voice, literary sources, and micro-history, and they told a story of a fractured, ambiguous, and dissident world populated by limited identities of class, gender, ethnicity, and region. In this kaleidoscopic context, however, historians of war and religion began writing their way back to the center of historical discourse. And, on their way, they encountered their critics moving to meet them, reclaiming language, narrative, and story-telling,

---

10. Cook, *Clio's Warriors*, 4, 176, 221.

11. Several of Canada's francophone historians, following the lead of their Annales colleagues, wrote exemplary Canadian socio-military history: Gravel, *L'Armée au Québec*; Gagnon, *Le 22e Bataillon*. A good discussion of the debate between social and cultural/linguistic historians is found in Sewell, *The Logic of History*. His dating of the arrival of Annales history on this continent (by which he means the United States) fails to acknowledge its earlier influence on Canada, largely through its francophone historians, such as Ouellet, *Histoire économique*.

and proclaiming the importance of character, power, ideas, and values in recounting the fractured history of change over time.

The story of Canada's religious minorities' response to the South African War was a conspicuous casualty of the linear, grand narrative of reducing a richer, variegated reality, to a simple, homogenized tale of essential ethnic, religious, and social identities, established and justified by a search for roots, continuity, logic, and meaning. Several years ago John Macfarlane alerted historians to how reading history backwards distorted our understanding of the South African and the Great War—how our search for the roots of the tragic conscription crisis of World War 1 in the South African conflict ignored French Canadians' contrastive and changing responses to the South African conflict.[12] Religious minorities suffered a similar fate during that conflict; they were ignored and marginalized in favor of a simpler, poorer tale. If so, how do we redress this lacuna and write minorities into the historical narrative? One way may be to enlarge the frame and re-examine the contexts in which they lived.

"Civilization Advances,"[13] Victoria's *Western Methodist Reporter's* headline announcing the beginning of the war in South Africa, underscored the close link between war and religion. The *Western Methodist Reporter* spoke for many of Canada's social gospel "high priests" of radicalism[14] who saw the war as a God-given opportunity to rescue Africa from medieval Dutch terrorism and bring another nation to the feet of Christ. Theirs was a message with which Rev. F. G. Scott and his Anglican divines at Quebec would have heartily endorsed. Perhaps the fullest, systematic Canadian justification for imperialism's Christian mission was Albert Richardson Carman's, *The Ethics of Imperialism: An Enquiry whether Christian Ethics and Imperialism Are Antagonistic*, published three years after the end of the South African War, in which the editor of the Montreal *Star* and son of the Superintendent of the Methodist Church of Canada argued a strong case for benevolent coercion to hasten the Kingdom of God.[15] His religious justification for military intervention was largely an elaboration of the assumptions underlying the rhetoric of many popular, contemporary, progressive war advocates. And they were not alone.

12. See MacFarlane, "'Ready Aye Ready?'"
13. *Methodist Reporter*, 18 October 1899.
14. Miller, *Paining the Map*, 17–18.
15. Carman, *The Ethics of Imperialism*.

Had Canadian soldiers or civilians needed to justify their participation in the war, they had not far to look for secular leaders, military and social, British and American, who were equally convinced of the conflict's Christian purpose. Most notable in Canada's very British world were Lord Frederick Roberts, the Commander-in-Chief of the British Army in South Africa, and his Second-in-Command, Lord Herbert Kitchener. They, like many distinguished British lady imperialists, boldly claimed a God-given personal mission to serve as secular "civilizers" and "evangelists," called "not only to be pure but to purify" the nations.[16] And had they needed a contemporary example to justify their self-appointed, God-given mission, they would undoubtedly have pointed to the popular contemporary Spanish-American War in 1898–1901 (in which some of Canada's Boer War recruits served before volunteering for service in Canadian forces), an example especially convincing to Protestants who saw the Spanish-American war as simply a "struggle between the open and closed Bible."[17]

To citizen soldiers seeking incentives for service in the South African War, advocates offered an array of additional reasons, material, patriotism, politics, blood, and belongings that appealed especially to Central Canada's English-speaking, urban middle class. A few fanatical pro-war advocates spiked their advocacy with accusations, hate, and bigotry, dismissing the Boers as an obstinate, "inferior race" of "slave holders,"[18] berating their Canadian anti-war opponents as "the barbaric yawp of . . . foreign yahoos,"[19] "priest-ridden, malcontents and enemies of the Empire," "traitors and conspirators" who had unwisely been given the franchise in Canada, and threatening that "if ballots failed to fix [their ideas] bayonets would."[20] Some "fanatics" went further: editors were silenced, teachers dismissed, curricula prescribed, and dissidents and minorities intimidated. Kruger and Canadian dissidents were burned in effigy and threatened by patriotic mobs.

Pervasive, vocal, persuasive, or abusive as were the Canadian pro-war advocates, dissenters were not silent, even though they were relatively few in number and were divided and unable to mount a concerted resistance. The Christian socialist editor of the Toronto based *Citizen and Country*,

---

16. Bush, *Edwardian Ladies*, 79, 80. See also Heath, "Passion for Empire."
17. *The Western Methodist Reporter*, November 1899.
18. *The (Toronto) Globe*, 14 October 1899.
19. Riley and Dahl, "Militarism, Anti-militarism, Imperialism."
20. Miller, *Painting the Map*, 18–19.

George Weston Wrigley,[21] looked in vain to progressive clergy to lead the opposition to "this wicked war." But he soon realized that the "Army of the Prince of Peace" was deeply "divided,"[22] a division he found noticeably and painfully conspicuous among his progressive clerical friends and his socialist fellow travelers. Wrigley, however, was not alone. In almost every religious minority in Canada (and every Canadian religious group might claim that numeric status), there were clergy and laity who opposed the war.[23] There were also institutional constraints to fanaticism and fair-minded persons ready to defend dissent and rebuke intolerance.

The sacred and secular opponents and their reasons, however, are not easily separated or examined in isolation, shaped as they were by mutual, overlapping ideological convictions, social commitments, and ethnic identities. Moreover, the relatively small number of Canadian war opponents, the varying intensity and durability of their opposition, their scattered geographic distribution, and their disparate arguments and objectives have made a concerted opposition difficult and unlikely. A crude general profile of Canadian opposition to the war and to Canada's participation would include French Canadians, farmers, radical labor, progressive Protestant clergy, Anglophobic Canadians of Irish and German descent as well as Quakers, Hutterites, Doukhobors, Mennonites, and other conscientious objectors. What divided them, however, seemed greater than what united them.

For example, neither of Canada's two prominent anti-war critics, Henri Bourassa (1868–1952), the eloquent, young, French Canadian Liberal, and Goldwin Smith (1823–1910), Toronto's opinionated author and former Oxford Regis professor of History, were obvious allies. Although Smith spoke of joining Bourassa in an anti-imperialist league, Smith's Anglo-Saxon racialist views would have made it a very fragile alliance. Nor would Smith have been comfortable for long with the socialism of George Weston Wrigley or of his outspoken, English-born, anti-war friend, Thomas Phillips Thompson (1843–1933), although both shared Smith's agrarian politics. On the other hand, the anti-war editors of the *Huntington Gleaner* and the *Regina Standard*,[24] who shared Smith's agrarianism and anti-Semitism, blaming the war on Jewish capitalists, might have caused Smith less dis-

21. See *Dictionary of Canadian Biography*, s.v. "Wrigley, George Weston."
22. *Citizen and Country*, 9 December 1899.
23. Miller, *Painting the Map*, ch. 2 n. 39.
24. *Regina Standard*, 1 Nov 1899.

comfort, even though neither editor exercised much influence outside his uncertain constituency.

The editor of the *Huntington Gleaner* would have been an even more uncommon ally of Bourassa, given the editor's previous intemperate, English, Protestant crusades. And, even Michael Donovan, the anti-war, Irish-Catholic editor of the *Antigonish Casket* would have had difficulty working with Bourassa and his anti-war allies who staked their Boer sympathies on their fanciful shared "Latin" racial affinities, and by extension, Catholic sympathies, forgetting that the Boers' "Latin" roots were Huguenots, not Catholic. Nor did Donovan hesitate to remind Bourassa that Kruger cared "not a fig" for Catholic rights. Donavan's opposition to the war was Irish-born, grounded in his antipathy to Joseph Chamberlain's imperialism and "maltreatment" of Ireland.[25] Solidarity was no more obvious among "workingmen's friends." Radical anti-war labor journals like the *New Denver Ledger,* the *Sandon Paystreak,* or *Nelson Miner* possessed but thinly veiled scorn for the *Winnipeg Voice* and Toronto's *Citizen and Country* and their concern for what Christ thought of imperialism or what Jesus might have done if he were still on earth. Fewer still were prepared to join the Montreal trade unionists' crusade to "Stop the War and arrest the Murderers."[26] Altogether, the ideological divisions among Canada's war's opponents offered little chance of a congenial or stable coalition. What their voices demonstrated, however, is a wide scattering of English-Canadian opposition to the war, a challenge to the Canadian simplistic, reductionist tale of French-English conflict. So, too, is an understanding of the more nuanced context in which they worked.

The war opponents' varying intensities and their fragility and evolution over time made concerted, sustained opposition even less likely. While several anti-war journals persisted in their criticism of the war with apparent impunity, others were silenced by their readers, owners, sponsors, or for more opportunistic reasons. For example, Martin Butler, the editor of Fredericton's *Butler's Journal* did not own "his" journal. Consequently, his anti-war views were quickly stifled by its owners.[27] Similarly, the *Regina Standard*, a Liberal journal edited by John Kenneth McInnis, a Prince Edward Island-born school teacher, who shared Goldwin Smith's agrarian sympathies, reluctantly dropped his opposition to the war as well,

---

25. Miller, *Painting the Map*, 22.
26. Miller, *Canada's Little War*, 16.
27. *Citizen and Country*, 2 December 1899.

shortly after Canada's decision to send troops, a causality of political pressure. However, his journal reported the activities of war opponents, and praised their courage.

The English-born printer and editor of Winnipeg's labor journal *Voice*, Arthur Puttee (1868–1957), had more pragmatic reasons to suspend his opposition. Although an early war opponent, Puttee dropped his opposition to the war upon his decision to become the Labor's candidate in Winnipeg's federal by-election. Not only did he announce, organize, and report his electoral campaign in popular military language, but he assured his constituency that, if he were elected, he would vote for war supplies, since the country was at war, and he was a patriot, adding significantly that he would not discuss the justice of the war on which he appeared to retain reservations. His strategy worked, and he was elected as a Labor Member of Parliament. Puttee's apostasy, however, did not impress George Wrigley or Phillips Thompson, even after the apostate attempted to revert to his previous reservations after his re-election in 1900. Clearly, Puttee's electorate was more convinced of his good faith or more tolerant of his temporary lapse than his socialist colleagues.[28]

Canada's minorities lived and worked in a more variegated environment than historians have often suggested, who were content to portray Canada's response to the war as a simple ethno-linguistic contest, fueled by the colorful or entertaining language of fanatical commentators and verbal bullies. After all, much of the early, over-heated rhetoric such as the *Galt Reporter's* threat of "war in Berlin" [Ontario] against the town's "disloyal" German-Canadians, "which the noble 29th battalion will be asked to quell," was largely bravado and verbal intimidation that soon lost its appeal. Unpleasant as the abuse and intimidation was, there is no reason to think it represented a wide constituency. Nor did it go unanswered and un-rebuked. For example, in January 1900 the venerable old Principal of Queen's University, the Rev. Dr. George Munro Grant, alarmed by the tactics and language of the fanatics, sternly reminded his readers that "if there is one thing more than any other which a free people must preserve as the indispensable price of freedom it is the liberty of speech, and that means not liberty to echo the cries of the hour . . . but the liberty to dissent."[29]

Moreover, even in the early, emotional stages of the war, Canada's prowar advocates employed more civil language and advanced more pragmatic

28. For additional information see, Miller, "English-Canadian Opposition," 431–32.
29. "Current Events," *Queens Quarterly*, January 1900, 154–55.

and political arguments for Canadian participation in the war. The pragmatists spoke of obtaining war contracts, gaining status in the community of nations, insuring British support for the defense of Canada's borders and providing military experience and training. In their view the war was not an ethnic or religious contest, and those "fanatics" who employed those arguments and language were an embarrassment to the cause they defended.

Of course, many of the early war advocates were political partisans who were out to discredit the government on the eve of a general election, and who were ready to use whatever argument might serve their cause. But a pluralistic political community partisanship cut both ways, restraining as well as inspiring excess. Consequently, many war partisans, sensitive to the adverse effects of verbal excess on sectors of their own electorate, rebuked the extremist in their own party and appealed for British "fair-play," explaining that abusive language and tactics were disloyal and disruptive of the war effort. They cooled the ardor of their followers, denounced "jingoism,"[30] and downplayed the influence of the racial agitation, confined largely to urban central and eastern Canada.[31]

Goldwin Smith endorsed their cheerfully analysis, explaining to one of his contemporary American correspondents that, in Canada, Toronto was "the center of jingoism and almost its circumference."[32] Although a vast over-simplification even if he had included English Montreal, Smith's assessment reminds us that Canada was still predominately a rural country, and that Central Canada's urban press may be an imperfect barometer of small town and rural Canada's response to the war. The relative silence of Canada's numerous rural weekly and monthly journals on the war suggests, but does not prove, a certain indifference or opposition to the war, or a preoccupation with other issues. Bowmanville, Ontario's *The Canadian Statesman's* masthead may have had it right when it defined its mission as "Our Town and Country First; the World Afterwards." In the early weeks of the war, the paper certainly remained, more or less, true to its words, absorbed as it was in local material issues, such as the weather, the crops, and the price of cheese.[33]

---

30. *Canadian Churchman*, 12 and 29 October 1899.

31. *Calgary Herald*, 14 October 1899; *Victoria Colonist*, cited in the *Vancouver Province*, 28 October 1899.

32. "Goldwin Smith to W. Bourke Cochran," *W. Bourke Cochran Papers*, 10 November 1899.

33. *Canadian Statesman*, 11 October 1899.

Granted that *The Canadian Statesman* was a Liberal paper and that party discipline restrained many Liberal (and Conservative) journals and partisans, especially before the party endorsed Canadian participation in the war. But once the government had endorsed the war, *The Canadian Statesman* assured its rural and small town readers that "Laurier would never be carried away by passion, prejudice, or enthusiasm," unlike the "ribald ravings of the senile leader of the Opposition and his discredited creator, the nest of traitors."[34] This journal's subsequent sparse and reassuring comments and preoccupation with local issues bordered on indifference to the war; certainly, it exhibited little enthusiasm.

A similar equivocal reaction stalked the *Sarnia Observer* and the *Moncton Transcript*, both Liberal papers. Their initial spirited opposition to Canadian participation in the war and their delayed reluctant acceptance of the government's decision to send troops suggest a more founded opposition than simply political discipline. Whatever the reason for their initial reluctance, they subsequently remained a voice of moderation.[35] The same might be said for other Liberal journals, such as the *Ottawa Journal*, the *Montreal Witness*, the *Quebec Telegraph*, the *Hamilton Herald*, the *Sherbrooke Record*, and even Toronto's fashionable *Saturday Night*, which, before the war, saw no need for Canadian volunteers, and above all, no reason "to rush" troops to South Africa. Clearly, minorities inhabited a more fluid, ambiguous, and less hostile world than we have often assumed.

Framing a minority is always hazardous, especially a community of multiple identities, interests, and ideologies. The Canadian Church of England's response to the South African War is a conspicuous example, largely because it arrogated to itself the appearance of a state church, as it did during the dispatch of the first Canadian contingent for South Africa; its high patriotic rhetoric assumed an official authority that neither its ecclesiastical, political, or practical power could execute or justify. Although Holy Trinity's display of clerical patriotism was echoed from many Church of England pulpits, other Anglican clerics appeared less convinced or convincing, and a few were decidedly opposed to the war—one was the Rev. Dr. William Wright, a former professor of Medicine at McGill University and assistant priest of Montreal's Anglo-Catholic parish of St. John the Evangelist, who chose the Church of England's solemn Sunday service of solidarity to denounce the war, informing his congregation that

---

34. *Canadian Statesman*, 18 October 1899.
35. *Sarnia Observer*, 13 and 20 October 1899.

he considered the war "inconsistent with the profession of Christianity." Amy Redpath (1868–1954), a poetess and member of one of Montreal's leading families, was delighted with his intervention, recording in her diary that she shared his views.[36] *Citizen and Country*'s editor and fellow Anglican, George Wrigley, would have agreed; so, too, would Canon William Reiner, the priest of the Church of England's Holy Trinity Church in Barrie, Ontario. Who, one might ask, speaks for this community? And how is representation determined?

Certainly, the Church of England's Toronto-based family journal, the *Canadian Churchman*, offered a much more guarded, moderate, and less urgent approach to the war than Quebec City's Holy Trinity's militant farewell call to arms. In fact, the Church of England's family paper went out of its way to assure its readership that, before the war, it had "countenanced no jingoism" and had prayed to the last that "England may be spared a war which ... cannot but bring in its train consequences so disastrous and so dishonoring."[37]

The Montreal-based *Presbyterian Record* adopted a similar cautionary tone, dismissing fanatical war advocates as "Canadian Boers" trading on "racial hatred." Given Montreal's significant Presbyterian francophone community at the time, the *Record* had good reason to be concerned with hateful, divisive advocacy based on ethnicity and language. J. D. McLeod, the editor of the *Presbyterian College Journal* (whose publications featured a full francophone page), went farther in his opposition to the war, as did one of the College's instructors, Rev. W. D. Reid.[38]

The Methodists' popular weekly, *The Christian Guardian*, too, wrestled with the question of war and peace; and if one can judge from a random list of Protestant clerical war opponents, opposition may have been strongest among Methodists.[39] In the *Christian Guardian*'s last edition before the war, its editor, the Victoria College graduate, Rev. Andrew Cory Courtice, an avowed peace advocate who only recently had endorsed the 1899 Hague Peace Conference's resolutions, seemed torn by indecision. He made no plea for Canadian participation in the war. He simply condemned the Jingoes

---

36. "Diary," *Amy Roddick Papers*, 11 February 1900.

37. *Canadian Churchman*, 12 and 29 October 1899.

38. *Presbyterian College Journal*, January 1900.

39. Miller, *Painting the Map*, 463 n. 39. According to William Magney, the Methodists were ambivalent to the war and were caught between their nationalism and historic rejection of war and a division between their hierarchy and "lesser clergy." Magney, "The Methodist Church," 46.

in "Great Britain and the Transvaal," and published side-by-side the "Case of the British" and the "Case of the Boers," as though they were of equal validity.[40] Later, pressed to take a more active stance, Courtice exonerated Canada from any responsibility for provoking the war, blamed the war on the Jamieson Raid, Cecil Rhodes, greedy mine owners, and speculators, and assured his readers that Canadian soldiers fought only for "just and honest government," and to rescue Black Africans from wicked, cruel, and "hard-hearted, selfish commercialism."[41]

A comparable ambiguity stalked the early issues of *The Canadian Congregationalist*, which "prayed that those Canadians [who were] called upon to serve in South Africa may never stain their hands with the blood of their fellow man."[42] The Rev. Morgan Wood, the minister of Toronto's Bond Street Congregational Church, however, was far from ambiguous in his denunciations of the war. War is wrong, he argued, as it is an outmoded Old Testament notion diametrically opposed to the teachings of Christ (strictures that were carried in the *Globe* and a dozen Ontario weeklies and some out of province papers).[43] Similarly, the Saint John's *Maritime Baptists Messenger and Visitor* condemned the immorality of the war.[44] And even the Rev. J. C. Speer, the Associate Editor of the *Western Methodist Recorder* who had welcomed the war as an advance of civilization, praised George Wrigley for his war against war, adding that "we admire his courage."[45] How then do we evaluate these voices? Who do they represent?

The extent and influence of clerical opposition to the war is difficult to measure, especially their congregation's reaction. The Rev. J. C. Herdman, the minister of Calgary's Knox Presbyterian Church, used his pulpit to denounce the sheer wickedness of the war, its butchery of brothers, cursing, coveting, and anarchy, with the full knowledge that his cause lacked popularity in the "great cathedrals," the "wealthy endowed colleges," and the "metropolitan churches." His parishioners appeared to agree; at least they did not object to their minister's interventions.[46] His Presbyterian col-

40. *Christian Guardian*, 4 October 1899.
41. Ibid., 17 January 1900.
42. *The Canadian Congregationalist*, 12 and 19 October, 2 November 1899.
43. *The Globe*, 6 November 1899; *Citizen and Country*, 25 November 1899; *The (Montreal) Witness*, 6 November 1899.
44. Moody, "Boers and Baptists."
45. *The Western Methodist Reporter*, November 1899.
46. *The Standard*, 1 November 1899.

league in Orangeville, Ontario, the Rev. M. Dickie, however, encountered strong opposition from members of his congregation who objected to his "pro-Boer" sentiments.[47] In Vancouver, the Rev. J. Herbert Bainton's anti-war sermons provoked organized resistance, leading to the founding of a rival Congregational church.[48] In other churches peace may have been purchased by silence, a strategy that Goldwin Smith claimed accounted for the Catholic Church's "dignified impartiality."

Extensive as a roll call of clerical and lay anti-war voices may appear, they were never numerous or an effectual opposition. Yet they were more than merely a little cult of cranks, foreign agitators, and chronic objectors. Some were persons whose anti-war critique a future generation considered remarkably sound, especially as that generation re-assessed Britain's methods of warfare, its scorched-earth policy and concentration camps.[49] Fueled by official inquiries into the causes and remedy of British failures, the public debate occurred largely after the British Army had reached Pretoria and the public was sufficiently confident of their victory; their criticisms would not be taken for a want of patriotism.

The South African War was a moving picture, though historians have tended to represent it as one or several snapshots. Canadian historians' snapshots of the war consist of (1) the acrimonious debate on the justice of the war and the necessity of Canada's participation, (2) the vindication of the government's decision by the success of Canadian arms, and (3) the war as a dress rehearsal for the Great War; the first two fashioned from the first half of the conflict, Canada's war.

By February 1901 Canada had no more units in South Africa. Canada's first three contingents had gone home, and had been feted and honored by their compatriots. Yet the war was only half over, and during the remaining sixteen months, Canada dispatched six more units to South Africa, representing over 60 percent of its total component of citizen soldier volunteers. In the remaining months of the war, the nature of warfare changed; so, too, did the public's response to the war. How, then, do we incorporate that period into our narrative? Canadian historians have all but erased this period from our historical record. For almost one hundred years after the war, only two contemporary books endeavored to tell the full story of Canada's Boer

---

47. *Ottawa Journal*, 7 November 1899.

48. Humphries, "Two B. C. Pacifists and the Boer War."

49. See "George Bryce" in Roberts, *A Standard Dictionary of Canadian Biography*, 50–51.

War; and both ended their account effectively with the return of Canada's first three contingents;[50] a history that mirrored their contemporaries' perception of the war. To understand their perspective, the war can be divided into three overlapping periods. The first confident, bombastic, and triumphant period began with the acrimonious debate in October 1899 and ended with a chastened British Empire, reeling from a series of defeats during Black Week, 10–17 December 1899. The second period began in January 1900 as a shaken British Empire replaced its commander and strategy, re-armed, re-equipped, and multiplied its ground forces to begin its slow, contested march to the Boer capitals of Bloemfontein and Pretoria. But since the war did not end with the capture of their capitals as European military textbooks had suggested, a dirty third period began, characterized by brutal guerrilla warfare, farm burning, and concentration camps that ended only in a negotiated peace on 31 May 1902.

The war that fired Canadians' initial enthusiasm belonged to the first period, a temporary emergency in which an imagined united empire marched triumphantly to Pretoria. Once that bubble burst, Canadians stayed the course until they reached Pretoria. They regarded the aftermath, the mopping up, as the responsibility of regular soldiers of the British Army, not citizen soldiers who had put their lives temporarily on hold. Moreover, few Canadian soldiers or civilians relished guard duty, concentration camps, and farm burning. Consequently, the recruitment of subsequent Canadian units lacked the public support and enthusiasm of the earlier units, and often incurred public resentment. Certainly, that was the case for the first of the last six units, the 1,208 Canadian constables recruited for Baden-Powell's South African Constabulary, a hybrid soldier-police force being recruited just as Canada's first three contingents were leaving South Africa. An important element of the Lord Milner's pacification of South Africa was that the Constabulary's soldier-policemen were to remain, settle, and marry in South Africa, and serve as a military reserve in the event of further conflict. The Canadian government resented Milner's attempt to poach Canadian settlers and undermine its efforts to settle the Canadian West. Even the *Canadian Military Gazette* denounced Milner's scheme as "virtual deportation."[51] Nor were the Canadian constables entirely happy with their mission; they served as constables, posted in small, African villages or isolated blockhouse. So unhappy did they become that at least 720

---

50. Evans, *The Canadian Contingents*; Marquis, *Canada's Sons on Kopje*.
51. *Military Gazette*, 19 February 1901.

of their number returned home before their terms expired, disillusioned and mutinous and poor advocates of imperial service.[52]

The 3,000 men who followed the Constables were civilian soldiers, not policemen. The first thousand, the Second Battalion Canadian Mounted Rifles, arrived in South Africa in February 1902 just in time to participate in one of the last engagements of the war, the famous Hart's River Battle, where they acquitted themselves with honor and distinction; one of the three renowned Canadian battles of the war. As for the remaining 2,000 Canadian volunteers recruited in the late winter of 1902, the Third, Fourth, Fifth, and Sixth Canadian Mounted Rifles arrived in South Africa only after peace had been proclaimed, and they returned with little to show for their efforts. None of these latter units enjoyed the farewell and welcome offered the first three Canadian units, even the Second Canadian Mounted Rifles, the heroes of Hart's River. Many of those men were disappointed with their treatment. They felt they had been forgotten even before they had returned, with the promises of post-war employment unredeemable, and the country preoccupied with other issues.

The Canadian public knew little of their exploits and appeared to care less; and until recently, these latter units were ignored by historians. The four Canadian war correspondents that accompanied the first contingent departed with that unit, and they were not replaced. Thereafter, Canadians were almost entirely dependent for news from British and American sources. Even the initial news of the costly, heroic Hart's River battle came from American sources! After Pretoria, several Canadian journals and periodicals confidently announced the war's end; and in a sense, they were right—after Pretoria, Canadians did not consider it their war. In fact, some journals debated the possibility of Laurier negotiating an end to the conflict, as though Canada were a non-belligerent, a possible, impartial arbiter.[53]

Much changed during the last half of the war in South Africa and in Canada, including the nature and intensity of Canadian support or opposition. For example, even before the departure of the Canadian troops, many French Canadians who initially had rejected official Canadian participation for constitutional, practical, and cultural reasons came to accept Canadian participation, especially after Britain's startling defeats of "Black week," defeats that a French-Canadian elite feared might signal the end of

---

52. Miller, "The Unhappy Warriors," 77–104.
53. Miller, *Canada's Little War*, 21–22.

imperial hegemony and compromise Britain's ability to protect Canada from American aggression.[54]

Similarly, Montreal's highly publicized three-day riot (1–3 March 1900), begun by McGill students celebrating the relief of Ladysmith, that pitched French Canadian against English Canadian students and hot-headed townsmen became a wake-up call for sensitive or pragmatic politicians to appreciate the perils of imperial engagements in a bi-national country. It was no coincidence that immediately after the Montreal Riot the foxy old Conservative leader, Sir Charles Tupper, anticipating an imminent federal election, began a campaign in Quebec claiming that he had broken up the old Imperial Federation League and that Sir Wilfrid Laurier was too imperialist for him!

The war, too, produced its cross-currents and ironies. A war that was both welcomed and feared as an opportunity and stimulus for imperial consolidation fueled the cause of autonomy for defensive and positive reasons. The searing debate on the cause and remedy of British military failures together with Canadian criticism of British leadership and Canadian pride in their own military accomplishments, notably at Paardeberg, Liliefontein, and Hart's River, fed a Canadian confidence, a sense of power, and a desire to control its own affairs and regenerate the Empire—captured so vividly by Jeannette Duncan in her novel *The Imperialist* (1904) and by the British journalist John A. Hobson in his *Canada today* (1906)—a cross-cutting debate from which religious communities could scarcely have remained immune, especially those whose social gospel was increasingly becoming a national, if not a nationalist, gospel.

The debate, however, was much more than a heated discussion on military leadership, strategy, tactics, and performance. Very shortly, it became a wider, more profound, and disturbing discussion of racial, physical, and moral decline, subterranean questions that the war brought to the surface and found expression in the Royal Commission on the South Africa War (1903), and more particularly, in its social Darwinian Interdepartmental Committee on Physical Deterioration (1904). This contemporary and ensuing debate preyed upon British fears of decline and loss of power, warnings that Rudyard Kipling had exploited in his poetry, and which the war critique appeared to confirm. Altogether, it challenged the cultural hubris and racial certainty incarnate in imperialism and missionary endeavor that had been expressed so dramatically in the confident Canadian headline

---

54. Ibid., 19.

"Civilization Advances" announcing the beginning of the war. Might it also have re-directed Canadian missionary energies toward home missions where the growing number of the *Strangers within Our Gates* appeared to pose a national danger to the emergence of progressive New Christianity?

The British military failures also created a new urgency for military preparedness in Britain and the empire, focused on youth, discipline, patriotism, morality, and physical fitness, initiatives in which churches played a conspicuous role. But in other quarters, it rejuvenated a peace movement, opposed to the militarization of youth. The British-scorched earth policy, with its farm burning and concentration camps and the public exposure of their shocking death rates, had revealed the ugly face of imperialism, and given voice and courage to the silent and timid, and vindication to the unorganized but fearless war objectors.[55] Two eloquent Canadian pacifist leaders, J. S. Woodsworth[56] and Nellie McClung emerged from this period to provide pacifist leadership within their denomination. At the same time, the Women's Christian Temperance Union that had courageously advocated peace and arbitration in the early months of the war before it fell silent, re-affirmed its commitment to peace. One cannot quite divorce the founding of the Canadian Peace and Arbitration Society in 1905, so soon after the war, from the example of the Christian Socialists, the Quakers, Mennonites, Hutterites, and Doukhobors whose leadership and witness for peace shaped the early years of the organized peace movement in Canada. Our challenge is to place Canada's religious minorities within a more variegated, dynamic, mobile context, with all its cross-currents and ironies, especially during the fraught last half of the South African War.

BIBLIOGRAPHY

Primary Sources

Personal Papers

Amy Roddick Papers, McGill University
W. Bourke Cochran Papers, New York Public Library

Newspapers

Calgary Herald
Canadian Churchman

---

55. McClung, *The Stream Runs Fast*, 27.
56. MacInnis, *J. S. Woodsworth*, 100–101.

The Canadian Congregationalist
The Canadian Statesman
The Christian Guardian
Citizen and Country
The Globe, Toronto
The Globe
Methodist Reporter
Military Gazette
The Mitre
The (Montreal) Witness
Ottawa Journal
Presbyterian College Journal
Queen's Quarterly
Regina Standard
Sarnia Observer
The Standard
Vancouver Province
Victoria Colonist
The Western Methodist Reporter

Secondary Sources

Borthwick, J. Douglas. *Poems and Songs of the South African War*. Montreal: Gazette, 1901.

Bush, Julia. *Edwardian Ladies and Imperial Power*. Leicester: Leicester University Press, 2000.

Carman, Albert Richardson. *The Ethics of Imperialism*. Boston: Herbert B. Turner, 1905.

Cook, Tim. *Clio's Warriors Canadian Historians and the Writing of the World Wars*. Vancouver: University of British Columbia Press, 2006.

Dechêne, Louise. *Habitants et Marchands de Montréal au XVIIe Siècle*. Paris: Plon, 1974.

Evans, William Sanford. *The Canadian Contingents and Canadian Imperialism: A Story and a Study*. Toronto: Publishers Syndicate, 1901.

Gagnon, Jean-Pierre. *Le 22e Bataillon (Canadien-francais) 1914–1919: Étude Socio-Militaire*. Vol. 1. Québec: Presses de l'Universite Laval, 1986.

Gravel, Jean-Yves. *L'Armee au Quebec (1868–1900), Un Portrait Social*. Montreal: Boreal, 1974.

Heath, Gordon L. "Passion for Empire: War Poetry Published in the Canadian English Protestant Press during the South African War, 1899–1902." *Literature & Theology* 16 (2002) 127–47.

———. *A War with a Silver Lining: Canadian Protestant Churches and the South African War, 1899–1902*. Montreal: McGill-Queen's University Press, 2009.

Humphries, Charles W. "Two B. C. Pacifists and the Boer War." *BC Studies* 45 (1980) 116–27.

MacFarlane, John. "'Ready Aye Ready?' French Canadians and the South African War 1899–1902." Paper presented at the Annual Meeting of the Canadian Historical Association, Ottawa, Ontario, Canada, 1998.

MacInnis, Grace. *J. S. Woodsworth: A Man to Remember*. Toronto: MacMillian, 1953.

Magney, William H. "The Methodist Church and the National Gospel, 1884–1914." *The Bulletin* 20 (1968) 3–95.

Marquis, T. G. *Canada's Sons on Kopje and Veldt*. Toronto: Canada's Sons, 1900.

McClung, Nellie L. *The Stream Runs Fast*. Toronto: Thomas Allen, 1945.

Miller, Carman. *Canada's Little War Fighting for the British Empire in Southern Africa 1899-1902*. Toronto: Lorimer, 2003.

———. "English-Canadian Opposition to the South African War as Seen by the Press." *Canadian Historical Review* 55 (1974) 431–32.

———. *Painting the Map Red*. Montreal: McGill-Queens University Press, 1993.

———. "The Unhappy Warriors: Conflict and Nationality among Canadian Troops during the South African War." *The Journal of Imperial and Commonwealth History* 23 (1995) 77–104.

Moody, Barry. "Boers and Baptists: Maritime Canadians View the South African War." Paper presented at the conference on Canada and the Boer War, Institute for Commonwealth Studies, London, U.K., March 2000.

Ouellet, Fernand. *Histoire économique et Sociale du Québec 1760–1850*. Montreal: Fides, 1966.

Riley, Barbara, and Ed Dahl. "Militarism, Anti-militarism, Imperialism, the Idea of Progress and the Sense of Mission in the Methodist Magazine and Review around the Time of the Boer War." Seminar paper presented for History 533, Carleton University, Ottawa, ON, 1969.

Roberts, Charles G. D. *A Standard Dictionary of Canadian Biography: The Canadian Who Was Who*. Vol. 2. Toronto: Trans-Canada, 1934.

Sewell, William. *The Logic of History*. Chicago: University of Chicago Press, 2005.

3

Canada's Non-Francophone Catholics and the South African War, 1899–1902

MARK G. MCGOWAN

WHEN LONGSTANDING GRIEVANCES BETWEEN the British government and the two Dutch Boer Republics in South Africa turned to war, non-Francophone Catholics in Canada were divided in their responses. Differences in ethnicity, class, nationalism, political affiliations, and region of origin prompted a variety of responses to the declaration of the war and the eventual participation of Canadian volunteers who would serve with the empire's forces so far away from home. Contemporary observers themselves would be hard pressed to identify a "Catholic" position on the war, since even some of the most noted leaders, lay and clerical, differed publicly in their approach to the conflict. If one had only heard the remarks of Charles Fitzpatrick, a Quebec-born Catholic of Irish descent, and the Solicitor General in Wilfrid Laurier's federal cabinet, one might think Catholics would enthusiastically rally to the colors. At the outbreak of hostilities, he told an audience of Toronto Liberals, "Wheresoever the British subject goes he carries with him all that is right, the might and power of the British Empire."[1] Here for all to see was a prominent Catholic offering a passionate defense of Britain's military campaign in South Africa, implying that those who enjoy the rights and privileges of the empire better be prepared to do their duty and defend it.

---

1. *The Globe*, 10 November 1899.

One could be forgiven for confusion, however, if one tried to square Fitzpatrick's speech with Patrick F. Cronin's editorial comments in Toronto that same week. In the pages of the *Catholic Register*, one of Ontario's prominent Catholic weeklies, the Irish-born Cronin was critical of Fitzpatrick's mixture of jingoism and religion, which sounded to the editor suspiciously like the rhetoric of hawkish imperialists at Westminster and in Canada. In disgust, Cronin exclaimed that the empire was engaged in a needless war. He also derided local imperialists for enthusiasm akin to the Solicitor General: "[Sam Hughes is] the cheapest talker in Canada . . . He insists upon taking command himself and of course he knows that except from the idiot asylums of the land, he could never get a corporal's guard to follow him across a potato patch."[2] In 1899, at least in Toronto, there was no unifying Catholic position on the war.

The experience of the South African War provides an opportunity to investigate and rethink the development of non-Francophone Catholic communities in Canada and their relationship to the British Empire. Described by Carman Miller as the "most significant public event" to Canadians in the twentieth century until the Great War (1914–1918), one is certainly tempted to see how one of Canada's largest religious minority groups responded to events unfolding in the Cape Colony and the adjacent Boer republics.[3] For Canada's Irish, Scottish, English, and European Catholics, the pathway to embracing the war was a slow and circuitous one, strewn with caution and struggle over issues of communal and individual self-identification, particularly in terms of their relationship with their Francophone co-religionists in Quebec. In 1899, non-Francophone Catholics did not approach the war as a united group, nor did they speak as one body through a single bishop, politician, or newspaper. The non-Francophone Church was characterized by differences in regional concentrations, occupations, political affiliations, and ethnicity, which was of mostly Irish with identifiable Scottish, English, German, and tiny Italian and Polish minorities. Those Catholics lived ordinary lives that diverged little from the communities in which they lived from the bustle of Halifax to the ranches and farms of the Northwest Territories, soon to be new provinces. Given the diversity of the non-Francophone Catholic community, it should not be surprising that lay leaders, clerics, and the press offered inconsistent mes-

---

2. *The Catholic Register*, 20 July 1899. Criticism of Fitzpatrick came 10 November 1899.

3. Miller, *Painting the Map Red*, xi.

saging that varied in tone, overt professions of loyalty, and timely criticism of government actions, the Canadian and Imperial. Few bishops, technically the official leaders of the Catholic Church in Canada, offered little clarity or unanimous opinion regarding the Church's formal position on sending Canadian troops to South Africa, although the prelates never retreated from the salient principle that the Catholic Church in Canada was steadfastly loyal to the Crown.[4] Within this context of conflict or silence from Catholic leadership, it is quite clear that Catholic laymen, whether out of loyalty to the empire, a sense of adventure, or seeking a steady paycheck, enlisted in significant numbers to defend British interests in South Africa. By war's end, however, there was less inconsistency in the Church's position on the war as greater coherence appeared in non-Francophone Catholic public attitudes. While some editors might still have questioned the meaning and purpose of the war, Catholic pundits were unequivocal that they "supported the troops" and were steadfast in their loyalty. In fact, when the Great War began in 1914, some clergy would draw upon the Catholic engagement in the Boer conflict as testament to both patriotism and a precursor to the Church's support of the empire in this new crisis.

At the turn of the century, Irish Catholics were the dominant ethnic group in the Church, behind the Francophone Catholics.[5] Most Irish migration to Canada, a movement of well over 500,000 people, took place between 1815 and 1845.[6] The famous Famine Migration, from 1846 to 1851, was in reality an endpoint to mass Irish migration to Canada and really did not significantly disrupt the pre-existing Irish settlement grid.[7] Thus, many of the Irish Catholics in Canada by 1900 were of Irish descent not of Irish birth, a fact that would be confirmed by the records of those Catholic men who enlisted. The epicenters of Irish-Catholic settlement were Halifax and parts of Cape Breton Island in Nova Scotia; the city of Saint John and the Mirimichi valley in New Brunswick; the rural areas of Prince Edward Island; Montreal, Quebec City, Pontiac County, and the Eastern Townships, in Quebec; and southern Ontario's farmlands and principal cities—Toronto, Ottawa, Kingston, and Hamilton. As a recent study of Irish-Catholic Halifax has demonstrated, each of those Irish communities

---

4. McGowan, "Canadian Catholics."
5. Houston and Smyth, *Irish Emigration*, 338–40.
6. See McGowan "Irish Catholics"; Elliott, "Irish Protestants."
7. There were some local variations, where famine migrants were visibly more significant. See Grace, *The Irish*; Nicolson, "Irish Tridentine Catholicism."

had distinctive characteristics, often shaped by their relations with other linguistic and religious groups in the area, the time of their arrival, the occupational opportunities specific to their locale, and the extent to which they participated in local political structures.[8] Although as Catholics they shared a common religious bond and sense of Irish roots, the levels of a feeling of "Irishness" often varied and could be more pronounced in places like Montreal or Ottawa, where Irish Catholics faced a "double minority" status—a linguistic minority among their French-speaking coreligionists and a religious minority within the local Anglo-Protestant community.[9] In 1900, no one region in Canada was representative of the life of all Irish Catholics, although the wars of the early twentieth century would expose their common commitment and loyalty to Canada and the empire.

It is estimated that at the turn of the twentieth century, there were over one-half million (580,229) non-French-speaking Catholics in Canada's provinces and territories, comprising just over 10 percent of Canada's people.[10] The Irish Catholic majority may have numbered as many as 480,000 nationally.[11] Within the non-Francophone Catholic group, the Irish were joined by clusters of Scottish Highlanders in Cape Breton, eastern Nova Scotia, Prince Edward Island, and the townships of Glengarry, Stormont, Lanark, and Dundas in eastern Ontario. Scottish Catholics, who in Scotland only account for one-ninth of the population, were disproportionally represented among the Scots migrants to British North America in the nineteenth century.[12] Many of the Catholic Scots who had migrated to Nova Scotia and Prince Edward Island in the late eighteenth and early nineteenth centuries had been forced to leave their tenancies during the highland clearances, had departed Scotland for better economic opportunities for their families, or had been involved in relocation schemes sponsored by Catholic clergy. Such

---

8. McGowan and Vance, *Irish Catholic Halifax*.

9. Moir, "The Problem of a Double Minority."

10. Estimates are based on *Fourth Census of Canada, 1901*, tables I, IX, X, XIX, and XI. See also Perin, *Rome in Canada*, 11–38.

11. "Population," *Fourth Census of Canada, 1901*, vol. 1. Numbers based on the total Catholic population 2,229,600 in Canada. Subtract French Canadians (1,649,371), Italians (10,834), Belgians (2,994), 25 percent of Germans in Waterloo (7,500), 66 percent of Austrians (12,000), PEI Scots (15,965), Glengarry Scots (5,075), and Eastern Nova Scotian Scots (44,742) for a rough estimate of the Irish Catholics. The estimate is approximate.

12. Bumsted, "Scottish Catholicism in Canada"; MacLean, "The Highland Catholic Tradition"; Hornsby, "Patterns of Scottish Immigration."

was the case in 1790, when eighty-six Catholic families from the Arisaig region boarded two ships bound for Prince Edward Island.[13] In central British North America there were other prospective Scots Catholic migrants who participated in military resettlement in available lands in the colonies. Loyalist refugees from the American Revolution also contained clusters of Catholic Scots. In the wake of the rebellion in Ireland, in 1798, the Glengarry Fencibles, and their chaplain (later bishop), Alexander Macdonell, assumed titles to land in the Ontario county that still bears their name.[14] With such a military pedigree, it was not surprising to find many Canadian-born Scots Catholics within the Canadian recruits for South Africa.

Although the Irish and Scots dominated clerical and lay leadership in the non-Francophone Catholic community in Canada, there were other small minorities including Catholics of English descent, Americans of a variety of backgrounds, and English-speaking converts from Protestantism. Non-Anglophones included German-speaking Catholic settlers who arrived in Upper Canada in the 1850s, especially in Waterloo and Bruce counties, Poles from the Kaszub region of the Baltic who settled in the upper Ottawa Valley in the 1870s, and single Italian men and some families who began arriving as sojourners and settlers in Toronto, Montreal, Hamilton, and Sydney as early as the 1890s.[15] The non-Francophone Catholics were rounded out by the presence of First Nations Peoples whose contact with Catholic missionaries dated back to French missionaries in the seventeenth century. These Ojibwa, Algonquin, Cree, Mohawk, and Odawa communities, living both on reserves and in unceded territory, were served primarily by members of the Society of Jesus (Jesuits) and the Oblates of Mary Immaculate. One common practice shared by many of the non-Francophone Catholics was their strong rates of regular church attendance, ranging from 73 percent in Charlotte County, New Brunswick, to 85 percent in Halifax, to allegedly 99 percent in Hamilton, Ontario.[16] Religion mattered to them, and the Church was a community hub where clerical leadership was respected.

13. SCA, University of Aberdeen, Oban Letters, OL/1/1/3, List of Emigrants from Highlands to Island St. John [PEI], 1790; OL1/3/16, Reverend A. Scott, Glasgow, to John MacDonald, Glenaladale, 17 August 1826.

14. McLean, "Peopling Glengarry County"; McLean, *The People of Glengarry*; Rea, *Bishop Alexander Macdonell*.

15. Zurakowska, *A Concise Guide*; McGowan, "Roman Catholics," 49, 56–57; Zucchi, *The Italians of Toronto*.

16. "Churches and Sunday Schools for Canada and the Provinces." *Fourth Census of Canada, 1901*, vol. 4, table XIX. Calculations are based on these figures of actual

Although the non-Francophone Catholic Church in Canada was diverse, the inescapable fact by 1900 was that the Irish majority were ascendant and, in most regions, dominant, in the Church. Irish Catholics could be found in all twenty-seven Canadian dioceses and vicariates apostolic, although those Catholics living in Ontario and the Maritime provinces would be the only ones administered by bishops of either Scottish or Irish descent.[17] West of the Manitoba-Ontario boundary, Irish Catholics were a very tiny minority, but this did not arrest their aspirations to control the Church in an effort to assure the French-Canadian Catholic influence that was contained outside of Quebec. The Irish and their Anglophone Scots colleagues would spend much of the early twentieth century solidifying their control of the Episcopal sees in the Prairies and British Columbia.[18] In this effort, Celtic Catholics were assisted by several Apostolic Delegates (Papal representatives in Canada), who believed that the future of the Church in North America was tied to the fortunes of the English language.[19] Battles within the Catholic leadership, between Francophones and Anglophones, over such issues as the allegiance of new Canadians in the Church, the language of separate publicly-funded Catholic schools, and the control of Catholic diocesan sees would create a cultural wedge in the Canadian Church, a side effect of which would be a strengthening of solidarity between Scots and Irish Catholics on a variety of political and social issues. The linguistic divide would be deepened within the Church as a result of the imperial wars of the twentieth century, when Francophone Catholics would show less interest, and even resistance, to the fight against the Boers and, later, to the struggle against Germany and its allies after 1914.

The weekly newspapers and literature generated in centers of Catholic settlement were dominated by Irish editors, by birth or descent, who, through their columns and news stories, reflected Catholic communities that appeared to be in a transitional period when the Boer War erupted. Political rhetoric, speeches by community leaders, and editorials in Catholic periodicals suggest that many Catholic readers in Canada were still concerned about politics in Ireland, particularly the century-old struggle for Home Rule, by means of the restoration of an Irish provincial parliament

---

participation when compared to basic rates of profession in the same census. See also McGowan, "Irish Catholics," 751.

17. McGowan, "Rethinking Catholic-Protestant Relations," 11–32.
18. Huel, "The Irish–French Conflict"; McGowan, "The Tales and Trials."
19. Fiorino, "The Nomination of Bishop Fallon."

in Dublin, autonomous from Westminster. Interestingly, Irish Canadian Catholic advocacy for Irish Home Rule prompted a greater process of reflection upon the nature and current state of Canadian governance and democratic institutions, which in turn, prompted Irish Catholic expressions of a profoundly deep attachment to the Dominion's semi-autonomous status within the British Empire. Canada's English-language weekly Catholics papers reflected a belief that Ireland ought to enjoy Canadian-style responsible self-government.[20]

Not surprisingly such comparisons were evident as Irish Catholic leaders expressed their affection for Canada, their thanksgiving for the rights enjoyed by Catholics in Canada, their appreciation of a neutral Crown, and their commitment to Canada's responsibilities within the empire.[21] In 1898, London's *Catholic Record*, which had a national circulation of 9,000,[22] called upon English-speaking Catholics to be active in the exercise of their patriotic duties:

> Every Catholic, we think should take practical interest in live questions—that is questions which concern them temporally, or spiritually . . . We do not insinuate for one instant that our taking part in public questions should make us aggressive in a way that would be calculated to arouse the enmity of our separated brethren . . . We should take our stand as Canadians interested in the welfare and progress of our country. It might get us out of the rut or the "don't care" habit, and might also convince us that we are not serfs but citizens.[23]

In a similar spirit, as early as 1896, *Walsh's Magazine* discussed the empire's involvement in South Africa, singling out Cecil Rhodes as "the greatest among energetic figures."[24] Membership in the empire was a topic of discussion and one that raised serious questions of Canada's responsibilities, military and otherwise. As the aforementioned joust between Fitzpatrick and the *Catholic*

---

20. Mannion, "'Halifax Catholic.'"

21. Some sources for this include McGowan, *The Waning of the Green*, 184–217; Shanahan, "The Irish Question"; Lyne, "Irish-Canadian Financial Contributions"; Horrall, "Canada and the Irish Question."

22. *McKim's Directory of Canadian Publications*, 1899.

23. *The Catholic Record*, 29 October 1898. Similarly, see Fitzpatrick's speech in *The Catholic Record*, 25 March 1899; *The Catholic Register*, 13 May 1897; Harris, "Our Own Land."

24. *Walsh's Magazine*, 2 April 1896, 5.

Register suggests, however, Catholics were still not of one mind on the "imperial question," when war actually erupted in South Africa.

One might expect that, given the hierarchical structure of the Catholic Church, the bishops of English Canada might have offered public comment, either negative or positive, on Catholic participation in the war. Given their outspoken positions on such political and religious issues as denominational schools in the Prairie West, the Manitoba Schools Question, the Jesuits Estates controversy in Quebec, Home Rule in Ireland, and the anti-Catholic elements within the Coronation Oath, few bishops made public statements concerning British activities in South Africa, the recruitment of a Canadian contingent, or the linguistic and cultural politics at play in Prime Minister Laurier's policies emanating from Ottawa. In 1900, when Canada's bishops reported to Rome on the nature of Protestant–Catholic relations in Canada, none mentioned the war as a factor in creating heightened sectarian tension. In fact, the bishops of the Maritimes and eastern Ontario reported peaceful relations between Protestants and Catholics, while the prelates of southwestern Ontario argued that there was more to fear in terms of subtle Protestant proselytization through private friendly relations between Protestants and Catholics than from public demonstrations or by overt discrimination by governments or the Protestant population at large.[25]

Such a muted hierarchy may be explained in part by the fact that, between 1899 and 1902, the non-Francophone Catholic hierarchy itself was in a time of transition. Bishops in a position to wave the flag or condemn the British war effort were hamstrung by a number of other considerations. Many bishops were young, inexperienced, and overly cautious about entering the public square with their guns blazing. Suffragan bishops and auxiliary bishops rarely took the lead in public debates without testing the waters first with their Archbishop. In the case of Ontario, Denis O'Connor, appointed Archbishop of Toronto in 1899, rarely made public appearances and eschewed any relations with politicians, although he was considered by

---

25. ASV-DAC, vol. 157.37, Archbishop Cornelius O'Brien of Halifax to Diomede Falconio, Apostolic Delegate, 29 November 1900; Bishop John Cameron of Antigonish to Falconio, 15 January 1901; Bishop James MacDonald of Charlottetown to Falconio, 19 November 1900; Bishop Thomas Barry, coadjutor Bishop of Chatham to Falconio, 5 December 1900; Bishop Alexander Macdonell of Alexandria to Falconio, 21 January 1901; Archbishop Charles Hugh Gauthier of Kingston to Falconio, 12 December 1900; Bishop Richard O'Connor of Peterborough to Falconio, n.d.; more anxious were Bishop Fergus McEvay of London to Falconio, 19 November 1900; Archbishop Denis O'Connor to Falconio, 20 November 1900; and Bishop Thomas J. Dowling to Falconio, 8 December 1900.

many to have Liberal-Conservative (Tory) political sympathies.[26] It is not surprising then that O'Connor's suffragan bishops in Hamilton and London, the latter of whom was newly appointed Fergus McEvay, balked at any public comment on political matters not directly related to the Church. Ontario's other metropolitan, Archbishop Charles Hugh Gauthier of Kingston, who was less than a year in his position when the war erupted, preferred private negotiations and deal making to public interventions on matters that did not relate directly to the faith or Catholic moral life.[27] For many in the episcopacy, if a political issue did not offend the faith and morals of the Church, silence was to be interpreted as consent.

Some bishops, however, possessed a high public profile and a personality suited to political engagement. This certainly appears to be the case in Halifax, Nova Scotia, where the metropolitan, the Prince Edward Island-born Archbishop Cornelius O'Brien, was a noted Tory and a member of the Imperial Federation League.[28] Even if O'Brien's suffragan bishops in New Brunswick, Antigonish, and Prince Edward Island, had opposed the war effort privately, which in a few cases seemed unlikely given their political sympathies, they would have not been prepared to cross O'Brien, who took an active interest in all his suffragan dioceses.[29] Soon after the outbreak of hostilities in South Africa, O'Brien issued a pastoral letter stating clearly his support for the "noble and just" imperial war effort.[30] His suffragans were publicly silent in their support or opposition for O'Brien's statement. Bishop John Sweeny of Saint John and James Rogers of Chatham were both elderly and inactive by 1899 and, their auxiliaries, given the nature of their subordinate positions, would not make public interventions of a political nature unless directly relevant to the life of the local Church. In another case, Bishop John Cameron of Antigonish was reticent to enter the political arena given the fact that Rome had severely reprimanded him for his

---

26. McGowan, *The Waning of the Green*, 63–66. NA, Laurier Papers, reel 815, 89419, Charles Fitzpatrick to Laurier, 7 September 1904.

27. Stortz, "Thomas Joseph Dowling," 100–102.

28. Burke, "The Irishman's Place," 230; Hughes, *Archbishop O'Brien*, 169, 172, 210; *Halifax Herald*, 10 March 1906.

29. ADC, Bishop James Charles MacDonald Papers, box 5, MacDonald to Cornelius O'Brien, 19 July 1901; MacDonald to Diomede Falconio, 31 August 1901; Stanley, "James Rogers," 893.

30. *Le Soleil*, 13 November 1899. O'Brien was in the public eye numerous times in the autumn of 1899, including the highly successful consecration of the new St. Mary's Cathedral in Halifax. See *Morning Chronicle*, 20 October 1899.

partisan involvement on behalf of the Liberal-Conservative Party in the election of 1896.[31]

Curiously, two French-Canadian archbishops, Joseph-Thomas Duhamel of Ottawa, and Louis Nazaire Bégin of Quebec City, who was also Primate of Canada, publicly endorsed the war effort in late 1899.[32] Likewise Archbishop Paul Bruchési of Montreal, in his New Year's Eve address, regretted that the year 1900 could not begin in peace, but he hoped for a speedy end to the war, "with the triumph of our great country."[33] Clearly, these public statements came at a time when Canadians were already actively engaged on the veldt and in the wake of "Black Week," when the British forces had suffered several setbacks at the hands of the Boers. Despite the large number of non-Francophone Catholics, primarily Irish, in each diocese, the Francophone archbishops' action appeared to be motivated more out of concern for the French-Canadian Catholic majority. Opposition to the war within the Liberal caucus, including public dissent by members Dominique Monet, Henri Bourassa, and Laurier stalwart, Joseph-Israel Tarte, in addition to anti-war sentiment in the French Canadian daily press, put the Church in an awkward position.[34] Since 1775, French-Canadian bishops had been visibly loyal to British Crown in time of war.[35] The angry reaction of many Anglo-Canadians to Bourassa and his colleagues necessitated that the Church in Quebec take a clear stand on the war and assert its loyalty. By contrast, there appeared to be no urgency stemming from charges of disloyalty to prompt prelates of Irish or Scottish descent to do the same.

Not necessarily constricted by the canons and protocols of episcopal office, many Catholic laypersons and some priests of Irish descent were less constrained in their support or opposition to the war. As has been noted, Laurier's Solicitor-General, the Honorable Charles Fitzpatrick, became an outspoken advocate of Canadian participation in the pacification of the Boer republics. Fitzpatrick had solid credentials both nationally and in Quebec; in 1885, he had been one of Louis Riel's counsels, and as an MP had worked hard to secure economic development in Quebec City. While

---

31. Perin, *Rome in Canada*, 65; LAC, Sir Wilfrid Laurier Papers, V, II, Pastoral, 20 June 1896, 4359; ASV-DAC, 13.0, "Antigonish"; MacLean, *Bishop John Cameron*, 152.

32 . Miller, *Painting the Map Red*, 155.

33. *The Catholic Register*, 4 January 1900; "Circulaire de Mgr L'Archeveque de Montreal au Clergé de son Diocese," 276–80.

34. Miller, *Painting the Map Red*, 154–55; Page, *The Boer War*, 16–19.

35. Moir, *Church and State*, 104–6.

respectful of the right of some of his French-Canadian Liberal colleagues' dissent from his position, Fitzpatrick nonetheless boldly laid out his reasons for his support in public addresses and in the House of Commons, condemning Boer injustices against British citizens in South Africa, and hinting that fulfilling one's imperial responsibilities would send a powerful message to Britain's European rivals:

> I say that the time had come, not only because of what was going on in South Africa . . . but because of mutterings on the continent for British subjects the world over to prove once and for all that the British Empire is no mere geographical expression for a number of sundered and disunited provinces—the time had come when it was necessary for the whelps of the lion to rally to the defence of the old land. The time had come when every man must be made to understand whether on the European continent or in South Africa, that blow for blow whensoever the blow might come, must be struck back by the British, and would be struck as freely from Australasia and Canada as from the heart of the Empire itself.[36]

No doubt Fitzpatrick may have been applauded by fellow jurist, William Wilfred Sullivan, Chief Justice of Prince Edward Island, who cheered the departure of Islanders in 1899, as they sailed off to do their duty for "the Great motherland,"[37] or by Senator Lawrence Geoffrey Power of Nova Scotia who, as early as October 1899, publicly endorsed the sending of a second contingent.[38]

Power's elder Irish Catholic colleague in the Senate, Sir Richard Scott, was not so ardent. A veteran legislator, who cut his political teeth in the bitter sectarian atmosphere of Canada in the 1850s and 1860s, Scott saw Canadian participation in South Africa as part of some jingoistic conspiracy hatched by Joseph Chamberlin and his Canadian supporters. As Laurier's Secretary of State, Scott jousted with Sir Edward Thomas Henry Hutton, the General Office in Charge of the Canadian Militia, over the latter's misplaced belief that he was to serve the British Government first and the Canadian second. While never as outspoken publicly in his views as was Fitzpatrick—certainly in deference to Laurier—Scott remained suspicious

---

36. *Hansard*, 63–64; Victoria, 20 February 1900, 668–69.

37. *The Morning Guardian* (Charlottetown), 24 October 1899. See Sullivan's obvious Tory connections in Morgan, "William Wilfred Sullivan," 985.

38. *Halifax Herald*, 2 November 1899.

of Canadian participation in the imperialist adventure.[39] Scott's attempt to secure a pro-Boer resolution from the Irish Literary Society of Ottawa was defeated, indicating that not all of the veteran statesman's colleagues shared his views, and underscoring clearly the lack of an Irish-Catholic consensus in the initial stages of the Boer War.[40]

Although Scott appeared atypical in his opinions, he was by no means an isolated "Irish" voice. There are fragments of evidence suggesting that other Irish Catholics suspected imperialist conspiracies or voiced outright opposition to British policies. There was at least one report of a pro-Boer resolution passed by the Ancient Order of Hibernians in Montreal,[41] although this action appeared uncharacteristic of the behavior of Catholic associations across the country.[42] There is no evidence to suggest that other branches of the AOH echoed the anti-Britishness of the Montreal group, nor did the larger Catholic men's associations—Catholic Mutual Benefit Association, St. Patrick's Society, Young Irishman's Literary and Benefit Society, Holy Name Society, and Knights of Columbus—make any significant public statements for or against the war effort. Young Catholic men of Irish and Scottish descent were prominent in militia units which were endorsed or financially supported by Catholic organizations, the most notable being the support given to the 63rd Halifax Rifles by the Charitable Irish Society of Halifax.[43] The behavior of the Montreal branch of the AOH, however, does confirm the presence of an ultra-Irishness among some Irish Catholics in Montreal, a city in which Irish Catholics were, religiously and linguistically, a double minority and tended to wear their Irishness as a principal badge of identity. As had been the case in the early nineteenth century, this double minority status made its imprint on recent Irish Catholic immigrants drawn to Montreal's buoyant economy, and, as a result, several vociferous Irish nationalist factions emerged in Montreal's Anglophone parishes. Nevertheless, even within Montreal's Irish Catholic community, there were variances in opinion. Prominent Irish Catholic judge, scion of the St. Patrick's Society, and future federal Minister of Justice (1911–1921),

---

39. Scott, "Sir Richard Scott," 59; Clarke, "Sir Richard Scott," 915.

40. Miller, *Painting the Map Red*, 24.

41. Ibid.

42. Miller, "English-Canadian Opposition," 435. AOH branches in Moncton and Saint John repudiated the action of the Montreal branch. See *St. John Globe*, 16 October 1899.

43. Crooks, "The Quest for Respectability."

Charles J. Doherty, continued to serve as honorary patron and officer of the 65th Mount Royal Rifles, a unit in which he served as a captain with other Irish and French Catholics during the Riel Rebellion of 1865.[44] Such contrasting attitudes towards the empire's wars make even clearer that neither Montreal, nor Toronto, nor Halifax for that matter, epitomized a common Irish Catholic engagement with imperialism for all of Canada.

The mixed reaction of Catholic lay leaders to the Boer conflict was also evident in the largest of Canada's English-language Catholic weekly newspapers—the London *Catholic Record*, and Toronto's *Catholic Register*, which had a national readership, and New Brunswick's *The Freeman* and Nova Scotia's *The Casket*, two weeklies that served regional subscribers. In the Fall of 1899, no English-language Catholic weekly in Canada offered a ringing endorsement of imperial policy in South Africa or supported unconditionally the sending of Canadian troops. In fact, it was reported that the small *Canadian Freeman* of Kingston, Ontario, a paper sometimes at odds with the local bishop, was openly hostile to British actions against the Boer republics.[45] Several papers even expressed a grudging admiration for the rugged Boer farmers and their considerable ability to carve a homeland for themselves in the African interior.[46]

Patrick Cronin, the Irish-born editor of the *Catholic Register* was suspicious that this was an unnecessary military action hatched by Joseph Chamberlain and Canadian "jingos." Most disturbing to the Toronto Catholic weekly was the fact that Parliament had not been called to decide upon the participation of a Canadian Contingent. "There is a deeper Canadian loyalty than assuming the bloody shirt of the jingo and yelling for imperialism," wrote Cronin, "the men who ignore our institutions of responsible government are necessarily the disloyal ones, if there be any disloyal ones among us."[47] As noted earlier, in addition to being critical of Laurier for circumventing Parliament on the question, the *Register* did not spare its barbs for either Charles Fitzpatrick or Father Francis Ryan, rector of St. Michael's Cathedral in Toronto, both of whom had offered enthusiastic support for British war effort and the recruitment of Canadian Contingent, justifying

---

44. LAC, MG 27 II D-6 I, Fonds Charles J. Doherty, vol. 1, biography file, 1–2; vol. 2, Nominal Roll of No. 7 Company of the 65th Battalion, "Fort Saskatchewan," May 1885.

45. Ibid.; NA, Laurier Papers, vol. 33, John F. Coffey to Laurier, 14 January 1897, 11015–11016.

46. *The Catholic Register*, 24 August 1899.

47. *The Catholic Register*, 19 and 26 October 1899, 28 December 1899.

their positions by claims that the Boers had trampled on the civil rights of British subjects and upon the religious rights of Catholics in Transvaal and the Orange Free State.[48] Cronin eschewed any connection between jingoism and Catholicism, and went so far as to support Henri Bourassa's position that Parliament should decide.[49]

While expressing misgivings about military action against the Boers, Thomas Coffey, editor of the *Catholic Record* was far more guarded in his criticism of Laurier. The paper had traditionally been sympathetic to the Liberal Party, and Coffey had been instrumental in recent efforts to rally Ontario's Irish Catholics to the Liberal Party banner.[50] Coffey was put in the dangerous position of criticizing the most vociferous advocates of Canadian intervention, while avoiding anything that smacked of overt criticism of the Laurier Government and such ministers of the crown as Fitzpatrick. Even Chamberlain was given the benefit of the doubt as the *Record* described his actions more as losing high stakes "international poker" with Kruger, as opposed to being at the heart of an imperialist conspiracy. While Coffey labeled the Boers as "unprogressive" and "intolerant" of Catholics in South Africa,[51] he also displayed admiration for the "stubborn pluck and unquestionable courage" of Britain's foe in the Transvaal.[52] Nevertheless, the paper stood by earlier claims that "Loyalty is better proved by acts than words," and so in times of emergency Catholics could be counted upon to rally to the defense of the empire.[53]

The *Casket*, a weekly serving the Scots and Irish Catholics of Nova Scotia, disagreed. Michael Donovan, the paper's editor, was a Nova Scotian of Irish decent. He had been at the helm of the *Casket* since 1889, and had been described by local Bishop John Cameron as a man of Liberal-Conservative Party sympathies, but who was determined to maintain a policy of

---

48. The issue of Boer anti-Catholicism was frequently mentioned in Catholic newspapers. See *Catholic Register*, 17 and 24 August 1900, 10 November 1900, 14 December 1899, 11, 18, and 25 January 1900, 1 February 1900.

49. *Register*, 26 October 1899.

50. LAC, Laurier Papers, vol. 33, John Coffey to Laurier, 14 January 1897, 11015–11016; reel 760, Thomas Coffey to Laurier, 5 October 1898; reel 781, Thomas Coffey to Laurier, 5 December 1900, 51451–51453.

51. *The Morning Guardian* (Charlottetown), 28 August 1899, 31 October 1899; *The Casket*, 10 August 1899; *The Catholic Register*, 14 December 1899.

52. *Catholic Record*, 25 November 1899.

53. *Catholic Record*, 9 April 1898.

strict neutrality regarding party politics.⁵⁴ The *Casket* shared the *Register's* suspicion of Joseph Chamberlain and the imperialist lobby and regarded the war as needless. Donovan was careful to point out that Britain's claims on the Boer Republics were dubious under the international agreements, and that any difficulties between Britishers and Boers could have been worked out without bloodshed.⁵⁵ Several readers objected to his editorials and, in a gesture of fairness and in keeping with the "non-partisan stance" of the paper, Donovan printed critiques of his editorials. Some readers thought it in poor taste for the paper to withhold support for the war effort, while others were concerned about the Boer treatment of Catholics.⁵⁶ Donovan, however, refused to endorse the British position in 1899, although he was equally adamant that he had no "favor" with Kruger and the Boers.⁵⁷ Donovan bristled at the suggestion that his paper was anti-British; in his eyes, the *Casket* had only doubted the claims of justly defending the political rights of Uitlanders, suggesting the war was merely another of Cecil Rhodes "money-grabbing" schemes and contrary to the principles of the empire.⁵⁸

If one were to limit oneself to just this snapshot of several Catholic weeklies in 1899, Canadian Irish-Catholic opinion on the war could be characterized in several ways: restrained support, hostility, suspicion, or ambiguity. Over time, however, the press slowly reversed its initial impressions on Canadian participation in the war, offering glowing tributes to Canada's troops which became more enthusiastic as the imperial forces gained the upper hand. The *Record,* tied as it was to Laurier, continually defended the principle of a Canadian voluntary force and even defended the confiscations of Boer property by British troops.⁵⁹ The *Register's* conversion to an open support of the war effort came by 21 December 1899 and became more clearly supportive in January 1900. Cronin and his staff became increasingly concerned that the war might drive a wedge between the French and English population of the country.⁶⁰ As had been the case

54. LAC, Sir John Thompson Papers, vol. 207, John Cameron to Thompson, 10 October 1889, 10486.

55. *The Casket*, 10 August 1899.

56. *The Casket*, 31 August 1899; "Sacerdos," *The Casket*, 26 October 1899, 2 and 26 November 1899, 14 December 1899.

57. *The Casket*, 10 August 1899, 14 September 1899.

58. *The Casket*, 19 and 26 October 1899, 21 December 1899.

59. *Catholic Record*, 18 and 25 November 1899, 16 December 1899, 24 March 1900, 29 September 1900, 9 February 1901.

60. *Catholic Register*, 21 December 1899.

in the immediate past and would be the case in the next thirty years, Irish Catholics, torn by competing linguistic, religious, and cultural affiliations, feared being caught in the crossfire between Canada's two cultural solitudes. The *Register* urged peace between the "races," asking editors on both sides of the war, whether English or French, question that they had a "duty to Canada, and to Canadian people as a whole . . . To go to stir up strife and racial differences, or hatred in a country where so many nationalities have to live together and work out their joint destiny does seem to us to be an overwise [sic] policy."[61] The transformation of the *Register* came in the wake of "Black Week," a series of embarrassing military setbacks to the Boers—when any further criticism of the British effort might appear to more ardent imperialists as an expression of grave disloyalty in Britain's time of need. Likewise, the *Casket*, reiterated its loyalty and eventually softened its stand, offering plenty of war news by 1900, and followed the actions of the Canadian contingent with some measure of pride.[62]

It is within this context that the comments of the *Freeman* of Saint John New Brunswick are best understood. Re-established in January 1900, bearing the same masthead as the nineteenth-century journal of politician and journalist Timothy Warren Anglin, the *Freeman* intended to serve the large Irish-Catholic population of Saint John, the Fundy shore, and the Mirimichi Valley in the northeastern portion of the province. Under its new editor, William K. Reynolds, the resurrected weekly completely endorsed the war effort, repeating the claims of Boer oppression and anti-Catholicism, offering profiles of local Catholic heroes, giving laud to Archbishop Cornelius O'Brien and his imperialist affiliations, and suggesting that the port of Saint John should be more aggressive in its participation as a transportation center for the war, lest Halifax monopolize the provisioning and outfitting of Canadian troop ships.[63] Reynold's staff kept local Catholics well informed about the recruitment and deployment of New Brunswick's Catholic volunteers; in the case of Harry Phillips, a local member of the Division No. 1 AOH, the paper reported his enthusiastic "send off," adding "He goes to join the 8,000 Irish Catholic soldiers who are fighting under the British flag in

---

61. Ibid.

62. *The Casket*, 2 November 1899; *The Casket*, 25 January 1900, 15 and 22 February 1900, 24 May 1900, 12 July 1900, 17 May 1901, 24 October 1901. See MacLean, *Casket*, 102.

63. *The Freeman*, 6, 13, and 27 January 1900, 3 February 1900, and 2 June 1900.

South Africa."[64] There was little doubt as to the "imperial" sympathies of the *Freeman*, when, upon Queen Victoria's death, the front page headline boldly proclaimed above her photo, "Demise of England's Greatest Constitutional Ruler, Her Gracious Majesty Queen Victoria."[65]

Perhaps the engagement of Canadian troops forced the hands of the Catholic weeklies, who in no way wanted to appear disloyal to the Canadians laying their lives on the line in South Africa. After 1900, and significantly after the Canadian heroics at Paardeberg, the *Catholic Register*, *Casket*, and *Record* joined the *Freeman* as enthusiastic boosters of the Canadian effort, highlighting in particular the role of Catholic heroes, such as Archibald H. Macdonell, J. H. Elmsley, James C. Mason,[66] and the courageous and much respected Quebec City priest, Father Peter O'Leary, a Catholic chaplain serving with the Canadian Contingent.[67] Those men were promoted as examples of Catholic manhood and symbols of Catholic loyalty. The *Register* was quick to remind its detractors that its initial criticism of the Canadian war effort was based upon Laurier's circumvention of Parliament, and was not to be interpreted as an expression of disloyalty to the nation or the empire.[68] All Catholic weeklies covered the war extensively until the end of the principal engagements concluding with the capture of Pretoria, expressing all the while a loyalty based on balancing imperial needs with respect for Canada's Parliamentary institutions. This was a war, commented one editor, in which Canada, "did herself proud."[69]

As to what effect the journals had on forming the minds of their English-speaking Catholic readers, or how they reflected the views of their readers, is difficult to determine. One way of measuring the response of ordinary rank-and-file Catholics to the South African War is to examine

64. *The Freeman*, 10 March 1900 (Patrick McCreary), 17 March 1900 (Phillips), 7 April 1900 (case of John M. Dermott).

65. *Freeman*, 20 January 1901.

66. Mason's letters home were reprinted in the *The Catholic Register*, 8 February 1900, and 15 February 1900. The Register contained regular features on war news, Canadian troop movements, and British military advances. See *The Catholic Register*, 11 and 18 January 1900, 1, 8, 15, and 22 February 1900, 22 March 1900, 10 May 1900.

67. *The Catholic Register*, 14 December 1899. A very proud rendition of the return of the second contingent can be found in *The Catholic Register*, 3 January 1901. See also *The Catholic Register*, 3 October 1901. On O'Leary, see the *The Catholic Register*, 12 April 1900; and Crerar, *Padres in No Man's Land*, 20–21. O'Leary was highlighted in *Le Soleil* as early as 2 November 1899 and *The Freeman*, 28 July 1900.

68. *The Catholic Register*, 28 December 1899.

69. *The Catholic Register*, 3 January 1901.

the rate of non-Francophone Catholic recruitment and the characteristics of the recruits themselves. Carman Miller has analyzed the files of 5,825 volunteers, and has created a formidable statistical context within which the participation of non-Francophone Catholics can be measured.[70] In aggregate terms, Miller's analysis reveals that approximately 12.2 percent of the Contingents was Roman Catholic. When one subtracts from this figure the roughly 3 percent of soldiers who were French Canadian, it leaves a non-French-speaking Catholic total of roughly 9.2 percent of the entire contingent, or perhaps as many as 536 men among those whose files have been preserved. These numbers suggest that the proportion of English-speaking Catholics in khaki, mostly of Irish, Scottish, English descent, were well represented in the South African contingents, although slightly lower than their roughly 10.7 percent share of the entire Canadian population, as was the case with several rival Christian denominations.[71] The analysis in this study is based on a sample of 264 of these men (randomly extracted from 2,496 scanned files), or almost half (49.1 percent) of the non-Francophone Catholic recruits.[72] For the purposes of this study, the data set has been divided into Irish, Scots, English, and other categories based on their attestation papers and, where applicable, the Dominion Census of 1901.

The data set of 264 is a substantial sampling of the non-Francophone Catholic recruits. Table 1 makes clear that Irish Catholics dominated this Catholic portion of the South African Contingent, which was characteristic of the Irish dominance nationwide among the non-Francophone Catholic group. It should be noted that, while Scots and English Catholics constituted roughly one quarter of the sample, this proportion was higher than their estimated share of the non-Francophone Catholic population across Canada. Donald Akenson suggests (speculatively, by his own admission) that Scots Catholics may have only constituted 3 percent of the Catholic population

---

70. Miller, "A Preliminary Analysis."

71. Derived from the appendices in McGowan, "Rethinking Catholic-Protestant Relations"; and *Census of Canada, 1901*.

72. The names were selected from thirteen reels of microfilm in the RG 38 series (reels T2069, 2079, 2080–2084) found in Library and Archives Canada. In total, the files of 264 non-francophone Catholics were discovered among the 2496 files scanned. The sample was analyzed by surname, given name, religion, place of birth, address, and next of kin to determine Irish origin. Of the 264, 192 (72.7 percent) were Irish, 47 (17.8 percent) were Scots, 18 (6.8 percent) were English, and 7 (2.7 percent) were other/unknown. Surnames were verified by use of Hanks and Hodges, *A Dictionary of Surnames*; Woulfe, *Irish Names and Surnames*; Whyte, *A Dictionary of Scottish Immigrants*; Glazier, *The Famine Immigrants*; Matheson, *Special Report on Surnames*; and *Census of Canada, 1901*.

of Ontario.[73] Even accounting for the deduction of Francophone Catholics from the total Catholic population, and allowing for the presence of large numbers of Scots Catholics from Prince Edward Island and Nova Scotia, the proportion of Scots Catholics in the current South African Contingent data set appears to be high. There is no simple explanation for this other than the strong military traditions within the Scots Catholic community, dating to the days of the Glengarry Fencibles, and perhaps, the strong representation of Scots in the sample from both eastern Ontario and the Maritimes. It should be noted that the only other group represented in the data set, outside of British and Irish Catholics, were three Catholics of German descent. Two of these Germans had previous military or policing experience, which may explain their interest in volunteering for the South African mission. Alvin Schwartz, for example, was a native of the German Catholic community in Neustadt in southwestern Ontario, and he had served two years in the 30th Regiment. He volunteered for the 6th Canadian Mounted Rifles in 1902. Fellow German Edward Reichert had been born in Manheim, Baden, Germany, and at the time of his recruitment to the Canadian Mounted Rifles, in 1900, he had been serving with the Northwest Mounted Police on the Prairies.[74] Other than this tiny group of Germans, there appeared to be no other significant Catholic ethnic minorities among these volunteers. It was simply a British and Irish affair for the defense of the empire, so far as the Catholic themselves appeared to be concerned.

Table 1: Non-Francophone Catholics by Attestation and Previous Service (N=264)[75]

Catholic Group	Number of Volunteers	Percentage
Irish	192	72.2
Scots	47	17.8
English	18	6.8
Other	4	1.5
Unknown	3	1.1
Total	264	100.00

73. Akenson, *The Irish in Ontario*, 43.

74. LAC, RG 38, Department of Veterans Affairs, South African War, Attestation Papers (reel T-2083), Private Edward Reichert, #259, Canadian Mounted Rifles, 6 January 1900; and Alvin A. Schwartz, #164, 6th Canadian Mounted Rifles, 22 April 1902.

75. Source: LAC, RG 38 Department of Veterans Affairs (reels T2069, 2079, 2080–2084)

The persons who were represented in this sample of Catholics were themselves an interesting blend of men from different regions and occupations. No single individual Catholic volunteer appeared to represent the sample in its entirety. James Cooper Mason was a thirty-three-year-old bank manager living with his parents in Toronto when he answered the call. Living on Madison Avenue, Mason's father was a military veteran, and upon his enlistment, the young Mason was commissioned as a Lieutenant and would serve with distinction in several theaters of the war, before demobilizing back to Canada at the rank of Captain.[76] Private Edward Francis "Ned" Murray was the pride of one of the Ottawa Valley's most prominent and influential Irish Catholic families. Born in Pembroke, 27 March 1880, the son of Margaret Foran and William Murray, a local merchant,[77] Ned's half-brother J. L. Murray was soon to become State Deputy of the Knights of Columbus, his uncle the Reverend W. L. Murray was a future chaplain during the Great War, and his siblings could be found in successful marriages or in religious life. Identifying his occupation as "gentleman," he served three years as a lieutenant in the 42nd Regiment of the Renfrew and Lanark Highlanders, based in Smiths Falls and Renfrew.[78] During the South African War, he enlisted in the 2nd Canadian Mounted Rifles and had a horse shot from under him while fighting at Hart River.[79] Ned survived the war and enlisted again in the Great War.

Murray's Irish Catholic colleague, Private Gerald Michael O'Kelly, a native of Dublin Ireland was not so lucky. O'Kelly had been serving in the NWMP when he enlisted in the Canadian Mounted Rifles at Calgary in 1900. He fought in the Cape Colony and the Orange Free State, but died, neither in action nor of battle wounds, but of dysentery in Johannesburg, just over six months after he had enlisted.[80] Scots Catholic James McDonnell, like O'Kelly, was also working in the west, but in McDonnell's case, it was in the mines near Fort Steele. A native of Alexandria, Glengarry,

---

76. *Fourth Census of Canada, 1901*, District 126, Ward 4, Toronto, 11; LAC, MG 30 E397, Fonds James Cooper Mason, Regimental Number 1153. *The Catholic Register*, 8 and 15 February 1900.

77. *Census of Canada, 1871–1872*, Ontario, Renfrew North, District 82, Sub-district Pembroke, microfilm C-10021, item 368796.

78. LAC, RG 150, 1992-93/166, box 6525, file 52, Edward Francis Murray, 811814, Attestation Paper; RG 38, South African War Personnel Files, reel T2079, Attestation Paper.

79. *Renfrew Mercury*, 30 August 1918.

80. LAC, RG 38, Attestation Papers, Gerald Michael O'Kelly, #242, reel T-2082.

Ontario, the twenty-two-year-old McDonnell served in four theaters of the war with Lord Strathcona's Horse, before demobilizing in 1901.[81] Fellow Scot and namesake Charles Robert McDonnell also found himself in the west and enlisted in Strathcona's Horse while in Nelson, British Columbia, working as a prospector. A native of Ottawa, and a strapping man at six foot one inch, Charles Robert served with distinction in three theaters, was promoted to corporal, was wounded in action, and was mentioned in dispatches because of his bravery in the field.[82] Finally, Halifax's Lewis Power was a career soldier and among one of the first Catholics to enlist in November 1899. Serving with the Royal Canadian Regiment, Power was wounded at Paardeberg in 1900, but returned to action and was promoted to corporal. Upon his demobilization, in 1900, he re-enlisted in the Canadian Mounted Rifles.[83] While there is little to bind these stories other than a common religion, and, perhaps, among some, a previous engagement in militia and policing, those Catholic men appear to be little different from those non-Catholics with whom they served and described so vividly in the work of Carman Miller.

When comparing the non-Francophone Catholics in the South African expeditionary force to their non-Catholic colleagues, however, a number of dissimilarities can be noted. First, more non-Francophone Catholics were born in Canada than their non-Catholic comrades. Table 2 indicates that almost 79 percent of the non-Francophone Catholics were Canadian-born, when compared to only 64 percent of the entire Canadian contingent. Of the foreign-born, Catholics counted just under 17 percent who were born in the British Empire, whereas nearly 30 percent of the entire contingent were born imperial citizens. The remaining Catholic recruits were born in the United States or Germany. The high incidence of Canadian-born Catholics reflects the fact that the Irish and Scots Catholic communities were long-settled in Canada, [84] and that the urges to volunteer reflected less the impulse of a recent British immigrant who might feel

---

81. LAC, RG 38, Attestation Papers, James McDonnell, # 451, reel T-2080.

82. LAC, RG 38, Attestation Papers, Charles Robert McDonnell, #337, reel T-2080.

83. LAC, RG 38, Attestation Papers, Lewis Joseph Power, #2500, reel T-2083.

84. Houston and Smyth, *Irish Emigration*, 38–42; McGowan, *The Waning of the Green*, passim; Akenson, *The Irish in Ontario*, 3–47. Bumsted, "Scottish Catholicism in Canada," 85–87. The Scottish Catholics in the Contingent had a rate of identifying a Canadian birth place at 92.7%, which was even higher than the number of Canadian-born Francophones which was at 95.5 percent. The general figure comes from Miller, "A Preliminary Analysis," 221.

compelled to promote the military interest of the land of his birth. Non-Francophone Catholic recruits, despite their rootedness in Canada appear to have had greater interest in imperial matters than might be assumed in those who lived far from the heart of the empire and even farther from the theatre of the Boer War.

Table 2 also suggests that the Canadian geographic origins of the Catholic recruits were similar to the nationwide dispersion of the entire contingent. Catholic recruits, however, were under-represented in the Prairies and in British Columbia, which stands to reason, given the lower Catholic population generally in these territories, when compared to the rest of the country.[85] Ontario appeared to be the principal source of both Catholic recruits and men in the entire contingent. Since Ontario had about as many Catholics as all the other provinces and territories combined, except for Quebec, it is not surprising that Ontario Catholics provide the largest pool of recruits in the non-Francophone Catholic sample.[86]

Table 2: Non-Francophone Catholics by Place of Birth, South African Contingent (N=264)[87]

Place of Birth	Non-Francophone Catholics	Percentage	South African Contingent	Percentage	Dominion Census of 1901
Canada	208	78.8	3710	63.7	86.9
Nova Scotia	51	24.5	435	11.7	
PEI	22	10.6	139	3.7	
New Brunswick	28	13.5	353	9.5	
Quebec	28	13.5	484	13.1	
Ontario	68	32.7	2110	56.9	
Western Canada	8	3.8	189	5.1	
Unknown Canada	3	1.4			

85. *Fourth Census of Canada, 1901*, vol. 1, Tables I–II and IX–X. BC had only 33,693 Catholics, or 18.8% of the province's population, while the Northwest Territories had fewer at 30, 073 Catholics or 18.9%. The other provinces included the following percentages of Catholics: Manitoba (14%); New Brunswick (38%); Nova Scotia (28.2%); Ontario (17.9%); PEI (44.4%); Quebec (86.7%); NWT (18.7%): Unorganized Territory (18.2%).

86. *Fourth Census of Canada, 1901*, vol. 1, Tables I–II and IX–X. Despite the fact that only 17.9 percent of Ontario's population was Catholic, the Province's 390,304 Catholics compares favorably to 410,090 Catholics in the rest of the country outside of Quebec.

87. Source: Miller, "A Preliminary Analysis," 221. The Contingents' numbers reflect 5,579 of 5,825 (95.8 percent) in which nativity is identified.

Place of Birth	Non-Francophone Catholics	Percentage	South African Contingent	Percentage	Dominion Census of 1901
British Empire	44	16.7	1710	29.4	7.8
Other	10	3.8	159	2.7	5.1
Unknown	2	0.8	246	4.4	
Total	264		5,825		

The real anomaly in the data set appears to be in the high numbers of non-Francophone Catholic volunteers who were born in Nova Scotia. Across the contingent as a whole, only 11.7 percent of the volunteers hailed from Nova Scotia, whereas Nova Scotians accounted for almost 25 percent of the Canadian-born Catholics and just over 19 percent of the entire non-Francophone data set. The high rate of Nova Scotian Catholic participation may be accounted for in a variety of ways, beyond just attributing high recruitment in Halifax as symptomatic of the military culture in Britain's key strategic naval installation on the North Atlantic. First, according to the 1901 Census, over 28 percent of the population of Nova Scotia was Roman Catholic, so there is no doubt about available Catholic men for service.[88] Secondly, Irish Catholics were heavily engaged in the Halifax militia units and their participation was eagerly supported by the Charitable Irish Society, the largest Catholic benevolent society in the city. At least half of this Halifax Catholic sample, both born in Halifax or living in the city (42),[89] had previous militia or military service, primarily in the 63rd and 66th regiments. The rate of such high previous militia service by Catholics in both Nova Scotia and across Canada is confirmed in Table 4. Thirdly, Archbishop Cornelius O'Brien and his clergy openly supported the war effort, and this may have assisted recruitment, particularly in the Halifax area. Finally, it might be argued that perhaps high levels of unemployment in the port city of Halifax might account for high recruitment as an alternative to unemployment. The *Labour Gazette* for Halifax for the war years reports no significant slowdown in employment for blue-collar workers, so that it would be difficult to argue that Irish Catholic simply sought army life as an alternative to unemployment or a significant decline in real wages.[90] When

---

88. *Fourth Census of Canada, 1901*, vol. 1, Tables I–II and IX–X.
89. The number "42" is the sample size.
90. Government of Canada, *Labour Gazette*, 636–37.

in November 1899, the *Halifax Herald* proclaimed that "Halifax is Intensely Interested in the War," this enthusiasm included its Catholic community.[91]

Table 3: Non-Francophone Catholic Canadian Troops by Occupation (N=264)[92]

Occupation	Non-Francophone Catholic	Percentage	South African Contingents	Difference
White Collar	55	20.8	22.9	- 2.1
Blue Collar	104	39.4	29.2	+10.2
Service	55	20.8	16.3	+4.5
Primary	40	15.2	27.4	-12.2
Unknown	10	3.8	4.2	-0.4
Total	264			

The Catholic sample also suggests that the idea of "vertical mosaic" when applied to Irish Catholics, particularly the negative image of the Irish worker in the Canadian social spectrum, may have been overplayed by historians.[93] While the number of blue-collar recruits was higher than the national average (39.4 percent to 29.2 percent), perhaps owing to urban recruiting patterns in eastern Canada, it should also be noted that the Catholic percentage of white-collar workers was just slightly under the contingent average (20.8 percent to 22.9 percent), while the percentage of Catholic recruits employed in the service sector was actually higher than the number for the entire contingent's (20.8 percent to 16.3 percent). Another area where one can note a significant difference was that only about half as many Catholics were employed in primary industries (15.2 percent to 27.4 percent).[94] Again, the low recruitment of Catholics from Western Canada and its frontier economy helps to account for this significant discrepancy in recruits coming from ranching, forestry, and mining industries. It appeared that, what Catholics lacked in terms of their participation in the manual tasks of the primary industries of the West, they compensated for in their blue-collar work in the cities of the East. Overall, the sample does reveal clearly that the non-Francophone Catholics serving in the South African

91. *Halifax Herald*, 2 November 1899.
92. Source: Miller, "Preliminary Analysis," 230–32.
93. Darroch and Ornstein, "Ethnicity and Occupational."
94. Figures for the entire contingent are derived from Miller, "A Preliminary Analysis," 230–32 (see Appendix 3).

Contingents could not be stereotyped simply as sitting at the bottom of the social order desperately searching for steady work, even if it meant joining the army. In fact, if they had chosen to do so, Catholics could have found abundant, gainful, and safe employment in Halifax, given its strong wartime economy,[95] rather than herding aboard the troop ships bound for the Cape Colony. Catholics appeared willing to volunteer, indeed eager in the case of Halifax, perhaps less for want of work, but more for want of adventure or a willingness to serve the empire in a time of perceived need.

Table 4: Non-Francophone Catholics by Attestation and Previous Service (N=264)[96]

Catholic Group	Enlistment 1899	Enlistment 1900	Enlistment 1901	Enlistment 1902	Previous Service	Total
Irish	57	21	22	92	127	127
Scots	10	13	5	19	24	24
English	3	5	2	8	11	11
Other	0	1	0	3	3	3
Unknown	0	1	0	2	1	1
Total	70	41	29	124	166	166

Nor could Catholics be regarded as newcomers to khaki or adverse to Canadian military traditions. The non-Francophone Catholic sample indicates that 62.9 percent of recruits had some military or militia background prior to enlistment; such a high number of men with experience challenges the impression that Catholics had only loose ties to the militia tradition in English Canada.[97] Some in the sample attested to the Canadian forces with records of longstanding service to local militia units, while others joined the militia units during the war, because these units were principally responsible for recruitment of the contingents themselves. In fact, the Irish Catholic soldiers in this data set, appear to have had more militia and police experience (66.1 percent) than their Scottish co-religionists (51.1 percent), whom historians have memorialized for their military traditions.[98]

    95. Government of Canada, *Labour Gazette*, 636–37.

    96. Source: LAC, RG 38 Department of Veterans Affairs (reels T2069, 2079, 2080–2084). Note that *previous service* includes regular army, militia, and Northwest Mounted Police.

    97. Crerar, *Padres in No Man's Land*, 17, 21, 27.

    98. See Bumsted, "Scottish Catholicism," 84–85. In my sample, 24 of 47 Scottish

In retrospect, when the strong Irish Catholic participation in the Boer War is situated within the broad context of the evolution of Catholic communities in Canada, it appears less a radical point of departure in terms of Irish Catholic loyalty and participation in the Canadian imperial story. One could make a case that it was one more step—an important step—in the Irish and Scots Catholic integration into the mainstream of English-Canadian life. The Boer War challenged Canada's Catholics of Celtic descent to define more clearly their focus of political loyalty and, should their decision veer in an imperial-national direction, to place themselves in the service of the Queen, country, and empire—and not always in that order. The Catholic elementary schools had already moved their curriculum in this "imperial" direction in both Ontario and the Northwest, where one inspector at St. Mary's School in Calgary, in 1900, when treated to a patriotic concert and rendition of "The Rose the Shamrock and the Thistle," could exclaim: "Nothing could be more admirable than the sight of those manly little fellows, pupils in a Roman Catholic school, looking you squarely in the eyes and singing a patriotic British song with all the enthusiasm imaginable."[99] The concert, while obviously an effort by the teachers to pander to the inspector, was nonetheless symptomatic of much broader changes in the civil indoctrination of Catholic youth.[100]

Similarly, as the press and clerical leaders lined up behind the war effort after the arrival of Canadian troops on the Veldt, the question of Canada's role in the empire came to the fore for many non-Francophone Catholics. Here the weekly Catholic press, at least in central Canada, advocated a vision of Canada as an equal partner in the British Empire.[101]

Catholics had previous militia or military experience compared to 127 of 192 for the Irish. Catholic military traditions could even be overlooked by Catholics themselves (see *The Catholic Register*, 3 September 1914).

99. *The Calgary Herald*, 15 February 1900.

100. Notable is the publication of the *Canadian Catholic Readers*, 1899, with their overtly Canadian and imperial selections of poetry and prose in the "Fourth Book" and the adoption of Public School readers and texts by many Ontario Catholic schools, a fact already played out for Catholic school children in the single publicly funded systems elsewhere in eastern English Canada. *The Catholic Register*, 24 August 1899; *Catholic Record*, 2 September 1899. ARCAT, Fergus McEvay Papers, copy of letter of Michael O'Brien to John Seath, Department of Education, 15 January 1909; O'Brien to McEvay, 8 March 1909.

101. *The Catholic Register*, 21 August and 16 October 1902, 15, 22, and 29 October 1903, 12 and 19 November 1903, 28 June 1917. NA, Charles Murphy Papers. vol. 10, Father James T. Foley to Murphy, 25 March 1913, 4134-35; Foley to Murphy, 13 June 1913,

There was little difficulty for non-Francophone Catholics to identify with Canada as a player in the empire, provided that it was clear that, in the words of Kipling's "Our Lady of the Snows," Canada would be "mistress in her own house." Such ideas would permeate Catholic communities, and would facilitate enthusiastic support for Canada's participation in the Great War and equally strong levels of Irish-Catholic recruitment in the Canadian Expeditionary Force after 1914.

In fact, in the decade and a half that separated the Boer War from the Great War, non-Francophone Canadian Catholics incorporated the South African experience into their own story of their contribution to Canada and the empire. In the period immediately leading up to August 1914 and throughout the first months of the Great War, Catholic leaders across the country would reminisce proudly of Catholic loyalty during the Boer crisis. The *New Freeman* of Saint John included the stirring remarks of Ottawa priest and future CEF chaplain, John J. O'Gorman, and his contention that, as in South Africa, Britain's engagement in the Great War was just and honorable.[102] Winnipeg's Catholic weekly, the *Northwest Review* was even more open in its imperial sentiment claiming that Canadians were "loyal to the Motherland. The spirit that animated their forefathers a century ago when invasion threatened this infant nation, the spirit which impelled her sons to brave the dangers of the African veldt—that spirit, the surest defence against aggression, animates them still."[103] Imbued with this sense of "national" purpose, it is not surprising that Catholic veterans of the veldt emerged as leaders during the First World War: Ned Murray of Pembroke, Captain Charles McGee of Ottawa, Generals J. H. Elmsley and A. H. Macdonell of Toronto, William Donovan of Quebec, and nurse Margaret C. MacDonald of Bailey's Brook, Nova Scotia, who went from nursing sister in South Africa to Matron-in-Chief of the CEF.[104] The fearless and beloved Father Peter O'Leary of Quebec City himself volunteered for the Canadian Chaplain service in the Canadian Expeditionary Force in 1914, and although he was physically and mentally a mere shadow of his former self and had to be discharged, his heroics during the Boer War became the rod by which all Catholic chaplains would be required to measure

4137–44; Foley to Murphy, 4145–49; and Foley to Murphy, 17 December 1913, 4158–61.
  102. *New Freeman*, 31 October 1914.
  103. *Northwest Review*, 8 August 1914. See also Burke, "The Irishman's Place," 225–32.
  104. NPRC, Ottawa, Attestation Papers and Personnel Files. Also, *Catholics of the Diocese of Antigonish*, 51–53. *Catholic Record*, 13 January 1917.

themselves.[105] These returning veterans, primarily of Irish and Scots origin, became identified by non-Francophone Catholics as powerful symbols and models of Catholic service and "undoubted" loyalty.[106]

The Boer War and Catholic participation in it was absorbed by the next generation of English-speaking Catholics whose direct links to Ireland and Scotland might be far weaker than those of their parents and grandparents. This was particularly true in the publicly funded Catholic schools of Ontario, where Catholic children drank deeply from the imperial sentiments of text books, young boys shouldered mock rifles and marched in school cadet corps, and girls and boys celebrated the imperial connection in poetry, art, and song on Empire Day each year.[107] After 1907, across the country, English-speaking Catholic youth joined the burgeoning Scout movement, founded by Lord Robert Baden Powell, the veteran of the siege of Mafeking and commander of the South African Constabulary. For Catholic youth in English Canada, the Boer War, according to Catholic Senator A. C. Macdonell, would form part of a much larger imperial tapestry in which Canada was perceived to play the role of "bridge" between the Great Anglo-Saxon peoples of America and Britain.[108] It would be these youth, nurtured on such memories, who would constitute the main body of the non-Francophone Catholic contribution to the Canadian Expeditionary Force, from 1914 to 1918.

Thus, the story of the non-Francophone Catholics and the Boer War is really two stories. When situated within the time of the conflict itself, it is a story of indecision and ambiguity, and of a people searching for a clearer understanding of their loyalties. In Fitzpatrick's words—words not unanimously received by his own constituency at the time—Catholic Canadians may have been "whelps of the lion," but they were truly "whelps" testing their legs as citizens, scampering about, playing with ideas, and tumbling

105. LAC, RG 9 III C 15, Canadian Chaplaincy Corps., Personnel Files, vol. 4637, C-O-4, Peter M. O'Leary. In 1914, O'Leary enlisted again at age 64 and served with the 12th Battalion and the 1st Canadian General Hospital. There were rumors afoot about his intemperance, although these were hotly denied and fellow Padres took up a petition in his favor (21 November 1915). In January 1917, he was promoted to Lieutenant-Colonel and several months later was demobilized on account of his age. His influence as a "faithful and gallant" padre in South Africa was noted by the ADCS-Catholic. His popular influence is confirmed in Crerar, "In the Day of Battle," 56.

106. *Catholic Record*, 26 July 1902.

107. McGowan, *The Waning of the Green*, ch. 4.

108. *Hansard*, Session 1917, vol. 3, 29 June 1917, 2854; LAC, Charles Fitzpatrick Papers, MG 27 II C1, vol. 81, "Canada and the Empire," 7-01-1901, 45154–58.

over one another. By the end of the war, with their own service having been done and the dead buried, the non-Francophone Catholic leadership appeared more clearly focused on Canada's role in the empire and their role within Canada. Even the *Catholic Register* praised Fitzpatrick's patriotism, recognizing in him a man who "commands the respect of all Canadians."[109] In the decade that followed, Irish and Scots Catholics, in particular, created a new narrative. This story drew on a selected memory of South Africa, unencumbered by the ambiguities evident in 1899. For their part, the Irish would not forget the struggles of Ireland for Home Rule, but this aspiration would be clearly situated within the context that Ireland should have what Canada already has, its own responsible government. Such notions of Home Rule, whether it be Irish or Canadian, did not detract from the idea that both nation could and should be active members of a larger British Empire.[110] In this way, the South African conflict set the stage for an even greater test to come between 1914 and 1918.

APPENDIX 1: CATEGORIES OF EMPLOYMENT[111]

White Collar

1. Professional: student, teacher, doctor, law student, professional engineer, dentist, medical student

2. Proprietorial: merchant, gentleman, owner/florist/outfitter, hotel/restaurant keeper, business owner manager

3. Sales/Clerical: salesman, traveling salesman, clerk, store clerk, traveler, bookkeeper, commercial traveler, chemist, messenger, bank clerk, druggist, merchant tailor, draughtsman, inspector, bill collector, grocer, agent/life insurance, surveyor, stenographer, law clerk, agent, civil servant, accountant

---

109. *The Catholic Register*, 16 October 1902.

110. See Sir Frank Smith's address in *The Catholic Register*, 7 October 1897, and Patrick F. Cronin's editorial in the *The Catholic Register*, 14 February 1901. A later example of "double duty" is noted in Rev. Captain J. J. O'Gorman's speech as recorded in *Ottawa Citizen*, 23 March 1917.

111. Source: Miller, "A Preliminary Analysis," 230–32.

Blue Collar

1. Skilled: artisan, baker, printer, cooper, miller, butcher, saddler, electrician, plumber, brickmaker, machinist, stone mason, shoesmith, painter, photographer, tailor, glass worker, cheese maker, black/tinsmith, carpenter, book binder, marble polisher, mechanic, brewer, wheel wright, watch maker

2. Un/semi-skilled: factory worker, laborer, stevedore, cotton worker, mill hand, bridge worker, packer

3. Service: (a) *Protective*: soldier, police, fireman; (b) *Transportation/communication*: conductor, line/brake/trainman, coachman, driver, telephone/telegraph; (c) *Personal*: gardener/servant, waiter/barman, janitor, cook; (d) *Miscellaneous*: barber, reporter, horse trainer, actor/artist, jockey, veterinarian

4. Primary: (a) *Agriculture*: farmer, farm laborer, rancher, ranch laborer/cattleman/cowboy, stablehand, dairy man; (b) *Mining*: miner, prospector; (c) Fishing: sailor, mariner; (d) *Trapping*: hunter/trapper; (e) *Lumber*: lumberjack, shantyman, teamster

BIBLIOGRAPHY

Primary Sources

Archives

ADC—Archives of the Diocese of Charlottetown
ARCAT—Archives of the Roman Catholic Archdiocese of Toronto
ASV-DAC—Archivio Segreto Vaticano, Delegazione Apostilica Canada (Secret Vatican Archives)
LAC—Library and Archives Canada
NA—National Archives
NPRC—National Personnel Records Centre
SCA—Scottish Catholic Archives

Periodicals

The Globe
The Calgary Herald
The Catholic Register
Catholic Record
The Casket
The Freeman
The New Freeman

Northwest Review
Halifax Herald
The Morning Guardian (Charlottetown)
Le Soleil
Morning Chronicle (Halifax)
Ottawa Citizen
Renfrew Mercury
St. John Globe
Walsh's Magazine

Other

Catholics of the Diocese of Antigonish, Nova Scotia, and The War, 1914-1919 with Nominal Enlistment Rolls by Parishes. Antigonish: St. Francis Xavier University Press, 1919.
Census of Canada, 1871-1872. Ottawa: I. B. Taylor, 1873.
Canadian Department of Labour. *Labour Gazette: The Journal of the Department of Labour* 2.11 (1902) 636-37.
"Circulaire de Mgr L'Archeveque de Montreal au Clergé de son Diocese," 14 fevrier 1900, *Mandements, lettres pastorales, circulaires et autres documents*. Montreal: Arbour et Dupont, 1908-1925, 276-80.
Fourth Reader. Canadian Catholic Readers. Toronto: Copp Clark, 1899.
Fourth Census of Canada, 1901.
Hansard: House of Commons Debates. 20 February 1900, 668-69. Ottawa, Canada.
Harris, Dean William Richard. "Our Own Land." Speech to the 'Old Boys' Meeting at Beamsville, Ontario, 3 September 1900.
McKim's Directory of Canadian Publications. Toronto: A. McKim, 1899.

Secondary Sources

Akenson, Don. *The Irish in Ontario: A Study in Rural History*. Montreal: McGill-Queen's University Press, 1984.
Bumsted, J. M. "Scottish Catholicism in Canada." In *Creed and Culture: The Place of English-speaking Catholics in Canadian Society, 1750-1930*, edited by Terrence Murphy and Gerald Stortz, 79-99. Montreal: McGill-Queen's University Press, 1993.
Burke, Alfred E. "The Irishman's Place in the Empire." In *Empire Club Speeches, 1909-1910*, edited by J. Castell Hopkins, 225-32. Toronto: Warwick and Bros, 1910.
Clarke, Brian P. "Sir Richard Scott." In *Dictionary of Canadian Biography*, 14:913-16. Toronto: University of Toronto Press, 1998.
Crerar, Duff. "In the Day of Battle: Canadian Catholic Chaplains in the Field, 1885-1945." *CCHA Historical Studies* 61 (1995) 56.
———. *Padres in No Man's Land: Canadian Chaplains and the Great War*. Montreal: McGill-Queen's University Press, 1995.
Crooks, Katherine. "The Quest for Respectability: The Charitable Irish Society of Victorian Halifax." In *CCHA Historical Studies* 81 (2015) 167-94.
Darroch, A. Gordon, and Michael Ornstein. "Ethnicity and Occupational Structure in Canada in 1871: The Vertical Mosaic in Historical Perspective." *Canadian Historical Review* 61 (1980) 305-33.

Elliott, Bruce. "Irish Protestants." In *Encyclopedia of Canada's Peoples*, edited by Paul Magocsi, 762–72. The Multicultural History Society of Ontario, 1999.

Fiorino, Pasquale. "The Nomination of Bishop Fallon as Bishop of London." *CCHA Historical Studies* 62 (1996) 33–46.

Glazier, Ira A., ed. *The Famine Immigrants: Lists of Irish Immigrants Arriving at the Port of New York, 1846–1851*. Vols. 1–4. Baltimore: Genealogical, 1984.

Grace, Robert John. *The Irish in Mid-Nineteenth Century Canada and the Case of Quebec. Immigration and Settlement in a Catholic City*. PhD diss., Université Laval, 1999.

Hanks, Patrick, and Flavia Hodges. *A Dictionary of Surnames*. Oxford: Oxford University Press, 1991.

Horrall, Stanley W. "Canada and the Irish Question: A Study of the Canadian Response to Irish Home Rule, 1882–1893." MA thesis, Carleton University, 1966.

Hornsby, Stephen J. "Patterns of Scottish Immigration to Canada, 1750–1870." *Journal of Canadian Historical Geography* 18 (1992) 397–416.

Houston, Cecil, and William Smyth. *Irish Emigration and Canadian Settlement: Patterns, Links and Letters*. Toronto: University of Toronto Press, 1990.

Huel, Raymond. "The Irish-French Conflict in Catholic Episcopal Nominations: The Western Sees and the Struggle for Domination within the Church." *CCHA Study Sessions* 42 (1975) 51–70.

Hughes, Katherine. *Archbishop O'Brien: The Man and the Churchman*. Ottawa: Rolla L. Crain, 1906.

Lyne, Daniel C. "Irish-Canadian Financial Contributions to the Home Rule Movement in the 1890s." *Studia Hiberica* 7 (1967) 182–206.

MacLean, Raymond. *Bishop John Cameron, Piety and Politics*. Antigonish: Casket, 1991.

———. *The Casket, 1852–1992: From Gutenberg to Internet, The Story of a Small-Town Weekly*. Antigonish: Casket, 1995.

———. "The Highland Catholic Tradition in Canada." In *The Scottish Tradition in Canada*, edited by W. Stanford Reis, 93–117. Toronto: McClelland and Stewart, 1976.

Mannion, Patrick. "'Halifax Catholic' 'Patriotic Work': Responses to Irish Nationalism, 1880–1923." In *CCHA Historical Studies* 81 (2015) 195–223.

Matheson, Robert. *Special Report on Surnames in Ireland*. Dublin: Printed for His Majesty's Stationary Office, 1909.

McGowan, Mark G. "Canadian Catholics, Loyalty, and the British Empire, 1763–1901." In *Loyalism and the Formation of the British World, 1775–1914*, edited by Allan Blackstock and Frank O'Gorman, 201–22. Woodbridge, U.K.: Boydell, 2014.

———. "Irish Catholics." In *Encyclopedia of Canada's Peoples*, edited by Paul Magocsi, 747–61. The Multicultural History Society of Ontario, 1999.

———. "Rethinking Catholic-Protestant Relations in Canada: The Episcopal Reports of 1900–1901." *CCHA Historical Studies* 59 (1992) 11–32.

———. "Roman Catholics (Anglophone and Allophone)." In *Christianity and Ethnicity in Canada*, edited by David Seljak and Paul Bramadat, 49–100. Toronto: University of Toronto Press, 2008.

———. "The Tales and Trials of a 'Double Minority': The Irish and French Catholic Engagement for the Soul of the Canadian Church, 1815–1847." In *Religion and Greater Ireland: Christianity and Irish Global Networks, 1750–1950*, edited by Hilary M. Carey and Colin Barr, 97–123. Montreal: McGill-Queen's University Press, 2015.

———. *The Waning of the Green: Catholics, the Irish, and Identity in Toronto, 1887–1922*. Montreal: McGill-Queen's University Press, 1999.

McGowan, Mark G., and Michael E. Vance, eds. *Irish Catholic Halifax: From the Napoleonic Wars to the Great War. Historical Studies.* Occasional Papers 81. Toronto: Canadian Catholic Historical Association, 2015.

McLean, Marianne. *The People of Glengarry: Highlanders in Transition.* Montreal: McGill-Queen's University Press, 1991.

———. "Peopling Glengarry County: The Scottish Origins of a Canadian Community." *CHA Historical Papers* (1982) 156–71.

Miller, Carman. "English-Canadian Opposition to the South African War as Seen through the Press." *Canadian Historical Review* 55 (1974) 422–38.

———. *Painting the Map Red: Canada and the South African War, 1899–1902.* Montreal: McGill Queen's University Press, 1993.

———. "A Preliminary Analysis of the Socio-economic Composition of Canada's South African War Contingents." *Histoire Sociale-Social History* 8 (1975) 219–37.

Moir, John S., ed. *Church and State in Canada, 1627–1867: Basic Documents.* Carleton Library Series 33. Toronto: McClelland and Stewart, 1967.

———. "The Problem of a Double Minority: Some Reflections on the Development of the English-speaking Catholic Church in Canada in the Nineteenth Century." *Histoire Sociale-Social History* 4 (April 1971) 53–67.

Morgan, Henry James, ed. "William Wilfred Sullivan." *The Canadian Men and Women of the Time.* Toronto: William Briggs, 1898.

Nicolson, Murray W. "Irish Tridentine Catholicism in Victorian Toronto: Vessel for Ethno-religious Persistence." *CHA Study Sessions* 50 (1983) 415–36.

Page, Robert. *The Boer War and Canadian Imperialism.* Historical Booklet 44. Ottawa: Canadian Historical Association, 1987.

Perin, Roberto. *Rome in Canada: The Vatican and Canadian Affairs in the Late Victorian Age.* Toronto: University of Toronto Press, 1990.

Rea, J. E. *Bishop Alexander Macdonell and the Politics of Upper Canada.* Ottawa: Ontario Historical Society, 1974.

Scott, W. L. "Sir Richard Scott, K. C." *CCHA Report* 4 (1936–1937) 46–71.

Shanahan, David. "The Irish Question in Canada: Ireland, the Irish and Canadian Politics, 1888–1922." PhD diss., Carleton University, 1988.

Stanley, Laurie C. C. "James Rogers." In *Dictionary of Canadian Biography* 13:893. Toronto: University of Toronto Press, 1998.

Stortz, Gerald J. "Thomas Joseph Dowling: The First 'Canadian' Bishop of Hamilton, 1889–1924." *CCHA Historical Studies* 54 (1987) 93–107.

Whyte, Donald. *A Dictionary of Scottish Immigrants to Canada before Confederation, Vol. 1.* Toronto: Ontario Genealogical Society, 1986.

Woulfe, Patrick. *Irish Names and Surnames.* Dublin: M. H. Gill & Son, 1923.

Zucchi, John. *The Italians of Toronto: Development of a National Identity.* Montreal: McGill-Queen's University Press, 1988.

Zurakowska, Anna. *A Concise Guide to the Canadian Kashuby.* Barry's Bay: Polski Instytut Kaszuby, 2008.

4

"This South African war does not affect all citizens in the [same] manner"

French Protestants in Quebec during the South African War

GORDON L. HEATH AND SID D. SUDIACAL

OCCUPYING THE UNCOMFORTABLE LIMINAL space between English Protestants and French Catholics were French-speaking Protestants in Quebec. The vast majority of Quebecers were French Catholics, but a small segment had embraced Protestantism—what was deemed to be the religion of the Anglais. Since they were neither French-Catholic Quebecers nor English Protestants, they were doubly-marginalized: Protestants in an overwhelmingly Catholic province, and French speakers of what was widely considered to be an English variety of Christianity.

The growth of Protestantism in Quebec can be traced to the early years of the nineteenth century, but missionary work began in earnest in the 1830s and 1840s. Protestant missionaries from Canada, the United States, and Europe had faced intense opposition from the Catholic Church but were nonetheless successful in winning converts and establishing a number of mission centers, educational facilities, and local churches southeast of Montreal.[1] However, only a small percentage of French Catholics actually

---

1. Zuidema, *French-Speaking Protestants*; Rocher, et al., *Huguenots et Protestants*; Hudon, "Family Fortunes," 138–66; Scorgie, "The French-Canadian Misionnary Society," 79–98.

found the message appealing, and, by the end of the century, estimates range from only 20,000–40,000 converts.[2]

This chapter focuses on war-related commentary in *L'Aurore*, a weekly newspaper published in Montreal for the French Protestant community.[3] Its contents were standard fare for religious newspapers, and included a range of items on local church news, theological issues, poetry, editorials, devotional material, letters to editor, as well as domestic and international news. How closely the material in the paper correlated with opinions in the pews is unknown, but for the paper to be viable, there needed to be a degree of correlation between readers and paper.[4] What is certain is that the published material was for public consumption, and it is the public nature of the paper that is of interest here. The paper was—among other things—constructing a public identity. In its pages, readers would get a sense of the French-Protestant reaction to the war, and, in turn, identify French Protestants with such views.

Historic mutual suspicions and animosities in Canada between French and English were further exacerbated by Canada's military involvement in South Africa. Providing modern-day readers with a sense of how a century ago that doubly-marginalized group understood its tenuous liminal status was a statement in *L'Aurore* (*The Dawn*):[5] "this South African war does not affect all citizens in the [same] manner."[6] The author went on to detail the differing loyalties and perspectives of both French and

---

2. Balmer and Randall, "'Her Duty to Canada,'" 66; Hudon, "Family Fortunes," 142.

3. Its chief editor was Théo Lafleur. Circulation figures are uncertain. The papers for this research were accessed at the Canadian Baptist Archives, McMaster Divinity College, Hamilton, Ontario. For a summary of the paper and its significance for studies of French Protestantism, see Lalonde, "*L'Aurore*, Voix et Miroir," 183–204. For details on Quebec papers in general, see Silver, "Some Quebec Attitudes," 441–60. For details on English Protestant papers, see Heath, "'Forming Sound Public Opinion,'" 109–59. English papers in Canada received their information about the war primarily from London-based wire services, whereas the French papers in Canada received their news primarily from Paris-based wire services. The origins of those cables influenced the reporting, and thus the papers' perspective. See Page, *The Boer War*, 17.

4. For further discussion of the correlation of newspapers and public opinion, see Paddock, *A Call to Arms*; Wilkinson, *Depictions and Images of War*; Franzosi, "The Press as a Source," 5–16; Beaumont, "*The Times* at War," 67–83; Hampton, "The Press, Patriotism, and Public Discussion," 177–97.

5. Not to be confused with the socialist paper of the same name published in Paris, France.

6. " . . . cette guerre sud-africaine n'affecte pas tous les citoyens de la mâme manière." See "Le Canada et l'Afrique," *L'Aurore*, 20 January 1900, 9.

English, recognizing that understanding their backgrounds of blood and history made sense of differing wartime loyalties and narratives. There is no way of knowing how convinced readers were with what seems today to be a commonsensical statement. Nevertheless, its value to contemporary historians is readily apparent. At the very least, it reveals the plight and position of Quebec's French-Protestants in the midst of polarizing rhetoric and racial and religious tensions. More importantly, it and other wartime commentary in *L'Aurore* provide a sense of how that doubly-marginalized community sought to construct its identity within a public forum. The difficulty, however, was the fact that French-Protestants had multiple—even competing—loyalties, and thus no uniform perspective on the war.

TWO SOLITUDES[7]

The history of harsh polemics between Catholics and Protestants dates back to the sixteenth-century religious reformations and imperial rivalries. The link between Protestantism and the British Empire was considerable, and the "strong link between imperial and anti-Catholic rhetoric" was shared in Britain, South Africa, Australia, New Zealand, and Canada.[8] Further exacerbating tensions was the evangelical distrust and dislike of Catholics.[9] Organizations such as the Orangemen and Protestant Protective Association formalized and mobilized those prejudices.[10] French Catholics were also deemed a legitimate target for Protestant missions. In Canada, that meant supporting missions in the province of Quebec in order to, in the words of John Webster Grant, "penetrate the very heart of darkness and destroy the citadel of Antichrist."[11] Methodists carried out extensive missions among native groups in Quebec, sometimes leading to protracted confrontations and legal battles with Catholic authorities. Presbyterians worked in Quebec in the shadow of the controversial Father Charles Chiniquy, while Baptists supported the Grande Ligne Mission just south of Montreal.[12]

---

7. Taken from Hugh MacLennan's novel, *Two Solitudes* (1945).

8. Wolffe, "Anti-Catholicism and the British," 43. See also McLeod, "Protestantism," 44–70; Miller, "Bigotry in the North," 289–301; Miller, "Anti-Catholicism in Canada," 25–48.

9. Wolffe, "Anti-Catholicism and Evangelical Identity," 184.

10. See Houston and Smith, *The Sash Canada Wore*; Watt, "Anti-Catholic Nativism," 45–58.

11. Grant, *The Church*, 83. See also Lalonde, "French Protestant," 163–90.

12. Semple, *The Lord's Dominion*, 291; Moir, *Enduring Witness*, 154–57. See also

French Catholics in Quebec, on the other hand, had a sense of their own national mission to spread Catholicism in Canada and beyond, what A. I. Silver coins "a sort of Quebec imperialism."[13] Not surprisingly, as Grant has noted, "two militant expressions of an exclusive claim to Christian truth could scarcely coexist in Canada without colliding."[14] The decades preceding the war, especially the closing decades of the nineteenth century, had been marked by "a series of inflammatory incidents" and "a continuing cold war" between Catholics and Protestants.[15] Those tensions were exacerbated by events during the war in South Africa. As Desmond Morton has noted, the conflict may have been a relatively small one, but the debate and controversy it engendered was not.[16] Not all Canadians were convinced that Canada should send troops to fight against the Boers in South Africa; there was an acrimonious political debate over the issue and no aspect of the war has received more attention from Canadian historians than that clash.[17] Some have seen the controversy as a political watershed issue, one that "split open the cleft between English and French Canadians, launched the twentieth-century French-Canadian nationalist movement, broke Laurier's power in Quebec, and served as a dress rehearsal for the First World War."[18]

Goldwin Smith, one of the war's most outspoken Canadian English-speaking critics, was often singled out for his opposition to the war. Israel Tarte, Laurier's minister of public works, was taken to task for his support for the Boer cause, as was Quebec MP Henri Bourassa for his anti-war, and seemingly anti-British, sentiments.[19] Certain daily newspapers gave Laurier a rough ride over his alleged hesitation to support Britain, and the religious press tended to defend the actions of the Prime Minister.[20] While

---

Zuidema, "Charles Chiniquy," 145–62; Renfree, *Heritage and Horizon*, chs. 14 and 25; Balmer and Randall, "Henriette Feller," 29–48. For an earlier assessment, see Balmer and Randall, "'Her Duty to Canada,'" 49–72.

13. Silver, "Some Quebec Attitudes," 441–60.
14. Grant, *The Church*, 82.
15. Ibid. See also Lougheed, "Clashes in Worldview," 99–117.
16. Morton, *A Military History*, 70.
17. Miller, *Painting the Map*, 16.
18. Ibid.
19. "Mr. Tarte in Paris," *Canadian Churchman*, 26 April 1900, 259; "Anti-British," *Religious Intelligencer*, 30 October 1901, 4; "Mr. Bourassa's Lost Opportunity," *Westminster*, 15 September 1900, 317.
20. For example, see "The *London Times* on Laurier's Great Speech," *Onward*, 7 April 1900, 106; "The Premier's Defense," *Christian Guardian*, 14 February 1900, 104;

secular newspapers and politicians often showed restraint when it came to criticizing the French for their alleged lack of patriotism during the war, some did act irresponsibly. The Toronto *Mail and Empire* and the Hamilton *Spectator* were the worst examples of partisan reporting.[21] Growing hostility between English and French Canadian eventually erupted into violence in Montreal. On 1 March 1900, McGill University students celebrated the relief of Ladysmith and the victory at Paardeberg.[22] After their parade had traveled through the streets, they attacked the offices of *La Presse*, *La Patrie*, and *Le Journal*, and caused damage at Laval University. The next day Laval students peacefully marched to McGill University, where they were stopped by the archbishop of Montreal and the principal of McGill. The next evening the hostile crowd returned to Laval University, where a confrontation with police turned ugly. Eventually the militia was called to aid the beleaguered police force. The riot was widely reported in Canada and around the world. For some, it was a simple prank gone bad. For others, it was the beginning of the end of French-English relationships in the new nation.

WAR COVERAGE

Despite the editorial decision to limit reports on the war,[23] *L'Aurore* provided coverage of general events and trajectories in the conflict. Rumblings of looming war in the summer of 1899 were briefly commented on, with no editorial opinion stated as yet as to who was in the right.[24] Once hostilities commenced, the paper satisfied readers' craving for war news with occasional articles on South African demographics, political developments, plans for peace, battles, and casualties.[25] There were also a number of

---

"Canadians Complimented," *Dominion Presbyterian*, 28 June 1900, 407; "Sir Wilfrid Laurier's Speech," *Westminster*, 24 March 1900, 330. See also Miller, *Painting the Map*, 21.

21. Miller, *Painting the Map*, 20. There is some debate over how disciplined were the smaller, independent presses. See Ibid.; Beaven, "Partisanship," 317–51.

22. The following description of the riots is taken from Miller, *Painting the Map*, 443–44.

23. "La Guerre au Sud de l'Afrique," *L'Aurore*, 5 May 1900, 6.

24. "Nouvelles et Faits Divers," *L'Aurore*, 19 August 1899, 14.

25. "La Guerre dans l'Afrique du Sud," *L'Aurore*, 4 November 1899, 5; "La Paix au Transvaal," *L'Aurore*, 2 December 1899, 6; "La Question sud-Afrique," *L'Aurore*, 13 January 1900, 4; "Pour les Boers," *L'Aurore*, 19 May 1900, 8; "Dernières Nouvelles de la Guerre," *L'Aurore*, 7 June 1900, 12–13; "Toujours du Sang," *L'Aurore*, 14 June 1900, 5; "Afrique du Sud," *L'Aurore*, 28 June 1900, 12; "Nouvelles et Faits Divers," *L'Aurore*, 15 November 1900,

articles that revealed a diversity of opinions on the war, ranging from pro-Boer and anti-war sentiments to support for the imperial enterprise and Canada's role within it. Clearly, there was a spectrum of views that makes it difficult to generalize about how the French Protestant community viewed the war. Examples of that range of opinion corroborate the aforementioned claim that the war did "not affect all citizens in the [same] manner."[26] As well, it challenges the view that the French Protestant community tended to side with English Canada on social and political issues.[27] The following traces that range of opinion.

While there was initial uncertainty over who to believe regarding whether the cause was just,[28] it was clear to some that Europe in general, and Britain in particular, was succumbing to the disease of militarism. That concern was not unique to French Protestants, for numerous others elsewhere had expressed concern over the rise of militarism and jingoistic celebrations after victories.[29] The growth of a desire for martial glory, imperial expansion, conscription, and the never-ending construction of armaments was considered to be a new, alarming, and deadly sickness that was spreading throughout Europe.[30] In the words of Jean D'Arvey, the "game of war" was an expensive and deadly scourge on civilization: "The game of war—the favourite game of these big children called men—results in rivers of blood, torrents of tears and avalanches millions. The tears leave the human beast insensible and the smell of blood leaves the human beast intoxicated: only the sight of millions of people up in smoke can one day, perhaps, succeed in convincing him of his madness."[31] The cost of the war thus far had simply been staggering:

13; "Nouvelles et Faits Divers," *L'Aurore*, 3 January 1901, 13; " Nouvelles et Faits Divers," 10 January 1901, 13; "Nouvelles et Faits Divers," *L'Aurore*, 10 January 1901, 13; "Nouvelles et Faits Divers," *L'Aurore*, 25 April 1901, 12; "La Guerre," *L'Aurore*, 2 May 1901, 9; "Nouvelles et Faits Divers," *L'Aurore*, 2 May 1901, 12; "Faits Divers," *L'Aurore*, 28 December 28, 1901, 12; "Faits Divers," *L'Aurore*, 1 February 1902, 6–8; "Faits Divers," *L'Aurore*, 15 February 1902, 6; "Faits Divers," *L'Aurore*, 15 March 1902, 8; "Faits Divers," *L'Aurore*, 19 April 1902, 7; "Faits Divers," *L'Aurore*, 3 May 1902, 9; "Faits Divers," *L'Aurore*, 10 May 1902, 7.

26. "Le Canada et L'Afrique," *L'Aurore*, 20 January 1900, 9.

27. Lougheed, "Clashes in Worldview," 113–14.

28. "Qui croire? Je ne puis vérifier, puisque les documents et les temps me manquent également. Mais je suis sûr de ne pas me tromper en faisant des voeux pour la paix." See "La Crise Sud-Africaine," *L'Aurore*, 24 February 1900, 1–2.

29. Heath, *A War with a Silver Lining*, 53–55.

30. Albert Grimaud, "La Paix Armée," *L'Aurore*, 21 October 1899, 7–8.

31. "Le jeu de la guerre—le jeu favori de ces grands enfants que sont les hommes—se

An English journal, *Home Magazine*, states that the money England spent on the South African war, and just at the end of March, was 2 billion 850 million dollars. If this was represented by 20 francs put side by side, it would be a gold column measuring 142 kilometers and 500 meters in height. In other words, 475 columns each attaining the height of the Eiffel Tower . . . This amount of money could have given retirement for all the poor elderlies in the United Kingdom, raised millions of children, supported all the indigenous people, reimbursed all the costs made by the country for services of all types like welfare and hospitals . . . the asylums for all convalescents, the libraries and the museums, training and maintaining thousands of professional schools . . . coal supply, covering medical bills of millions of people, and it would still leave enough abundant resources for other useful works . . . The truth, the scary truth, is that we will all die because of the war—by what we have done and what we have prepared to do. The money thrown at this monster by England in South Africa is a small part of the incalculable sum devoured by the scourge of war at the end of the last century . . . Year after year, Europe feels the increasingly heavy weight on its shoulders the budget of future slaughters . . . Who is foolish enough not to hear it? Ah! The good we could have done, even with the small part of the millions that men spent for their criminal massacres.[32]

---

solde par des fleuves de sang, des torrents de larmes et des avalanches de millions. Les larmes laissent ensensible la bête humaine et l'odeur du sang l'enivre: seule, la vue de ses millions envolés en fumée réussira peut-être un jour à la convaincre de sa folie." Jean D'Arvey, "Guerre à la Guerre!" *L'Aurore*, 5 July 1900, 5–6.

32. "Un journal anglais, le *Home Magazine*, compte que l'Angleterre a dépensé pour la guerre sud-africaine, et seulement jusqu'à la fin du mars, la somme de deux milliards 850 millions. Cela représente, en pièces de 20 francs mises les unes sur les autres, une colonne d'or de 142 kilomètres 500 mètres de hauteur, autrement dit 475 colonnes atteignant chacune à la hauteur de la tour Eiffel . . . 'Il suffisait pour assurer une retraite à tous les vieillards pauvres du Royaume-Uni, élever des millions d'enfants, soutenir tous nos indigents, rembourser toute somme dépensée dans notre peys pour les missions de toute espèce et pour les oeuvres de bienfaisance, doter nos hôpitaux . . . pourvoir aux dépenses de nos asiles pour convalescents, de nos bibliothèques et de nos musées, équiper et maintenir des milliers d'écoles professionnelles . . . fournir du charbon, des couvertures et des soins médicaux à des millions de personnes, et laisser encore des réserves abondantes pour d'autres oeuvres utiles' . . . La vérité, l'angoissante vérité, c'est que nous mourons tous de la guerre—celle que nous avons faite et celle que nous préparons. L'argent jeté au monstre par l'Angleterre dans le sud de l'Afrique n'est qu'une faible partie des sommes incalculables dévorées paa le fléau de la guerre dans le siècle qui finit . . . D'année en année, l'Europe sent peser toujours plus lourdement sur ses épaules le budget des boucheries futures . . . Insensé qui ne l'entend pas! Ah! que de bien l'on

Other attitudes towards the conflict were similar. The horrendous and ultimately pointless suffering in former wars was lamented.[33] The escalating violence and expenses of the guerilla war were alarming, and the costs of the conflict were deemed simply too much.[34] Elsewhere the alleged glory of war was undermined by a stark reminder of the true reality of war: "It is true that we do not hear the shock of these two human troops who tear each other apart, who writhe, who hurl at each other like two groups of desert kings who want to obliterate each other. We do not hear the howls and roars of the dead. We do not feel all the unbelievable horrors that would make us shudder. All the pain, all the fear, all the tears."[35]

For ardent supporters of the imperial cause, those critical comments on war would have been a source of concern. Equally distressing would have been the positive portrayals of the Boers that undermined notions of British superiority that undergirded the imperial war effort. The Boers were portrayed as a simple, Christian, pastoral, and valiant people who heroically fought against aggressors just as early Americans did under George Washington.[36] They were a small minority simply trying to survive like other smaller nations with large and aggressive neighbors—a narrative that would naturally resonate with French Quebecers chafing under English rule.

Other commentary went even further and declared that the British cause in South Africa was unjust. Various authorities were cited in order to provide an argument for the injustice of the British cause. Well known Canadian anti-imperialist Goldwin Smith's disapproval of the war was noted.[37] American Andrew Carnegie's criticism of both the US involvement in the Philippines and the British in South Africa was also highlighted.[38] Testimo-

---

pourrait faire, même avec une faible part des millions que les hommes dépensent pour leurs criminelles tueries!" Jean D'Arvey, "Guerre à la Guerre!" *L'Aurore*, July 5, 1900, 5–6.

33. "Revue Très Sommaire du XIXe Siècle," *L'Aurore*, 3 January 1901, 1.

34. "Un Coup d'Oeil Rétrospectif," *L'Aurore*, 24 January 1901, 4.

35. "Il est bien vrai qu'on n'entend pas le choc de ces deux troupes humaines qui se déchirent, qui se tordent, qui s'élancent comme feraient deux bandes de ces rois du desert qui veulent s'anéantir. Nous entendons pas les hurlements et les mugissements de la mort. Nous ne sentons pas toutes ces émouvantes horreurs qui nous font frissonner. Toutes ces douleurs, toutes ces angoisses, toutes ces larmes." "La Guerre," *L'Aurore*, 7 March 1901, 7–8.

36. "Les Boers," *L'Aurore*, 4 November 1899, 6.

37. "Pour Les Boers," *L'Aurore*, 19 May 1900, 8.

38. "Opinion de M. Carnegie," *L'Aurore*, 18 November 1899, 4.

nies from a variety of other denominational sources were also provided.[39] The conclusion to be drawn from such opinions was that the much-touted justice of the imperial cause in South Africa was mere propaganda; the war was a blatant act of imperial aggression against the Boers.

A few months into the war the treatment of Catholics in the Boer republics was raised as further evidence that the conditions in the Transvaal were not as politicians had described it. According to one author, Catholics were doing quite well in the Transvaal: gaining converts, experiencing liberty, and enjoying constructive relations with the Boers. Such a positive experience, it was concluded, meant that "it would be unjust and misleading of us to describe [the Boers] as a small backward people and intolerant, whose suppression by England would have been good for Christian civilization."[40] In similar fashion, it was argued elsewhere that the experience of Catholics in South Africa was evidence that "freedom of religion still exists at Transvaal." As a result, the author declared, "We do not understand why Mr. Laurier stubbornly asserts that Canadians are going to war in South Africa for religious freedoms."[41]

Along with concerns expressed over issues related to the justice of the imperial cause was commentary over what Canada's involvement in its first overseas imperial engagement meant for future generations. Had a precedent been established by sending troops to support Britain's imperial wars? The larger Protestant denominations had expressed similar concerns, but had nevertheless remained generally supportive of the war effort.[42] In the case of some French Protestants, the issue seemed to be a rationale for opposing the war, or at least remaining guarded and skeptical about what Canada's role would be in the future. The specific concern was that the empire's responsibilities were growing, England's need for assistance mounting, and any sending of Canadian troops would set a precedent for obliging Canada to transport troops to any and every imperial conflict: "England,

---

39. L. M., "Quelques Témoignages Anglais de Dénominations Bein Différentes," *L'Aurore*, 24 March 1900, 9–10.

40. "il serait injuste autant qu'inexact de nous les représenter comme un petit pauple arriéré et intolérant, dont la suppression par l'Angleterre serait un bien pour la civilisation chrétienne." "Le catholicisme au Transvaal," *L'Aurore*, 13 January 1900, 8.

41. "La liberté des cultes existe donc au Transvaal . . . On ne comprend guère, dès lors, que M. Laurier s'obstine à affirmer que les Canadiens vont combattre au Sud de l'Afrique *pour la liberté religieuse*." "Les Catholiques au Transvaal," *L'Aurore*, 27 January 1900, 4.

42. Heath, *A War with a Silver Lining*, 53–55.

whose property extends all over the world, from now on, needs help from all her colonies to defend itself. Today, they need contingents of voluntary Canadians and Australians for Transvaal. Tomorrow, perhaps it will be for India, or for China, or for Europe. New politics will result in many changes in the relations of the other colonies with Britain. That which is optional is bound to become mandatory."[43] A few months later a similar sentiment was expressed: "Great Britain, with all her power, does not have the right to demand from us a man nor even a [cent]."[44]

For ardent supporters of the war effort, such tepid support and even hostile public commentary against Canada's participation in the war was alarming. One alarmed reader felt the need to remind the editor that not all were in favor of the general tenor of the paper's commentary: "Don't forget, Mr. Editor, that if there are L'Aurore readers who are sympathetic to the Boers, there are also many who share the [opposite] opinion."[45] That particular reader had a highly selective approach to reading the paper, for there had been early commentary expressing sympathy and even support for British claims,[46] including fairly derogatory portrayals of the Boers.[47] Apparently that was not enough. Perhaps in response to such concerns of sensitive readers—and realizing the heated domestic climate—the paper printed in the coming months arguments for the British imperial cause. Testimonies from a number of sources were printed that corroborated the

---

43. "L'angleterre, dont les biens s'entendent par tout le monde, a besoin désormais du concours de toutes ses colonies pour se défendre. Il faut ajuourd'hui des contingents de volontaires canadiens et australiens pour le Transvaal. Il en faudra peut-être demain pour les Indes, ou pour la Chine, ou pour l'Europe. Politique nouvelle qui entraînera bien des modifications dans les rapports des colonies avec la Grande-Bretagne. Ce qui est facultative ne peut manquer de devenir obligatoire." "L'Imperialisme," *L'Aurore*, 11 November 1899, 4.

44. "La Grande-Bretagne, avec toute sa puissance, n'avait pas le droit de nous demander un homme, ni un centin." D., "Le Canada et L'Afrique," *L'Aurore*, 20 January 1900, 9.

45. "N'oubliez pas, M. le Rédacteur, que s'il y a des lecteurs de l'Aurore qui sont sympathiques aux Boers, il y en a aussi beaucoup qui partagent l'opinion de l'évêque de Kimberley." "Lettre de St-Hyacinthe, Qué," *L'Aurore*, 31 March 1900, 12.

46. "La Guerre," *L'Aurore*, 25 November 1899, 4; "Quelques Raisons qui Justifient l'Angleterre," *L'Aurore*, 2 December 1899, 7–8; "L'opinion d'un homme de lettres," *L'Aurore*, 20 January 1900, 10.

47. "La Religion des Boers," *L'Aurore*, 6 January 1900, 8; "Les Boers," *L'Aurore*, 27 January 1900, 6.

British claim of Boer incompetence and injustice.[48] As one such article declared, Britain's cause was completely justified:

> The Boers wanted the war, and they prepared long beforehand in secret; they are conspirators. They bought the European press with their agents. The South African republics are not real republics, they are tyrannical oligarchies. They do not fight for independence, but to maintain slavery, like the states of Southern America during the Secession. The Boers wanted to drive out England from Cape colony. The offer of arbitration was nothing but a sham. They do not constitute a nationality.[49]

If anyone was guilty it was Transvaal President Kruger and those who misled him, and the only mistake Britain made was "showing too much clemency."[50]

Opinion on the war was sharply divided, as the above noted pages of *L'Aurore* indicate. One writer sought to alleviate the tension by explaining to readers why differences existed: "This South African war does not affect all citizens in the [same] manner."[51] The contributor went on to argue that the disparate views and loyalties could best be understood if history and "the voice of the blood" were considered:

> It does not affect the citizens who are of English origin in the same way as the citizens who are French in origin. For the citizen with an English origin, it is the voice of the blood which speaks. When he hears the battle cries of his mother country; his blood boils; his heart beats, and it is only natural that he would want to come to the rescue of his compatriots struggling against the enemy. But this is not the same voice that speaks in our hearts; it is not the voice of the blood; it is the voice of knowing which speaks to us,

48. "Lettre de St-Hyacinthe, Que," *L'Aurore*, 31 March 1900, 12; "Nouvelles Religieuses: Afrique du Sud," *L'Aurore*, 21 April 1900, 11.

49. "Les Boers ont voulu la guerre, et ils s'y sont prepares de longue main, en secret; ce sont des conspirateurs. Ils ont acheté la presse européenne par leurs agents. Les républiques sud-africaines ne sont pas de varies républiques, ce sont des oligarchies tyranniques. Elles ne combattent pas pour l'indépendance, mais pour le maintien de l'esclavage, comme les Etats de l'Amérique du Sud pendant la guerre de la Sécession. Les Boers voulaient chaser l'Angleterre de la Colonie du Cap. L'offre d'arbitrage n'était qu'un leurre. Ils ne constituent pas une nationalité." "M. Tallichet sur la Guerre Africaine," *L'Aurore*, 31 May 1900, 4.

50. "Si l'Angleterre a commis une erreur, elle l'a commise en se montrant trop clémente." "Contre les Boers," *L'Aurore*, 31 May 1900, 11.

51. "Le Canada et l'Afrique," *L'Aurore*, 20 January 1900, 9.

the voice of national solidarity that unites us as a country, the voice of institutions under which we live.[52]

Canadians of English background would naturally be supportive of the war because of historical and familial connections with the empire; Canadians whose origins were French neither felt enthused nor compelled to run to the defense of the imperial cause in Africa—or anywhere else for that matter. Protestants of predominately French Quebecois background were not—at least in this case—drawn to fight in Africa by "the voice of the blood," nor did Protestantism seem to override their historic and familial bonds with French Quebec.[53] However, even though there was understandable antipathy for the war among some, the author then appealed to both idealistic and pragmatic reasons for French readers to express their loyalty and support for the war:

> We said: this war is unjust. The time to ask the merits of the question has passed. The war is declared, and is ongoing against our mother country. This will have to do. As for the cause, we know that it is to safeguard civil justice, and also the religious and civil liberties; and if the Republic of Transvaal had given the same religious and civil liberties that we in Canada have, there wouldn't be a war. We could not but admire the courage of the Boers. But truth is always truth—whatever their courage or values. They do not recognize religious liberties: they do not want equality.[54]

52. "Elle n'affecte pas les citoyens d'origine anglaise comme elle affecte les citoyens d'origine française. Pour le citoyen d'origine anglaise, c'est la voix du sang qui parle. Quand il endtend le bruit des batailles de la mère patrie; son sang bout; son Coeur bat, et il est tout naturel qu'il veuille voler au secours de ses compatriots aux prises avec l'ennemi. Mais ce n'est pas la même voix qui parle dans nos coeurs; ce ne'est pas la voix du sang; c'est la voix de la reconnaissan ce qui parle en nous, la voix de la solidarité nationale qui nous unit dans ce pays, la voix des institutions sous lesquelles nous vivons." "Le Canada et l'Afrique," *L'Aurore*, 20 January 1900, 9.

53. This may be evidence that supports Christine Hudon's claim that relations between French Protestants and their Catholic kin remained somewhat intact after conversion. See Hudon, "Family Fortunes," 160.

54. "On nous dit: Cette guerre est injuste. Le temps d'entrer dans le mérite de la question est passé. La guerre est déclarée, engage avec la mère patrie. Cela doit nous suffire. Quant à la cause, nous savons qu'il s'agit de sauvegarder la justice civile, ainsi que les libertés religieuses et civiles; et que si la République du Transvaal avait accordé à ceux qui se sont établis chez elle les libertés religieuses et civiles que nous, au Canada, accordons à ceux qui viennent s'établir chez nous, il n'y aurait pas eu de guerre. Nous ne pouvons qu'admirer le courage des Boers. Mais la vérité est toujours la vérité—quelque soit leur courage, leur valeur. Ils ne reconnaissent pas la liberté religieuse: ne veulent pas d'égalité." "Le Canada et l'Afrique," *L'Aurore*, 20 January 1900, 9.

While that statement may have appeared lukewarm to patriots fired up over the war effort, it was a statement of loyalty and patriotism nonetheless. But, it was a patriotism to Canada and not to the empire. There were competing visions of Canadian nationalism during the war: English Protestant versions were decidedly imperial, and French Catholic versions were not. The pages of *L'Aurore* illustrate those competing visions, and also provide one example of an attempt to mitigate tensions and propose a unified way forward amid heated domestic tensions.

CONCLUSION

The conflict had long drifted from the front pages of newspapers by 1902, but its conclusion had been anticipated, as had a British victory. The end of the "long and sad" war on 31 May 1902 was noted by *L'Aurore*, with expressions of sorrow for the immense financial cost and loss of life.[55] The paper's commentary was decidedly muted, devoid of jingoistic expressions regarding how blessed the Boers would be under British rule. Rather than a spirit of optimism, fear was expressed over the inevitability of future wars and rising militarism.[56] Lost opportunities were also noted, for, as one commentator stated in regards to the immense sums spent by the combatants, "If the hundredth part of this large sum was given to establish the reign of the Prince of Peace on earth, who can tell what good that would have resulted in the world?"[57]

The paper's disparate responses are noteworthy for a number of reasons. First, they make it clear that there was no uniform position on the war among French Protestants, for both criticism and support for the war effort adorn the pages of *L'Aurore*. It would be interesting to know the impact of demographics on such views, what the abovementioned author called "the voice of the blood." For instance, were pro-British articles written by French-speaking Protestants (English-born), and pro-Boer ones by French-speaking Protestants (French/Quebec-born)? Since the authors of most articles remain unknown, such questions remain unanswered. Second, there was a distinct lack of anti-Catholic rhetoric, something often

---

55. "La Guerre est Finie au Sud de l'Afrique," *L'Aurore*, 7 June 1902, 3–4.
56. "Aurons-nous la Paix?" *L'Aurore*, 7 June 1902, 5.
57. "Si la centième partie de cette somme fabuleuse avait été donnée pour établir le règne du Prince de la Paix sur la terre, qui peut dire le bien qui en serial résulté pour le monde entire." "Ce Que la Guerre a Couté," *L'Aurore*, 28 June 1902, 9.

associated with alleged French Protestants' antipathy to French Catholics.[58] If anything, there was an affinity expressed towards Catholics, and attempts were made at explaining to readers the French Quebec ambivalence to the war. Possible motives for such articles was to ameliorate relations with the Catholic Church and thus relieve its restrictions and attacks on French Protestants and/or address accusations of disloyalty made by their English Protestant coreligionists. Such a strategy often made sense for communities on the margins. Third, the nature of the wartime commentary in *L'Aurore* reveals the plight and position of Quebec's French Protestants in the midst of polarizing rhetoric and racial and religious tensions, and provides a sense of how that doubly-marginalized community sought to construct its identity within a highly-charged public forum.

BIBLIOGRAPHY

Primary Sources

L'Aurore
Canadian Churchman
Christian Guardian
Dominion Presbyterian
Onward
Religious Intelligencer
Westminster

Secondary Sources

Balmer, Randall, and Catharine Randall. "Henriette Feller, The Spirit and Mission to Canada." In *French-Speaking Protestants in Canada: Historical Essays*, edited by Jason Zuidema, 29–48. Leiden: Brill, 2011.

———. "'Her Duty to Canada': Henriette Feller and French Protestantism in Québec." *Church History* 70.1 (2001) 49–72.

Beaumont, Jacqueline. "*The Times* at War, 1899–1902." In *The South African War Reappraised*, edited by Donal Lowry, 67–83. Manchester: Manchester University Press, 2000.

Beaven, Brian. "Partisanship, Patronage, and the Press in Ontario, 1880–1914: Myths and Realities." *Canadian Historical Review* 64.3 (1983) 317–351.

Franzosi, Roberto. "The Press as a Source of Socio-Historical Data: Issues in the Methodology of Data Collection from Newspapers." *Historical Methods* 20.1 (1987) 5–16.

Grant, John Webster. *The Church in the Canadian Era*. 1972. Reprint, Vancouver: Regent College, 1988.

---

58. Lougheed, "Anti-Catholicism," 161–80.

Hampton, Mark. "The Press, Patriotism, and Public Discussion: C. P. Scott, the *Manchester Guardian*, and the Boer War, 1899–1902." *The Historical Journal* 44.1 (2001) 177–97.

Heath, Gordon L. "'Forming Sound Public Opinion': The Late Victorian Canadian Protestant Press and Nation-Building." *Journal of the Canadian Church Historical Society* 48 (2006) 109–159.

———. *A War with a Silver Lining: Canadian Protestant Churches and the South African War, 1899–1902*. Montreal: McGill-Queen's University Press, 2009.

Houston, C. J., and W. J. Smith. *The Sash Canada Wore: A Historical Geography of the Orange Order in Canada*. Toronto: University of Toronto Press, 1980.

Hudon, Christine. "Family Fortunes and Religious Identity: The French-Canadian Protestants of South Ely, Quebec, 1850–1901." In *Households of Faith: Family, Gender, and Community in Canada, 1760–1969*, edited by Nancy Christie, 138–66. Montreal: McGill-Queen's University Press, 2002.

Lalonde, Jean-Louis. "French Protestant Missionary Activity in Quebec from the 1850s to the 1950s." In *French-Speaking Protestants in Canada: Historical Essays*, edited by Jason Zuidema, 163–90. Leiden: Brill, 2011.

———. "*L'Aurore*, Voix et Miroir de la Communauté Franco-Protestant," In *Huguenots et Protestants Francophones au Québec: Fragments D'Histoire*, edited by Marie-Claude Rocher, et al., 183–204. Montreal: Novalis, 2014.

Lougheed, Richard. "Anti-Catholicism among French Canadian Protestants." *Historical Papers: Canadian Society of Church History* (1985) 161–80.

———. "Clashes in Worldview: French Protestants and Roman Catholics in the 19th Century." In *French-Speaking Protestants in Canada: Historical Essays*, edited by Jason Zuidema, 99–117. Leiden: Brill, 2011.

MacLennan, Hugh. *Two Solitudes*. Toronto: Macmillan, 1945.

McLeod, Hugh. "Protestantism and British National Identity, 1815–1945." In *National Religion*, edited by P. van der Veer and H. Lehmann, 44–70. Princeton: Princeton University Press, 1999.

Miller, Carman. *Painting the Map Red: Canada and the South African War, 1899–1902*. Montreal: McGill Queen's University Press, 1993.

Miller, J. R. "Anti-Catholicism in Canada: From the British Conquest to the Great War." In *Creed and Culture: The Place of English-Speaking Catholics in Canadian Society, 1750–1930*, edited by Terrence Murphy and Gerald Stortz, 25–48. Montreal: McGill-Queen's University Press, 1993.

———. "Bigotry in the North Atlantic Triangle: Irish, British and American Influences on Canadian anti-Catholicism." *Studies in Religion* 16.3 (1987) 289–301.

Moir, John S. *Enduring Witness: A History of the Presbyterian Church in Canada*. 2nd ed. Burlington, ON: Eagle Press Printers, 1987.

Morton, Desmond. *A Military History of Canada*. 5th ed. Toronto: McClelland & Stewart, 2007.

Paddock, Troy R. E., ed. *A Call to Arms: Propaganda, Public Opinion, and Newspapers in the Great War*. Westport: Praeger, 2004.

Page, Robert. *The Boer War and Canadian Imperialism*. Historical Booklet 44. Ottawa: Canadian Historical Association, 1987.

Renfree, Harry A. *Heritage and Horizon: The Baptist Story in Canada*. Mississauga, ON: Canadian Baptist Federation, 1988.

Rocher, Marie-Claude, et al. *Huguenots et Protestants Francophones au Québec: Fragments D'Histoire*. Montreal: Novalis, 2014.

Scorgie, Glen G. "The French-Canadian Missionary Society: A Study in Evangelistic Zeal and Civic Ambition." In *French-Speaking Protestants in Canada: Historical Essay*, edited by Jason Zuidema, 79–98. Leiden: Brill, 2011.

Semple, Neil. *The Lord's Dominion: The History of Canadian Methodism*. Montreal: McGill-Queen's University Press, 1996.

Silver, A. I. "Some Quebec Attitudes in an Age of Imperialism and Ideological Conflict." *Canadian Historical Review* 57 (1976) 441–60.

Watt, James T. "Anti-Catholic Nativism in Canada: The Protestant Protective Association." *Canadian Historical Review* 48.1 (1967) 45–58.

Wilkinson, Glenn R. *Depictions and Images of War in Edwardian Newspapers, 1899–1914*. New York: Palgrave Macmillan, 2003.

Wolffe, John. "Anti-Catholicism and Evangelical Identity in Britain and the United States, 1830–1860." In *Evangelicalism: Comparative Studies of Popular Protestantism in North America, the British Isles, and Beyond, 1700–1990*, edited by Mark A. Noll, et al., 179–97. Oxford: Oxford University Press, 1994.

———. "Anti-Catholicism and the British Empire, 1815–1914." In *Empires of Religion*, edited by Hilary M. Carey, 43–63. London: Palgrave Macmillan, 2008.

Zuidema, Jason. "Charles Chiniquy: The Meta-Denominational and Protestant Presbyterian." In *French-Speaking Protestants in Canada: Historical Essays*, edited by Jason Zuidema, 145–62. Leiden: Brill, 2011.

———, ed. *French-Speaking Protestants in Canada: Historical Essays*. Leiden: Brill, 2011.

5

Canada's Salvation Army and War

The War Cry, Soul Saving, and the South African War

ERIC CROUSE

THE CANADIAN *WAR CRY* clarified that Christ's love and the salvation of souls was the primary focus of the late-nineteenth century Salvation Army, even in times of war. When the denominational magazine discussed the South African War, emotional patriotism for British interests in South Africa was missing. And *War Cry* commentary of Canadians fighting was remarkably sparse in an era when the public discourse of the war was intense and widespread in Canada.[1]

The message for Salvationists residing throughout South Africa, the Transvaal, and Orange River Colony was to be friends to both the British and the Boers. As the *War Cry* explained in the early stage of the war, "so far as actual combatants are concerned our position is one of the strictest neutrality, with the strongest disposition to effect the largest possible amount of good among both the opposing forces."[2] All lives mattered, and thus, it was paramount to seek God's will, spiritual revival, and "peace

---

1. For more on Christianity and war, see Heath, "Canadian Churches and War." On the profound impact of the war on Canadian society, see Miller, *Painting the Map Red*, xi.

2. "The War," *War Cry*, 20 January 1900, 13. Also, see "Tales of the Veldt," *War Cry*, 3 November 1900, 10. Salvationist Ensign Hurley desiring to serve South Africa during the war wired Commissioner Kilbey for his permission. Kilbey's response was: "Yes, if you stand on neutral ground."

and goodwill amongst men."[3] This was on a higher level than the goal to "integrate 'our brother Boer' into the imperial family."[4] Salvationists laboring in South Africa were to "push on, through storm and tempest, and amid seas of difficulties, assured as ever that God, even our own God, will bestow upon us His continued blessing."[5] Winning souls for Christ trumped all concerns.

The history of the Salvation Army began in 1865 when Methodist preacher William Booth (1829–1912) organized the Christian Mission, a group devoted to bringing the gospel of Jesus Christ to the unchurched in London, England. With his wife Catherine (1829–1890) at his side, Booth renamed the group the Salvation Army in 1878. The strategy of adopting military ideas to reach people with a message of sin and salvation was a successful one in an age when military order garnered significant respect in western society. With General Booth as head, military-attired Salvation Army preachers were officers, congregations were corps, and corps community centers were important sites for religious activities, with a clear focus in the early years on preaching the gospel. Salvationists kept it simple, "not wasting time in the discussion of minor points of doctrine, which can easily wait until we have the last sinner saved."[6]

The Salvation Army spread internationally, including to Canada in 1882.[7] At the start of the South African War, Booth's daughter Evangeline (1865–1950) was the Commander-in-Chief of Salvation forces in Canada, Newfoundland, and North-Western America, committed to war against "His Blackest Majesty King of the Nethermost Regions of Hell."[8] The key source for communicating the activities of the Salvationists was the *War Cry*, a weekly magazine published in Toronto that provided fourteen

---

3. See "The War! Salvationists, Beware!" *War Cry*, 11 November 1899, 9. Almost a year before the start of the Boer War, this was the message of the General when he referred to the peace proposals of the Czar of Russia. He encouraged more prayer for "the noble, beneficent and Christlike proposals." See "Reflections," *War Cry*, 21 January 1899, 7. Also, see "Peace or War," *War Cry*, 3 June 1899, 8; "Peace on Earth," *War Cry*, 10 June 1899, 8.

4. Miller, *Painting the Map Red*, xii. This imperialism theme was strong following the war. On Canadian Protestant churches, imperialism, and the idea of good coming out of the war, see Heath, *War with a Silver Lining*.

5. "The War in South Africa," *War Cry*, 12 May 1900, 5.

6. "Why Should I Become a Soldier?" *War Cry*, 18 March 1899, 2.

7. Marks, *Revivals and Roller Rinks*, 142. "Our 17th Birthday," *War Cry*, 21 October 1899, 1.

8. See "Manifesto," *War Cry*, 11 February 1899, 3.

pages packed with news and Bible-related stories, most of which contained regional and local Canadian material. At least one page gave accounts of Salvation Army work internationally, with news of Europe, South America, Asia, and Africa broken down into specific nations. As far as editorial policy, there was a clear lack of Canadian content which in part explains the absence of commentary on Canada's role in the South African War. In fact, R. G. Moyles's history of the Salvation Army in Canada gives no mention of the South African War, a notable absence given that over 7,300 Canadians served in the war.

Before war broke out in October 1899, much of the early accounts of Salvationist activities in South Africa in Canada's *War Cry* were brief.[9] Encouraging were reports of the open-air attendance and souls saved at revival meetings, of new halls opened, and of the work of Commissioner William Ridsdel who served in South Africa from 1896–1899. His duties included traveling throughout the region where the Salvation Army conducted day school operations and reached the unchurched "natives." There was an international flavor to Salvation Army efforts in South Africa, which helps explain its disposition for peacekeeping. Salvation of individual souls was the ultimate concern as Salvationists served in many different ways.

In South Africa, any Salvationist able to understand languages—ranging from Albania to the Zulu tongue—was considered to be an answer to prayer. One example was the French-speaking Salvation candidate preparing to reach the French foreign women in Cape Town "who parade the streets nightly."[10] Salvation Army work earned the respect of many belonging to other denominations. One supporter was imperialist Cecil Rhodes (1853–1902), former prime minister of the Cape Colony. In April 1899, Rhodes addressed an audience in London, praising the work of the Salvation Army in South Africa. He backed his words that day with a $1,000 donation to the Army.[11]

Satan was deemed formidable, but the Salvation Army served notice of its fight against the deception of Beelzebub found in city streets at home, abroad, and on the battlefront. The first *War Cry* report of "Boer troubles" was in late July 1899 with Salvationists desiring "a peaceful settlement."[12]

---

9. There was a South African *War Cry* published that included a page in Dutch for the Boers.

10. "South Africa," *War Cry*, 21 January 1899, 12.

11. "Cecil Rhodes and the Salvation Army," *War Cry*, 6 May 1899, 12.

12. "South Africa," *War Cry*, 29 July 1899, 9.

By October, the magazine wrote of "the horrors of bloodshed" and "the cheap bravado" of the masses clamoring for war. The scales were "trembling" as politicians weighed the correct action to take with the conflict in Transvaal.[13] Carman Miller notes that Canadian Methodists, Presbyterians, and Anglicans, in pulpit and press, "generally condoned and inspired the growth of imperialism."[14] However, in the *War Cry* coverage of the "Boer troubles," British imperialism gained little or no sway.

As for the signs of war, the expectation was grave consequences. But it would not be Commissioner Ridsdel at the helm to face escalating miseries. His replacement boarded the "Norman" at Southampton on 23 September and was on his way to South Africa.[15] Commissioner George A. Kilbey, previously the Chief Secretary for the United Kingdom, was the new leader of the South African Salvationists as they faced the problems of a war which various observers expected to last "for some months."[16]

Days before the war began, there was much fearful uncertainty in South Africa with businesses paralyzed and homes closed down, both causing a rise in paupers and refugees. The *War Cry* could see no justification for war between the "so-called Christian nations" of Great Britain and the South African Republic (Transvaal), and irresponsible British politicians risked the glory of the British Empire by choosing war against a weaker nation "to justify their own schemes." If the British decided "to sow the seed of death to national greatness," the Salvation Army leaders knew where they stood.[17] When the "cleverest spirits" from Hell agitated for evil "in the smoldering fire of war," the ultimate and highest service for Salvationists was "seeking the salvation of the individual soul." A greater triumph than any army defeating its foe was reclaiming "from the power of Evil and Darkness to the love of Truth and Right, one soul."[18]

After the war officially broke out on 10 October, the *War Cry* began informative reports on the conflict, beginning with a historical overview of the region from the days of Portuguese Bartholomew Diaz in 1486 to the demands of British subjects living among the Boers in Transvaal in

---

13. "Peace or War?" *War Cry*, 21 October 1899, 2.

14. Miller, *Painting the Map Red*, 9.

15. "South Africa," *War Cry*, 30 September 1899, 8; "South Africa," *War Cry*, 21 October 1899, 5.

16. "The Way of the World during 1899," *War Cry*, 6 January 1900, 9.

17. "Let Us Have War!" *War Cry*, 21 October 1899, 4.

18. "Peace or War," *War Cry*, 30 September 1899, 8.

the late 1890s.[19] The Salvation Army appointed Adjutant George Stevens, editor of the South African *War Cry*, as its special war correspondent. The Canadian *War Cry* gave Canadian readers detailed military news. As early as 4 November it reported on 500 British and many more Boer soldiers killed early into the "hapless war." Deadly engagements and land ravished by war meant ample work for Salvationists providing accommodations for "disabled soldiers and distressed refugees" of both sides.[20]

Early into the war it became obvious that the Salvation Army in Africa encountered many serious difficulties. Constant migrations of refugees poured into Cape Town, Salvation Army finances diminished in many depopulated districts, and Salvation operations in Johannesburg, Pretoria, and other communities, cutoff by the war, suspended their work.[21] The situation was grim, articulated in Salvation Army war reports by Stevens: "We fervently pray that something will speedily happen which shall put an end to these cruel and bitter struggles, which are maddening thousands and turning men's minds from thoughts of purity and righteousness to things worthy only of the heathen and the brute."[22] However, with darkness came light. Salvationists took courage, "fully confident that 'Yesterday, today, forever, Jesus is the same!'"[23] The Salvation work in Cape Town was portrayed as heroic: "All refugees come to us, and while we look after their bodies we do not forget the starving souls around us."[24]

On 30 December, the *War Cry* announced the arrival of the Canadian contingent which received orders to proceed to Orange River Station, south of Kimberley. Other British forces engaged the Boers at various locations and the Salvationist assessment at the end of the year gave little hope of a speedy conclusion of the "dreadful slaughter."[25]

In the New Year, the *War Cry* continued its close coverage of war developments, including an interview of Commissioner Kilbey who began his

19. "The South African War," *War Cry*, 4 November 1899, 13.

20. "The War in South Africa," *War Cry*, 11 November 1899, 4. Other commentary indicated this trans-national perspective: "As Salvationists, we are cosmopolitans and citizens of the One Country where war is an impossibility." See "The War in South Africa," *War Cry*, 28 November 1899, 4.

21. "The War in South Africa," *War Cry*, 2 December 1899, 12; "Side-Lights on the War," *War Cry*, 9 December 1899, 9.

22. "South Africa," *War Cry*, 30 December 1899, 5.

23. Ibid.

24. "South Africa," *War Cry*, 9 December 1899, 13.

25. "The South African War," *War Cry*, 30 December 1899, 9.

introductory tour of the eastern region of South Africa with a visit of Port Elizabeth where his entourage "had a good time, with a fair share of blessing for soldier, saint, and sinner."[26] They experienced some drama when their departure from Port Elizabeth by railroad was cut off by British authorities fearing Boer military operations. Their only alternative was boat travel to East London and on to King William's Town and Queenstown, which was close to actual military fighting. At a virtual continuous pace, mule-teams loaded with British provisions poured into Queenstown. There was a flood of soldiers at the railway station, looking much like a military depot. Continuing his tour from Queenstown to Stormberg, Kilbey found the region all but deserted with the exception of the natives. It was an unhappy situation for the Commissioner that, Salvationists, including Boer Salvationists who had been commandeered by leaders to fight, were at risk on the military front.[27] Despite his best effort to get a military permit for travel, Kilbey would have to wait almost two years later before he could visit Johannesburg and the Transvaal.[28]

Already within weeks of the start of the war there were reports of fallen Salvationists on both sides, slain on the battlefield. But, again, it was their duty to follow the Commissioner's direction and "hold themselves ready at all time to do the most menial thing possible, if it is likely to give them the opportunity to benefit either British or Boer."[29] The *War Cry* reported that only the Salvation Army had permission to conduct meetings in the military camps.[30] Pursuing the salvation of sinners, a typical Salvation Army procedure was a revival-type meeting at soldiers' camps near the front. At one meeting in January 1900, soldiers brought candles from their tents and used their bayonets as candlesticks to illuminate the gathering: "From the moment we began the presence of God was felt, and conviction was stamped on many faces."[31] One soldier confessed that he was "the biggest sinner in the camp," and many others "begged us to come again."[32] On the battlefield, men saw little glory of war, and many "cried like children"

26. "The War in South Africa," *War Cry*, 6 January 1900, 13.
27. "The War in South Africa," *War Cry*, 6 January 1900, 13.
28. "South Africa," *War Cry*, 2 November 1901, 9.
29. "South Africa," *War Cry*, 13 January 1900, 4; "The Double Soldiership," *War Cry*, 20 January 1900, 6.
30. "From the South African Battlefield," *War Cry*, 3 February 1900, 6.
31. "The War," *War Cry*, 20 January 1900, 13.
32. Ibid.

when they lost their mates. The Salvation meetings offered hope. Salvationists themselves witnessed the "evils of war" with many heart-breaking stories passed on to *War Cry* readers such as the following: "One of the Guards, a big fellow, thrust his bayonet through the body of a Boer, who, with his dying strength shot him through the head, both men dying almost simultaneously!" In contrast, the Salvation Army's "soul-saving work" was salvation after battle—a time of hallelujah proving that "God lives."[33]

Canadian readers learned that the Salvation Army also faced strong secular forces, notably in the cities. Sundays in Cape Town and other South African centers were "much like any other day."[34] Newspapers hit the streets, soldiers marched, and Christianity held "a very secondary place in many minds."[35] On the minds of people far from the battlefield were the problems brought by a disrupted economy. The basic law of supply and demand meant that oil, meat, butter, eggs, and vegetables were very expensive. With the end of the war nowhere in sight, people were desolate. [36] In gloomy times, the Salvation Army continued to fight: "We, as warriors of the Cross, must not think lightly of the enemy's opposition. The devil is strong and shrewd for unaided human skill, but, with the Holy Spirit's aid, enthused with Divine compassion, our Siege will be a decided success."[37] War correspondent Stevens wrote of the unwavering courage of the Salvation Army: "assured that in His own good time all shall be well, and the dear old Army shall yet advance from victory unto victory, even in quarters where now all is chaos and dire confusion."[38] One notable act of commitment, reported in April 1900, was a revival meeting held in a mine 1,400 feet underground for women who had retreated from the heavy bombardment of Boers during the siege of Kimberley.[39]

Told in South Africa and shared with Canadian *War Cry* readers were stories of "providential escapes" where "God's protecting arm" surrounded Salvationists exposed to the dangers of war.[40] Periodically, the *War Cry*

---

33. "From the South African Battlefield," *War Cry*, 3 February 1900, 6; "The War," *War Cry*, 20 January 1900, 13.
34. "From the South African Battlefield," *War Cry*, 3 February 1900, 6.
35. Ibid.
36. Ibid.
37. "The Siege," *War Cry*, 10 February 1900, 8.
38. "From the South African Battlefield," *War Cry*, 3 February 1900, 6.
39. "South Africa," *War Cry*, 28 April 1900, 12.
40. "The South African Battle Field," *War Cry*, 5 May 1900, 5.

referred to Leaguers who were members of the Salvation Army Naval and Military League created in 1894 to communicate with Salvationists in the armed forces. These Salvationists represented a different group than those belonging to the national group in Canada called the League of Mercy which specialized in hospital, prison, and shut-in visits. In a letter to his mother, a Canadian Salvationist of the Naval and Military League wrote of one fierce Boer attack: "The bullets whistled all around me. I can tell you, dear mother, it was a near shave for me; but our God did not see fit that I should be hurt, praise Him for evermore! I can say, 'I love Him best of all,' and if He sees fit, His will be done. I believe He will take me home."[41] Shortly after, many Canadians fell in the Battle of Paardenburg. The Canadian participation at Paardenburg, which resulted in the surrender of over 4,000 Boers, and thus, constituted an important victory for the British and earned the praise of many in the England and Canada. But any talk of the battle representing "a symbol of Canadian prowess" found no traction in the *War Cry*.[42]

Yet there were stories of heroism, of various Salvationists who died in the war, and were thus promoted to heavenly glory. One *War Cry* story of death, told by Adjutant Murray, drew the most important lesson for Salvationist serving in the war in the hospitals, kitchens, and halls, and near the battles. As she recounted, "Then we heard of Magersfontein and Bob Wilson, the Salvation hero. Oh, we lost many Leaguers, but I felt as I heard, 'If I can only help one man to die as our Bob Wilson died, with the water of Life in his soul, it is worth anything!'"[43] A Salvationist for several years, Wilson received two serious wounds to his head. As recounted by Murray, "When offered a drink of water he refused, saying, 'Give it some other lad; I have the Water of Life,' and so passed away to be with God."[44]

Canadian *War Cry* readers received many examples of Boers tenacity and British might. Slowly, the Salvation Army took advantage of British success against the Boers, since any advance towards the Transvaal enabled Salvationists to make contact with other Salvationists "long isolated"

---

41. "A Letter from One of Our Leaguers now on the South African Battlefield," *War Cry*, 5 May 1900, 5.

42. On Canadian participation at Paardeberg and the response at home, see Miller, *Painting the Map Red*, 105–12.

43. "Tales of the Veldt," *War Cry*, 3 November 1900, 10.

44. "The S. A. in the Boer War," *War Cry*, 14 September 1901, 3.

from the beginning of the war.[45] But British military victory did not alter the neutrality of the Salvationists. Months into the war, Salvation Army concern for the Boers remained steadfast with Salvation officers proclaiming "the glad tidings of salvation wherever and whenever the opportunity presents itself."[46]

Attending to all soldiers, the Salvationists believed that the Salvation Army was "the organization best able to do individual visitation and deal with these men about spiritual things ... They are our people, and, it would be wrong if we were not on the spot to minister to their eternal welfare."[47] And there were testimonies of soldiers under the fire of bullets "coming thick and fast" who remembered and found peace in the blessings spoken at Salvation Army meetings. After a half year of war, soldiers continued to flock to meetings: "An open-air here in camp is a sight not easily forgotten. Each means an audience of about three hundred. The men seem eager to hear the truth, and openly acknowledge that they have been blessed. We loan the troops song books and pick the songs that are mostly known, it is beautiful to hear the men sing."[48] Evidence of trust was that many soldiers gave the Salvationists postal addresses of their wives in the event of their death on the battlefield.[49]

General Booth continued to speak against the evil of war, "pleading with God for His intervention, and entreating my people to stand true to their principles as peace-makers between man and man, as well as between man and God."[50] It was not lost to many of the real possibility of a Salvationist succumbing on the battlefield at the hands of a Salvationist of the opposing army.[51]

The *War Cry* news on Canadians varied: there were reports of Canadians setting sail for South Africa, requests that people send financial donations to Evangeline Booth in Toronto, and word of victories scored when such Toronto soldiers captured a Boer camp near Sunnyside.[52]

---

45. "The War," *War Cry*, 20 January 1900, 13.
46. "The War in South Africa," *War Cry*, 3 March 1900, 7.
47. Ibid.
48. Ibid.
49. Ibid.
50. "The General on the War," *War Cry*, 19 May 1900, 3.
51. This certainly was the case during the First World War. See Moyles, *The Blood and Fire*, 171.
52. "The South African War," *War Cry*, 13 January 1900, 9; "The South African War,

But any mention of Canadian soldiers active in the war was often only a sentence or two. One report in mid-1900 stated that the Canadian soldiers, of which 200 were dead and wounded, were "very brave men" who "would make good Salvationists."[53] A month later a report gave 101 as the exact number of dead of the Canadians Contingent with many more who were sick and wounded.[54]

By the middle of 1900, some saw signs of the war ending soon, and General Booth wrote, "We have admired the courage and skill of the Boer Farmer Volunteer, and the endurance and dash of the British Soldier. Who now will go and dare and suffer in the Cause of Christ, the Cause of Righteousness, and the Cause of Universal Love?"[55] Other conflicting reports suggested that the war would continue for many more months. News of President Matinus Theunis Steyn of the Orange Free State, considering his willingness to surrender, included General Christiaan Rudolf De Wet's threat that he would shoot the president.[56] The *War Cry* gave reports of British success taking Pretoria, but there were reversals as the Boers scored victories elsewhere.[57] Whatever the state of the war, encouraging reports continued of "earnest prayer, vigorous singing, and red-hot testimonies" at open-air and indoor meetings. Accompanying such labor was the establishment of homes in Kimberley and Cape Town corresponding to the interests of Tommy Atkins (the common British soldier).[58]

There were harvests of souls at many locations, including a "spiritual awakening" at Kimberley. When British forces took control of Johannesburg, Salvationists voiced their excitement of expanding their "red-how campaigns" and social work, and at meetings for Boer prisoners of war, men came out for salvation.[59] Salvation Army Captain Bainbridge wrote of weekly meetings for Boer prisoners on the Island of St. Helena: "We have had some very nice meetings among the men; over 200 round us listening, in fact, there are meetings going on various parts of the camp all day

---

War Cry, 20 January 1900, 8; "The War," *War Cry*, 10 February 1900, 8.
53. "War as He Sees It," *War Cry*, 23 June 1900, 10.
54. "The South African War," *War Cry*, 4 August 1900, 4.
55. "Peace in Prospect," *War Cry*, 30 June 1900, 9.
56. "The South African War," *War Cry*, 28 July 1900, 8.
57. "The South African War," *War Cry*, 23 June 1900, 8.
58. "The War in South Africa," *War Cry*, 7 July 1900, 9.
59. "The Prospect in South Africa," *War Cry*, 21 July 1900, 5.

long, so it is not dull for them."[60] One Boer prisoner held elsewhere told a Salvationist nurse: "God bless you and the Salvation Army for what you are doing."[61] At a meeting for Boer prisoners in Ceylon it was a treat to hear 600 Dutch voices singing "The Lion of Judah."[62]

Faced with living in mostly rough conditions—a poor diet and pitiful sleeping arrangements—and struck down with fever and other illnesses, Salvationist nurses provided much comfort and care to all soldiers. In return, there was much love for the nurses as one nurse testified: "[T]he men were beautiful to us everywhere we went. When I was down with enteric fever, they gave quite a large sum to Ensign for delicacies for me. Our Leaguers upheld the honor of God and the Salvation Army."[63]

Such inspiring reports for Canadian readers were fewer in the remaining months of 1900, since overall coverage of the war lessened. It was the same with content of Canadian involvement in the war—it remained in short supply. In November 17, the *War Cry* briefly referred to the return of a large Canadian contingent of soldiers from South Africa and the subsequent "patriotic demonstrations" in Halifax, Quebec, Montreal, and Toronto.[64] A month later, Salvationist readers learned that Colonel Otter and 300 Canadians who fought the Boers were in transit to Canada, arriving home on Christmas Day.[65] The war was far from over, but it entered a new phase with Lord Roberts handing over the command of British troops to Lord Kitchener who "unexpectedly displayed a very conciliatory policy," according to the *War Cry*.[66] Having avoided capture, key Boer military leaders continued to fight, though mostly with fewer heavy engagements. One notable exception was in late 1900 when a force of 2,500 Boers took control of a British garrison manned by 550 troops near Pretoria in December.[67] Given the stubborn resistance of the Boer, over 40,000 men were sent to South Africa in the first three months of 1901, bringing the total number to

---

60. "South Africa," *War Cry*, 28 July 1900, 4.
61. "Tales of the Veldt," *War Cry*, 3 November 1900, 10.
62. "Among the Boer Prisoners in Ceylon," *War Cry*, 19 October 1901, 7.
63. "Tales of the Veldt," *War Cry*, 3 November 1900, 10.
64. "The Week," *War Cry*, 17 November 1900, 8.
65. "The Week," *War Cry*, 15 December 1900, 8; "Other War Items," *War Cry*, 12 January 1901, 8.
66. "General Kitchener's Policy," *War Cry*, 19 January 1901, 4.
67. "The South African War," *War Cry*, 29 December 1900, 13.

275,000 British troops. By June there were 18,000 Boer prisoners of war.[68] Unlike the first year of the war, a good part of the *War Cry*'s international news focused on other stories, notably the Boxer Rebellion in China and famine in India.

Some of the more interesting accounts in the *War Cry* were by Salvationists who gave personal accounts of their fighting experience. Despite three major wounds, one Leaguer held strong against a superior Boer force before his capture. Giving him "great credit for the stand" that he and others made, the Boers gave him water and took him to the Boer Field Hospital. He eventually fell in the hands of the British: "No matter what the devil may say or do, I am determined to fight for Him under the Yellow, Red, and Blue till I see my Saviour's face in Glory."[69] At the battle of Magersfontein, six Salvationists lost their lives, including two who sang "Safe in the arms of Jesus" before perishing.[70]

In 1901, there were occasional accounts of revival activity in South Africa. One report of the Leaguers of the 2nd Worcestershire Regiment shared information on the fruit of holiness meetings: "It is months since the dear old Canadian *War Cry* had any news of us. Praise His name, we are rising in the Arms of Faith, and our numbers are swelling."[71] In South Africa, soul-saving campaigns continued in many centers, and Salvationists also did their best to serve the needs of Boer refugees, numbering over 60,000, in British camps.

The *War Cry* presented a number of articles critical of war in general. Before the South African War reached its first year, one Salvationist predicted that, when the soldiers returned home, they would not be "better men individually and collectively . . . but rather worse. This Kingdom of God upon earth will not be any nearer than before."[72] Other *War Cry* statements pointed to the "greatest cruelties" of war. For example, when Lord Kitchener issued a proclamation in the final stage of the war that Boers captured in British uniform would be shot, General Louis Botha reportedly responded that every armed soldier captured would be shot.[73]

---

68. "The South African War," *War Cry*, 20 April 1901, 8; "The Week," *War Cry*, 1 June 1901, 8.
69. "A Prisoner of War," *War Cry*, 27 July 1901, 13.
70. "The S. A. in the Boer War," *War Cry*, 14 September 1901, 3.
71. "From South Africa," *War Cry*, 8 June 1901, 6.
72. "What Can Make War Impossible," *War Cry*, 1 September 1900, 4.
73. "The Week," *War Cry*, 23 November 1901, 8.

The Salvation Army consistently pointed out the misery of war, but there was also an awareness of the greater evil of sin in the human heart, day in and day out, that many people did not acknowledge. In one commentary on the war, the *War Cry* explained: "It is quite possible that in the view of the Almighty the ill-will, the evil eye, the secret spite, envy, uncharitableness, the dishonesty and over-reaching, the impurity and seduction, open to His all-searching gaze in the space of twenty-four hours, within one hundred miles of Charing Cross is more vile and abominable than the bloodiest battle, which we so much and so justly deplore."[74] Canadian readers also learned of lessons from war, including how soldiers faced and conquered major endurance tests whether it was fighting or thirst and hunger. Now if only "men would endure for Christ like they do for their country, what an Army we would be!"[75]

As far as British imperialism in general, Salvationists saw that all people benefited more than not from British power. This positive view of empire makes sense given the dominating British component of the Salvation Army; in fact, most of the Canadian leaders were from England.[76] Upon the death of Queen Victoria, the *War Cry* wrote of the British Empire leading "the van of civilization in the cause of liberty and commerce, as well as the propaganda of the Gospel among the heathen nations of the world."[77] One theme was Salvationists pursuing two duties. A letter to the *War Cry* from a Captain Stoakes indicated his willingness to fight and give his life for King Edward VII and win "precious souls" for the King of Kings.[78]

It was the spiritual component that gave the *War Cry* war reports a universality that Canadian readers or any Christian believer could appreciate. News of actual Canadians remained sparse, including the guerilla-fighting phase of the second half of the war. Three examples of the *War Cry* giving one-sentence reports of the Canadians are that of Major Howard killed by the Boers in early 1901, the death of Lieutenant Cecil Moore of Winnipeg in mid-1901, and, reported in 10 May 1902, the injury of Corporal Wilkinson of Guelph, who "lost his right eye and part of his arm."[79]

74. "War," *War Cry*, 4 August 1900, 5.
75. "A Lesson of the War," *War Cry*, 3 August 1901, 8.
76. Moyles, *The Blood and Fire*, 36.
77. "The Queen is Dead," *War Cry*, 2 February 1901, 8.
78. "A Letter from One of Our Comrades in South Africa," *War Cry*, 26 April 1902, 2.
79. "South African War," *War Cry*, 9 March 1901, 9; "South African Situation," *War*

One brief report in October 1901 was of a steamer that left Montreal for Cape Town, but it was 1,800 horses not soldiers on the way to the war.[80] Of the more than 7,000 Canadians who served in the South African War, there were only a handful of names identified in the *War Cry*.

CONCLUSION

The Canadian *War Cry* gave little coverage of the end of the war. For Salvationists, it was "extremely pleasing" to witness the conclusion of a war costing $1,100,000,000 and 21,000 lives.[81] The two editorials of the peace signing, published in June, said nothing of the Canadian contribution, in fact, they only mention Canada when noting the bells and whistles heard in most Canadian cities that celebrated the news of peace. The Canadian *War Cry* made no progress in providing "Canadian Salvationists with any sense of a Canadian identity."[82] At the end of the war, the more pressing issue was the solemn reality of Salvationists losing their lives on both sides of the conflict. Yet there was hope for South Africa as Salvationists prepared to "share in the opportunity of the future, when abundant opportunity will be given the people of that sunny land to hear the Gospel messages from the lips of our blood-washed warriors . . . "[83] The Salvation Army served faithfully during the war, and it was set to do its part in South Africa's future— "to win Boer, Briton, and Ultlander for Jesus."[84]

BIBLIOGRAPHY

Primary Source

War Cry (Toronto)

Secondary Sources

Heath, Gordon L. "Canadian Churches and War: An Introductory Essay and Annotated Bibliography." *McMaster Journal of Theology and Ministry* 12 (2010–2011) 61–124.

Cry, 7 September 1901, 8; "Canada," *War Cry*, 10 May 1902, 4.

80. "The South African War," *War Cry*, 26 October 1901, 8.
81. "Terms of Peace in South Africa," *War Cry*, 16 June 1902, 5.
82. Moyles, *The Blood and Fire*, 36.
83. "Peace in South Africa," *War Cry*, 16 June 1902, 8.
84. "South Africa," *War Cry*, 21 June 1902, 8. There was also success in Canada in the following decade, when the number of Canadian Salvation soldiers grew 55 percent. See Moyles, *The Blood and Fire*, 174.

———. *A War with a Silver Lining: Canadian Protestant Churches and the South African War, 1899–1902*. Montreal: McGill-Queen's University Press, 2009.

Marks, Lynne. *Revivals and Roller Rinks: Religion, Leisure, and Identity in Late-Nineteenth-Century Small-Town Ontario*. Toronto: University of Toronto Press, 1996.

Miller, Carman. *Painting the Map Red: Canada and the South African War, 1899–1902*. Montreal: McGill-Queen's University Press, 1993.

Moyles, R. G. *The Blood and Fire in Canada: A History of the Salvation Army in the Dominion 1882–1976*. Toronto: Peter Martin Associates, 1977.

6

"A Daughter in Her Mother's House"

Congregationalist Responses to the South African War, 1899–1902

JAMES TYLER ROBERTSON

THE BEGINNING OF THE twentieth century was a time of heightened optimism for Canada, and participating in an international conflict only multiplied this enthusiasm. In his turn-of-the-century address to the gathering of Ontario Congregationalists, Edmund Yeigh looked back in his nation's history and forward to his nation's future. Looking back, he argued that entering into the war was just one more way that Canada honored its loyal adherence to Britain. Looking forward, he saw that loyalty coupled with a new sense of national pride and development existed independently of the Crown. Such independence possessed much more nuance than the American definition of the term, so Yeigh attempted to capture his sentiments through the use of a familial analogy. For the chairman of Ontario and Quebec Congregationalists, Canada remained a "daughter in her mother's house," but her distance from the motherland and her own inherent strengths meant that she was also a "mistress in her own."[1]

Such a description must not be brushed past too quickly because it grants us insight into an understanding of Canada and the war from a unique Protestant perspective. This chapter argues that Canadian

---

1. "This Canada of Ours—'A daughter in her mother's house, but mistress in her own.'" Yeigh, "Chairman's Address," 75.

Congregationalism supported the British position almost unanimously based on three reasons specific to the culture of the denomination. First, the small denomination's polity created financial and practical obstacles that limited its ability to expand within Canada. Continued reliance on British missionary agencies meant that Canadian Congregationalists had a vested interest in supporting imperial goals both at home and abroad. Second, Congregationalist emphasis on mission saw advantages to the Kingdom of God if the empire was successful in the Transvaal. Third, the empire's stated desire to increase South African civil and religious liberties was seen as being closely aligned with core Congregationalist beliefs. Although there were a few pacifist voices that arose during the war, such sentiments did not last long and found no lasting home within Congregationalism. All of this must be read against the backdrop of Yeigh's comments about Canada's growing autonomy at the start of the twentieth century. While Congregationalism had been comfortable developing slowly with the "daughter" of empire, the smallness of the denomination and its ongoing reliance on Mother England meant that it was struggling to keep up with Canada's growing identity as "mistress."

CANADIAN CONGREGATIONALISM

By the time of the Boer War, Congregationalism was a small but established expression of faith in Canada.[2] While J. William Youngs quips that it was not theology but "Polity [that] gave Congregationalism its name," the denomination's sixteenth-century origin came as a result of like-minded individuals rejecting the Church of England as a false religion.[3] In Canada at the beginning of the nineteenth century, Congregationalism's integral teaching that "Standards of worship could not be fixed by the State" and that any true church should embody only those elements that "had been determined by the Gospel" made them a threat to the established church's colonial hegemony.[4] Coupled with their Dissenters' status was the un-

---

2. The following statistics for Canadian Congregationalism in 1900 come from the 6 June 1900 Annual Meeting. Canada and NFLD: 2 unions, 5 associations, 122 churches, and 105 ministers, 17 of whom not in pastoral work 5 in foreign missions; England and Wales: 54 associations, 2,890 ministers (seating accommodation for 1.6 million), and 4,592 churches and mission stations; US: 5,604 churches, 5,614 ministers, 1,959 of whom not in pastoral work, 629,000 members, 682,000 members of Sunday School, and 191,000 in endeavor societies.

3. Youngs, *Congregationalists*, 17.

4. Huxtable, et.al., *Book of Public Worship*, vii.

fortunate timing of the first official mission to Upper Canada. When the amiable missionary John Roaf arrived to begin work, he found that he had entered the province just days after the cessation of hostilities now known as the '37 Rebellion.[5] Although the land was thought to be ripe for a Congregationalist harvest, Roaf's fledgling congregation found itself "involved in the serious consequences" of rebellion.[6] The missionary reported that some of his congregants came under suspicion of belonging to those who had recently "broken into insurrection," and he lamented that the troubles included one of his most influential members being "banished" while another "had a price set upon his head."[7]

While this might not seem germane to the topic at hand, this story highlights the importance of loyalty in the colony and the dangers a denomination faced if the authorities suspected it of sedition. The origins and evangelical nature of Congregationalism did little to endear them to the established Church of England in Upper Canada; so, if they desired to remain, they needed demonstrable proof of their loyalty. Despite an active presence in the United States, Canadian Congregationalism developed closer ties to their English coreligionists and looked to London for supplies and support. This meant that essentials like Bibles, funds, and even ministers were slower to arrive, and usually in a smaller quantity, but the loyalty issue was assuaged by the connection to Britain. By the middle of that century, contentious issues like education (a cause very close to the Congregationalist heart) and funds from the Clergy Reserves were settled in a manner more equitable to all recognized forms of Protestantism in Canada.[8] However, by that time, the Congregationalists had

---

5. While I am using the term "official" in the preceding sentence, it should be noted that a small Congregational presence was already established. However, this was the first real push to advance the Congregationalist cause in the land. Here follows a brief timeline of some of the Congregationalist communities present in the Canadas and the Maritimes: 1775—first Congregational Church founded in St. Johns NFLD; 1795—London Foreign Missionary Society Founded; 1801—First Lower Canadian Congregationalist Church founded in Quebec; 1805—Quebec's first Sunday School founded; 1819—Upper Canadian Congregationalist Church established in Frome, Ontario.

6. Brown, *Colonial Missions*, 28.

7. Ibid., 30.

8. Further to the comment regarding the role of education in Congregationalism, each one of their annual yearbooks contained a page that described the distinguishing characteristics of Congregationalism as a passion for education (founded almost all New England colleges) and missionary zeal (founded, according to them, the first foreign missionary society in America). The missionary zeal factored prominently in their views on

missed out on financial resources that could have been used to grow their denomination along with the nation it served.⁹ Much of the discourse in the denominational meetings from 1899–1902 lamented the inability to promulgate "our doctrinal and ecclesiastical principles" due to a lack of money and the "failure on the part of many to see and to realize that the West is the strategic ground of Canada."¹⁰

While Yeigh's analogy celebrated Canada as a mistress, his denomination was finding the mistress's house a bit too large to manage effectively. By 1900, a Congregationalist presence could be found in Ontario, Quebec, New Brunswick, Nova Scotia, and Newfoundland, but the vast western expanses remained largely neglected. Therefore, Rev. Dr. George of New Brunswick was dispatched to London to express the "great needs of the work in the West" to the Colonial Missionary Society. Apparently, he was successful in his assignment and the CMS not only donated a "handsome grant" of money but gladly "co-operated with our Society in making the work in Vancouver and Victoria a success." Unlike other Canadian evangelical groups at that time, Congregationalists had yet to form a self-sustaining mission dedicated to national evangelization. As such, and to borrow from Yeigh again, they remained a dependent "daughter" at the turn of the century, rather than a capable "mistress." It could be stretching Yeigh's analogy in unfair ways, but "daughter" is a title that the Congregational leadership of 1900 seemed to embrace gladly. The report on western evangelization ended by stating that the "active sympathies" of the London-based CMS "ring the Empire round, and knit motherland and daughterland in true and sacred bonds."¹¹ While thankful to London, the

---

the South African War and is addressed in a subsequent section of this chapter.

9. It is interesting to note how many Congregationalist organizations begin to spring up in Canada in the latter half of the nineteenth century as more people, and more money, found its way into the church coffers. However, it should be noted that any Congregationalist union was based on voluntary principles as church autonomy was a prized trait of the denomination. Such independent versions of Christianity always lag behind the traditions with a more hierarchical polity. 1847—Union of Nova Scotia and New Brunswick formed; 1853—Canadian Congregational Missionary Society formed from societies "previously existing in Upper and Lower Canada." Union of Ontario and Quebec formed; 1886—The Canada Congregational Women's Board of Missions formed; 1891—First International Congregational Council, London; 1899—2nd International Congregational Council, Boston.

10. Brown, *Colonial Missions*, 31, and *47th Annual Report of the Canada Congregational Missionary Society*, 94, respectively.

11. Gerrie, "Preface to the 1900 Year book," *Congregational Year Books*, 1.

leadership was also displeased with this development, as is evidenced by W. McIntosh's chastisement of Canadian Congregationalists for being short-sighted, and for either forsaking or failing to understand "their privilege" and duty to serve the Kingdom of God on the west coast of Canada.[12] The Colonial Missionary Society stepped in to help fund and supply western expansion with some success, but the necessity of George's trip revealed a much deeper problem for the denomination.

The polity of Congregationalism defended the autonomy of the local church and a strictly voluntary fellowship between such church bodies. That very lack of an overarching structure meant that missionary endeavors, ever so central to Congregational identity, were funded solely by the membership. That system could work in places like England, or even America, but the sheer geographical vastness of Canada was proving too expensive for such a small collection of people. In order to address this uniquely Canadian dilemma, 1900 witnessed the birth of a committee appointed for the sole purpose of strengthening the "bond of fellowship between the churches." It was argued that this group could discover ways to increase communication, share resources, and engage in concerted missionary efforts to make Canadian Congregationalism "more effective in extending the Kingdom of God."[13] The need to bring the Congregational message from coast to coast was deemed of the highest urgency due to the manifestation of the South African War.

While largely supportive of "mother" England and the empire, there remained a growing concern that war, regardless of the morality of its cause, was a violent external indicator of a rampant, internal corruption.[14] In light of this, Canada was faced with an important task: the burgeoning nation needed to find a way to eschew the mentalities of Europe—and the Republic to the south—and make choices that were more indicative of a true Gospel spirit.[15] The importance of the so-called "New World"

---

12. McIntosh, "48th Annual Report of the Canada Congregational Missionary Society," as found in *47th Annual Report of the Canada Congregational Missionary Society*, 72.

13. Gerrie, "Preface to the 1900 Year book," *Congregational Year Books*, 1.

14. Roland Bainton wrote the following reflection on the content of one of his father's sermons during the Boer War: "War blunts the moral feeling of the nation because it slays sympathy. We grow insensitive to human feeling and we hear of the slaughter of hundreds, perhaps thousands with less sorrow than we do of the death of a single friend. Compassion is in danger of dying when a nation is at war." Bainton, *Pilgrim Parson*, 69.

15. One of the first Canadians to relate the social gospel to international affairs was C. S. Eby, a Methodist missionary to Japan. He wrote in his treatise *The World Problem*

mentality upon the Congregationalist churches at that time should not be minimized.[16] Being a peaceful light of British civilization and Christianity could be Canada's role within the empire. A country that embodied all that was great about Britain without the violent past would prove to be a tremendous benefit to all the nations of the world. Such patriotism and pride in Canada's potential meant that the Congregationalists had a role to play if Canada was to succeed in so grand a calling.[17] Yeigh believed his denomination and nation were so aligned that "One would naturally conclude that Congregationalism would be indigenous on Canadian soil," because both mandated and embodied "the widest personal, church and religious liberty of thought and action." Yeigh admitted that, while "we have no national heroic deeds of self-sacrifice with which to incite our membership to loyalty," the national character proved that his denomination's influence was "felt in Canada" and that it needed to be maintained.[18] This desire to remain as a positive influence over the immense geographical territory meant that the missionary endeavor to the west needed to be understood as not only serving denominational goals for the advancement of national character, but that it also served imperial concerns as well.[19]

Despite such lofty goals, only one year later, the committee "appointed to consider the formation of a Congregational Union for Canada" had come to nothing and was abandoned. The distance between the various bodies of Congregationalists made any hope of a national union from

---

and the Divine Solution the following: "Canada is beginning a career which is bound to be epoch-making in the history of the world. Is Canada to be carried into this destructive flood, under which all old nations have perished? Must we keep up the dance of death with all mature nations now heading in the same direction of moral failure? Or is it possible that we may find a better way and influence other nations for the common good? Underneath the bad in every land there is the fundamental desire for the good: underneath the war-attitude there is the everlasting profession of a desire for peace: underneath the universal exploitation of man by man there is the universal protestation of the desire to do right." Eby, *The World Problem*, 24–25.

16. "For the first sod of the Canadian Pacific Railway was turned on the 2nd of May, 1881, and the last spike driven on the 7th of May, 1885. These facts achieved, the new era may be said to have dawned." Brown, *Colonial Missions*, 46.

17. "[That] Canada constitutes an important and integral portion of the British Empire is a fact never so clearly recognized as now." Yeigh, "Chairman's Address," 76.

18. Ibid., 81.

19. "It is easier to state these facts than for the mind to realise [sic] their full significance, for they really meant that a new world was being called into existence." Brown, *Colonial Missions*, 46.

coast to coast "impracticable."[20] Despite a denominational culture that celebrated missionary zeal, Canadian Congregationalism found itself unable to achieve a substantial national presence. While Canada was coming into her own as mistress, Congregationalism had to remain dependent on "mother" England if it held out any hope of having an ongoing presence. Such transatlantic reliance seemed more like a vestige of nineteenth-century Canadian Christianity; so, if the small collection of like-minded souls could not find a way to remain relevant in this new Canada, there was a real concern that the unique voice of Canadian Congregationalism would be lost. Those concerns influenced all of the responses and writings that pertained to the South African War. Somewhat ironically, one of the most troubling opinions regarding the war came from the West, the very place that the denomination had been so desperate to evangelize.

ANTI-WAR SENTIMENT

Pacifism in the periphery of empire is always a tricky endeavor. Famed historian Roland Bainton wrote on this issue as it pertained to the Boer War from both an academic and personal standpoint. Bainton's father, Rev. James Herbert Bainton, served a Congregationalist community in Vancouver, and, early into his tenure as pastor, the recent English immigrant offered up a prayer beseeching the Almighty to "look with compassion on the British and Boer alike."[21] This incensed some influential members of the congregation—men Roland termed "super patriots"—to the point that they demanded an official wartime stance from their religious leader.[22] The elder Bainton, while sympathetic, lamented the war and referred to it as a "deplorable" turn of events for both physical and moral reasons. He concluded the sermon with the "assertion that any war was incompatible with Christianity" and that in his "heart of hearts" he did not believe "Jesus Christ would have countenanced war of any description."[23] Many of James Bainton's 125-person congregation agreed with him, but the aforementioned super-patriotic faction felt the position untenable and seceded from the community.

---

20. Anon., "*47th Annual Report*," 48.
21. Bainton, *Pilgrim Parson*, 48.
22. "[These] prayers incensed the 'super-patriots' of the congregation." Ibid.
23. Ibid., 70.

The fallout from this episode impacted Mrs. Bainton's health and the family, seeing that "all of Canada [was] involved in the war," and decided that it was better to emigrate to the United States where they could live out their convictions without risking further harm to the struggling Vancouver congregation.[24] Roland Bainton referred to his parents' ordeal as the "Bainton experience" and wrote that theirs was just one example among many of a "Christian minister's pacifist conscience in conflict with the popular position" that would be "repeated in Canada again and again during the course of the century."[25]

In Toronto, Rev. Morgan Woods of Bond Street echoed similar ideas. Preaching on the first Sunday after the Canadian deployment to South Africa, Woods did not mince words when he declared war to be wrong. He extolled his people to talk about the ramifications of war and how such violence was antithetical to the teachings of Christ. He encouraged his adherents to remember that the Christian's role was to pray and "create a sentiment that will muzzle the cannon."[26] Both Bainton and Woods were well within their theological and denominational rights to express such opinions, but both men were confronted by the reality that their message of peace was met with either disdain or indifference.

While such experiences could be dismissed as isolated, anecdotal or, especially as it pertains to the Baintons, biased, they are not without support in wider academic research into this topic. Peace Movement scholar Gary Moffatt states that, while "[f]ew of those who opposed the South African war left archival material or attained any degree of public recognition," he is aware of "a few Protestant ministers [who] denounced the war."[27] Thomas Socknatt sees the Bainton account as indicative of a larger trend within Canadian culture during the war. Writing on Canadian pacifism in the first half of the twentieth century, he states that even Christian-inspired pacifism "remained far from popular in the tide of emotional imperialism

---

24. Ibid., 71.
25. Ibid.
26. Miller, "English-Canadian Opposition," 433.
27. Moffatt, *History*, 5. Moffatt would go on to write that he was aware of only two official pacifist organizations at the time: The Society of Friends and the Women's Christian Temperance Union. His assessment of attitudes toward pacifism in Canada during the war was grim, to say the least: "The general pattern of society was to shout down dissenters, silence editors, dismiss teachers, proscribe curriculae, threaten minorities and subject dissenters to physical violence." Ibid.

that swept the country."[28] However, looking at the example of Rev. James Bainton, the question should be raised: if Canada was so imperialistic, how did a minister, born and raised in the heart of the empire, fall victim to charges of being unpatriotic?

Perhaps ironically, his place of birth might actually be to blame. Canadian imperialism has always been a shifting collection of nuanced concepts. In the 1880s, for example, Prime Minister John A. MacDonald famously acknowledged that he was born a British subject and would die in the same category. Robert Page's work on the development of Canadian imperialism argues that MacDonald "was appealing to the deep intellectual, emotional, and political traditions of Loyalism in Canada" rather than being blatantly pro-empire.[29] That is an incredibly important piece to recognize and one that Bainton failed to take into account. Simply put, it was relatively easier to critique the war in England than it was in Canada.[30] Bainton came from the metropolis of power, a place and culture secure enough to withstand, and sometimes even encourage, alternate viewpoints; the same was not true of life in the distant periphery of western Canada. Returning to Yeigh's personifications of the nation and the empire, it is one thing for mother to be a little self-critical of her actions and rationale, which might even indicate a balanced and healthy psychology, but it is a different matter entirely when the daughter raises such challenges and concerns.

This is not to say that Canadians espoused a uniform and blind adherence to the empire. The heightened patriotism and increased emphasis on militarism brought on by the South African contest, "raised profound concerns . . . about the long-term implications of imperialism and their cost to Canada." While Bainton's and Woods's concerns were influenced by Christian convictions, they were aligned with other critics of the war effort who believed there were "far more appropriate ways of using [Canada's] human and financial resources than on imperial adventures." And that is why Page's statement regarding "loyalty" in the time of the South African War is so integral.[31] What Bainton encountered was Canadian Congregationalism with an emphasis on the first word in that two-part moniker. With its geo-

28. Socknat, *Witness*, 37.

29. Page, *The Boer War*, 3.

30. Roland Bainton would make this claim himself in his book on the subject of his father: "it was more difficult to criticize the Boer War in Canada than in Britain." Bainton, *Pilgrim Parson*, 67.

31. Page, *The Boer War*, 3.

graphical location on the remote western coast, its dependence on the CMS for funds and ministers, and its lack of connection with co-religionists, it is likely that the "super-patriots" put so much emphasis on the "British" part of British Columbia because it gave them a sense of connection. If the minster from Ilkeston, England had uttered those words in his homeland, he might have been considered controversial. However, in Vancouver, British Columbia, during a time when the empire was struggling for the freedoms of an oppressed people, they bordered on being seditious.

Quebec politician Henri Bourassa also felt the sting of pro-war imperialism as his criticisms of the war created even greater tensions in the already volatile relationship between English and French speaking Canada. While the English papers drew their information about the war from sources in England, the people of Quebec drew from French papers that were clearly anti-British and spoke of the atrocities that the Imperial military committed. There were certain French sections in which "sympathy developed for the Boers, who were facing the ignominy of conquest by Britain just as Quebec had in 1759."[32] While Denominational publications kept their political discourse to a minimum, increased tensions had the potential of being very disruptive to the substantial number of Congregationalists in Quebec. The Montreal-based "Leaflet of the Canada Congregational Woman's Mission Board" showed concern about that as well as a perceived increase in racial rhetoric. In the 1902 Chairman's Address to Ontario and Quebec, Bradley Hyde reminded Congregationalists that believers are not permitted to adopt an attitude of racial superiority. "Is it true that 'God has made of one blood all nations of men to dwell on all the face of the earth'?" he posited rhetorically before going on to lament that human beings seemed to be "so slow to learn the lesson which God took such trouble to teach Peter."[33] Citing the Apostle's famous vision found in Acts 10, Hyde taught Congregationalists to reject the belief that some races are lesser than others and reminded the readers of "the message that 'what God hath cleansed, that call not thou common.'"[34] This was an important

---

32. Ibid., 18. Bourassa was at odds with the more popular conceptions of Canadian alliance in that he wanted Canada to rely fully on America, rather than Britain, for protection. Under the Monroe Doctrine, this was not such an outlandish idea, but, as stated earlier, this did come into conflict with the majority who viewed America as an aggressor and Britain as the natural choice for military protection and support.

33. Hyde, "Chairman's Address," 67.

34. Ibid.

and timely message, not just as a foil against racism but also for the social realities of the Congregationalists of Quebec.

In agreement with Hyde was Dr. A. Yale Massey, who had spent some time in Africa, and who chose to correct feelings of racial superiority through an historical, rather than theological, lesson. Concluding his brief explanation of some of the atrocities the Portuguese Empire committed against the people of Africa (specifically, the Congo), Massey put a poignant question to the readers of the Leaflet: "is it any wonder that the black man has sworn hatred to the white man?" He acknowledged that there were, in that part of the world, two sides to the story, but stated his opinion that "possibly, from a natural sympathy for the weaker side," he chose to side with "our black brothers." War was always a complicated matter, a fact proven by French and English Canada's own divided loyalties on the issue. However, Massey's letter was intended to remind the readers that, whatever the outcome, it was the black inhabitants that deserved the greatest consideration due to their long and tragic past with another, supposedly Christian, global empire.[35]

In addition to such social concerns, the *Missionary Herald* also lamented the fate of missionary endeavors in the south of Africa days before the war broke out. In 1899, a peace conference had recently ended in The Hague, and this was deemed all the more tragic, since it appeared that, right on its heels, "the demons of war will involve all the South African colonies." There were concerns that missions in Natal would be compromised, and a missionary by the name of Goodenough was reported to be "holding on at his post in Johannesburg, in the hope that peace will prevail."[36] The report concluded with the simple plea for God to "hear the prayers of Christendom and avert the long conflict, which to human view now seems inevitable."[37] Despite the prayer, the *Missionary Herald's* assessment that war in South Africa was "inevitable" turned out to be sadly accurate. Even with concerns about the horrors of war, the inconsistency of violence with the Christian message, the potential evils of unreflective patriotism, or the racism that formed much of the backdrop of the entire Boer affair, pacifist sentiment was almost non-existent within Canadian Congregationalism. The denomination threw its support behind the war effort and invested

---

35. Massey, "Letter," 6.
36. Anon., *Missionary Herald*, November 1899, 448.
37. Ibid.

the imperial cause with objectives that were considered in alignment with Congregationalist beliefs.

IN SUPPORT OF THE WAR

Nowhere is the imperial tone of Congregationalism heard stronger than in the pro-war rhetoric. With favorable reports coming in regarding the war effort, Yeigh offered "gratitude to God" that British victories meant the end of "the Boer oligarchy . . . founded on ignorance and superstition" in favor of the imperial "advance of civilization and freedom."[38] The Protestant, English desire to civilize and evangelize the world witnessed an "unprecedented upsurge of emotional and financial support for missionary efforts."[39] Such an upsurge necessarily meant that peoples' eyes were looking beyond national boundaries and towards the larger world beyond. Canadian Congregationalists would easily embrace such ventures as perfectly in keeping with their service to the Kingdom of God. Considering that one of the two self-stated characteristics of their denomination was missionary zeal, the fact that the Congregationalists of Canada enthusiastically embraced their nation's growing international evangelical concern should not be a surprise.[40]

Robert Page is again useful in his explanation of the religious component of Canadian imperialism: "The spread of the gospel under the protective arm of the British Empire would open up the way for a new golden age of peace and prosperity. The Pax Britannica would lead to the Pax Christi."[41] However, Page remains skeptical and a little caustic in his explanation that such attitudes meant that "imperialism was merely the secular arm of Christian expansionism."[42]

Congregationalists did not share Page's concerns, but they did see the war as beneficial if it meant that more people would be introduced to the Gospel.[43] Missions were an essential spiritual and social component of the faith, and one that every person aligned with Britain had to thank for their own freedoms. Writing in 1901, an anonymous author in the monthly

---

38. Yeigh, "Chairman's Address," 76.

39. Page, *The Boer War*, 4.

40. The pragmatic advancement of such missionary mindsets was seen in 1891, when the first International Congregationalist Council was organized in London.

41. Page, *The Boer War*, 5.

42. Ibid.

43. For more on this, see Heath, *Silver Lining*.

"Canada Congregational Woman's Mission Board" penned the following explanation of how the early churches' program of missions lifted "our forefathers in Britain from similar heathen habits and customs into the dignity of a Christian people." The article then went on to explain the valuable social benefits that the faith had brought. English Christianity, it was argued, was the only source "capable of producing . . . a Cromwell, a Gladstone, a Florence Nightingale and a Queen Victoria" and reminded the people that through "the same power, it is the mission of the Church to-day to carry on the same transformation already begun."[44]

The Missionary Board saw the spread of the gospel and civilization as going hand in hand with the general betterment of the world.[45] As missionaries went out they brought not only biblical teachings, but also the opportunity for greater technological advancement and civilization. These advancements, in turn, made the spreading of the gospel even more conducive to more people around the globe.[46] Practically speaking, as churches and schools were built, "steam and electricity appear as servants upon the scene" which bring about increases in "[c]ommerce, politics, science, literature" so that humans "in Asia and Africa" can enjoy the peace and prosperity of the Western world. Chief among the advancements of modern technology was, not surprisingly, the increased ability of remote and disparate people to hear the word of God. Under the reign of Queen Victoria, a Bible was telegraphed from New York to Chicago, "a distance of over a thousand miles" and "the longest message ever wired."[47] Singing the praises of the Bible House of the British and Foreign Bible Society, the author stated the printing presses insured "the words of a Nazarene peasant" would

---

44. Anon. "Monthly Leaflet," May 1901, 6.

45. Further to this point, news of a British victory was seen as a cause for celebration that was deemed a worthy enough interruption of the missionary meeting: "During the [missions] meeting our proceedings were interrupted by the ringing of bells and other sounds of rejoicing, occasioned by the good news from South Africa. Needless to say, the Convention joined heartily in the enthusiasm, singing the National Anthem, and offering praise for the probable speedy termination of the war." Anon., "Monthly Leaflet," July 1900, 3.

46. On the theme of scientific, medical, technological, and cultural advances of the past century that increased the ability for communication, "It is only two decades since I took part in the initial experiments made by Prof. Bell while perfecting the telephone, and now its commercial value cannot be approximated." Yeigh, "Chairman's Address," 78.

47. Anon., "Monthly Leaflet," Feb 1900, 4–5.

influence and "dominate the lives and social system[s] of one hundred and fifty million of the world's most advanced peoples."[48]

For John Robertson, the Congregationalists of Brantford were always an outward looking people. Their "missionary spirit" not only served the Kingdom and defined their faith community, but as well had a commercial component that saw Brantford's "mills, engines and agricultural implements well known in the centre of Africa, at Chisamba and Dondi in the Portuguese settlements."[49] Reflecting on the importance of the war, Robertson did not lament the fact that Canadians had gone to fight for the British cause in South Africa. He believed that this was not just the duty of Canadians, but was a cause that resided close to the hearts of the Congregationalists of his community. Building on the biblical theme that "to whom much is given, much is required," he stated that part of his community's Christian charity necessitated the willingness "to fight and die that others may be free, safe and prosperous also as they are."[50] Dr. Massey, writing in 1901, was in total agreement with statements like the one made by Robertson. As the war was waning, Massey recorded his thankfulness for the cessation of hostilities but then went on to celebrate the "dawn of the day of peace, when there will be extended to another land the fullest civil and religious liberty, a boon for which Congregationalism as ever fought, not by force of arms, but by the power of truth itself."[51]

The benefits of the war were felt within, as well as beyond, national boundaries. Returning to the concern regarding distance and division in the land, Yeigh reported his belief that "Canada has made rapid strides towards that unity that should obliterate the last vestige of racial cleavage in our fair Dominion." His argument was that the "bravery and self-sacrificing loyalty of our sons, of all races and divergent creeds" united Canadians in a cause greater than their petty pre-war rivalries and "won the respect and admiration of the world."[52] Perhaps due to their concentration on missions and education, Congregationalists adamantly and publicly abhorred cultural strife in any setting and celebrated the sacrifice made by Canadians, regardless of ethnicity, to bring liberty to a foreign land. Yeigh drew from an episode in Canadian Congregationalist history in order to demonstrate

48. Ibid., 5.
49. Robertson, *History*, 61.
50. Ibid., 62.
51. Massey, "Letter," 61.
52. Yeigh, "Chairman's Address," 76.

that Congregationalists had always been dedicated to the cause of unity. He recalled one of Canadian Congregationalist founders, the Rev. James Nail, who came to Canada in the late 1830s and set about building a church "in which all creed lines were obliterated."[53]

The future of Canada was to be found in such unity. Congregationalism's proven track record of combating division was one of the most important ways that the denomination could serve the land that was "cradling an empire" within its vast domain.[54] Although concerns remained that an ongoing imperial connection could involve Canada in more international wars, Yeigh remained steadfast in his assertion that "we ought to be profoundly grateful that we possess so rich an inheritance."[55] The inheritance he spoke of was two-fold: first, as this comment followed the story of Nail, the chairman was sounding a clarion call for contemporary Congregationalists to pick up the message of unity that the religious pioneer had left for them. Second, it celebrated the ongoing blessings imperial connections brought to the people of Canada. In his address, Yeigh summarized his belief about the benefits religion offered to the land: "churches and educational institutions are also indispensable adjuncts to national growth . . . the farmer, miner and stock-grower of the far west are demanding the advantages of education and religious instruction with as keen a perception of their value as the residents of the most highly favored cities of the east."[56] Education and mission remained to be the two intrinsic qualities of Canadian Congregationalism, and the arguments were put forward that these two qualities were advanced, both abroad and at home, by the war in South Africa.

---

53. Ibid., 77.

54. Yeigh's argument that Congregationalists were fans of unity is more than a little biased. After all, there is plenty of record of dissension within the denomination as well as their desire to remove the Church of England from the privileged status of establishment. Yeigh was clearly pleased that Canada was being governed in ways that were more conducive to Congregationalist beliefs: "That a salutary and powerful influence has been exercised by our church already is patent to all who are familiar with the history of the clergy reserve . . . our ministers took an active part . . . which resulted in the recovery of one-seventh of the public lands of Upper Canada." Ibid., 80.

55. Ibid., 78.

56. Yeigh, "Chairman's Address," 79–80.

THE DEATH OF VICTORIA AND THE END OF THE WAR

Arguably, the most shocking death to take place during the entirety of the war was that of Queen Victoria. The Union of New Brunswick and Nova Scotia printed the following tribute from their annual meeting:

> the Union remembers with profound regret that during the year that is past the hand of death was laid upon Her Gracious Majesty, Victoria—Queen and Empress—noble Christian woman and friend of religious liberty—our beloved Sovereign . . . This resolution was moved and carried by the audience rising unbidden and singing, "God Save Our Gracious King."[57]

The Forty-Seventh Annual report of the Canada Congregational Missionary Society echoed those sentiments and displayed their unequivocal respect and admiration for "the long and honored reign of our late sovereign, Queen Victoria," before going on to re-assert their "continued loyalty to the crown, and the new King, Edward VII."[58] Queen Victoria would not live long enough to see the end of the war, and Canadian Congregationalists lamented this fact and remained steadfast in their support for the woman who had done so much for their land. Under her guidance education had been brought "within reach of the humblest"; she had enacted and enforced "sanitary laws" and saw to it that "civil and religious liberty is enjoyed by all" by reducing the unfair benefits "of a State-sustained church."[59] Thanks to her government, Canadians could say "we are as happy, free and prosperous as any people on earth."[60] Those social benefits had blessed Canada and the hope remained that a British victory in the Transvaal would bring similar blessings to the people of South Africa.

A year and a half later the war ended, and the people rejoiced. The Ontario and Quebec Congregationalists of 1902–1903 recorded their "deepest gratitude" for "the conclusion of the prolonged South African war." J. P. Gerrie, the editor for that year, recalled to the mind of the readers the two-year old hope that the war would usher in "the dawn of the day of peace, when there will be extended to another land the fullest civil and religious liberty." In that statement dwelled the heart of Congregationalist support

---

57. Anon., *The Union of New Brunswick and Nova Scotia, 1901*, 159.

58. Various, *47th Annual Report of the Canada Congregational Missionary Society*, 49. For commentary on how other Canadian Protestants reacted to her death, see Heath, "Were We in the Habit of Deifying Monarchs."

59. Yeigh, "Chairman's Address," 79.

60. Ibid.

for the war. Gerrie reminded the people that liberty was "a boon for which Congregationalism has ever fought, not by force of arms, but by the power of truth itself."[61] Congregationalism was, first and foremost, a response to tyranny masquerading as genuine faith. From the time of its conception in England, like-minded people had seen the threat state-sponsored religion posed to the bodies of souls of all who lived within the land. Education was required to free people from the superstitions that kept them oppressed, and missions were vital to make sure as many people as possible heard the good news of the Gospel. While it might seem hypocritical for the Congregationalists to be so supportive of the British crown, the Canadian version of the faith—especially as it pertained to the British rejection of church establishment—had grown close enough to the crown that they could cheer for the monarchy's victories, arguing that they were in alignment with the traits that Congregationalists prized above all others.

In 1901, Yeigh had challenged his co-religionists with a lofty goal—to "show our faith by earnest work along the lines indicated as necessary to the building up of a free, educated and consecrated citizenship."[62] In such ways, Yeigh argued, could their denomination spread the Kingdom of God in Canada, a land united with the British Empire to spread civilization and Christianity to the farthest reaches of the globe. He believed that "God's calls are always to go forward and not backward, upward and not downward, and towards the light of a higher civilization."[63] Gerrie echoed this idea in his report and, with such opportunities for higher civilization available to the people of South Africa, wrote that it was time for "Congregationalists of all communions . . . to acknowledge gratitude to Him who maketh wars to cease."[64] Immediately following this call to prayer, Gerrie wrote a one-sentence reference regarding the recent death of Yeigh, the man who, perhaps more than any other, had helped shape Canadian Congregationalists' understanding of the war they had just come through.

CONCLUSION

Congregationalists, like most Protestants in Canada at that time, were optimistic and supportive of their government. The blessings Canada enjoyed were seen to be a direct result of its ongoing connection to Britain, even

61. Gerrie, "Annual Report, 1902–3," *Congregational Year Books*, 45.
62. Yeigh, "Chairman's Address," 85.
63. Ibid.
64. Gerrie, "Annual Report, 1902–3," *Congregation Year Books*, 45.

if that connection was beginning to wane. While most other denominations no longer relied on British institutions for support, the small Congregationalists still leaned heavily on their Colonial Missionary Society for funds and leadership; this only strengthened their attachment to the crown. While others had found that connection to Britain slowed their progress in Canada, Congregationalism's only hope for an ongoing presence was to look beyond their national communities for help from abroad. That reality demonstrates that, at the turn of the century, Congregationalism was being left behind as Canada moved ever increasingly into a more independent, though loyal, *milieu*.

One English-born minister rejected the military endeavor, but his stance proved so much at odds with certain members of his flock that he left for the United States. While his criticisms were influenced by no less than Jesus, the cultural realities of his increasingly "super-patriotic" adherents meant that his words were not well received. The vast majority of Canadian Congregationalists supported their nation's role in their empire's war, believing the people of South Africa would benefit from a British victory. However, the violence of war left Canadians with the thought that, perhaps, the newly formed Dominion could offer up a peaceful apologetic for the British way of life. Displaying the blessings of civilization to the world meant that Congregationalism needed to maintain a voice in the national discourse. This denomination believed its focus on freedom, education, and missions made it uniquely suited to speak into the cultural morals of the Canada of its time.

The war was framed as a struggle against superstition and oppression and, as such, many Congregationalists had no issue supporting the cause. Missionary endeavors were seen to bring the Gospel as well as technological advancements to various cultures, and British control of South Africa meant greater chance for both. Commerce also played a role as some Canadian Congregationalists looked forward to their products finding new markets under the banner of the empire. While the papers spoke about the horrors of war and shared concerns about divided loyalties in Canada and increased prejudice, none of these ever translated into anti-war teachings. The death of Queen Victoria only spurred the Congregationalists into greater professions of loyalty as they credited her reign with numerous blessings and advancements in Canada.

The most prolific Canadian Congregationalist writer during the war, Yeigh, described his country's relationship to the British Empire through an analogy. When it came to global affairs, like the war in the Transvaal, Canada was happy to be a loyal and dutiful daughter in her mother's house. She would answer the call to war and send her own to the aid of the mother, as any good child would. However, that picture was tempered by the demonstrable national desire to alter British institutions to better fit the Canadian context. Canadian loyalty did not mean recreating a little Britain, and the ways in which Canada was carving out a destiny unique to its own setting made her, in the words of Yeigh, the mistress of her own home. The same analogy could not be applied to Canadian Congregationalism. During the war, the small denomination was, at best, a young maiden who was dreaming of leaving the family home but who lacked the resources or opportunities to make such dreams a reality. History tells us that Canadian Congregationalism was never able to truly unify, despite the hopes that the post-war era would put aside dissensions. In fact, it was less than twenty-five years away from joining up with Methodists and Presbyterians to form the first truly Canadian denomination: The United Church. While they argued that they were uniquely situated to speak into the Canadian culture, it appears that even their ardent support for the British War effort was not loud enough to raise their voice above the clamor of the other loyal, but larger, Canadian Christian denominations.

BIBLIOGRAPHY

Primary Sources

Periodicals and Publications

Missionary Herald, November 1899.
47th Annual Report of the Canada Congregational Missionary Society. United Church of Canada Archives.
The Union of New Brunswick and Nova Scotia, 1901. United Church of Canada Archives.

Other

Anonymous. "Monthly Leaflet of the Canada Congregational Woman's Mission Board." December 1899–September 1901. United Church of Canada Archives.
Eby, C. S. *The World Problem and the Divine Solution.* Toronto: Briggs, 1914.
Gerrie, J. P., ed. *Congregational Year Books, 1899–1902.* United Church of Canada Archives.
Huxtable, John, et al. *A Book of Public Worship: Compiled for the Use of Congregationalists.* London: Oxford University Press, 1948.
Hyde, Bradley. "The Chairman's Address: The Redemption of the Commonplace." 1902, As found in *Congregational Year Books, 1899–1902.* United Church of Canada Archives.
Massey, Yale A. "Letter from Dr. Massey." In "Monthly Leaflet of the Canada Congregational Woman's Mission Board," September 1901, 5–6. United Church of Canada Archives.

Yeigh, Edmund L. "Chairman's Address: Making an Empire." In *Congregational Year Books, 1899–1902*. United Church of Canada Archives.

Secondary Sources

Bainton, Roland H. *Pilgrim Parson, the Life of James Herbert Bainton (1867–1942)*. New York: Thomas Nelson & Sons, 1958.

Brown, John. *The Colonial Missions of Congregationalism: The Story of Seventy Years*. London: Colonial Missionary Society, 1908.

Heath, Gordon L. *A War with a Silver Lining: Canadian Protestant Churches and the South African War, 1899–1902*. Montreal: McGill-Queen's University Press, 2009.

———. "'Were We in the Habit of Deifying Monarchs': Canadian English Protestants and the Death of Queen Victoria, 1901." *Canadian Evangelical Review* (Fall 2005–Spring 2006): 72-97.

Miller, Carman. "English-Canadian Opposition to the South African War as Seen through the Press." *The Canadian Historical Review* 55.4 (1974) 422–38.

Moffatt, Gary. *A History of the Peace Movement in Canada*. Ottawa: Grape Vine, 1982.

Page, Robert. *The Boer War and Canadian Imperialism*. Ottawa: Canadian Historical Association, 1987.

Robertson, John. *History of the Brantford Congregational Church 1820 to 1920*. Brantford: Renfrew Mercury Print, 1920.

Socknat, Thomas P. *Witness Against War: Pacifism in Canada 1900–1945*. Toronto: University of Toronto Press, 1987.

Youngs, J. William T. *The Congregationalists*. New York: Greenwood, 1990.

7

Canadian Quakers and the South African War

ROBYNNE ROGERS HEALEY

THE RELIGIOUS SOCIETY OF Friends (Quakers) is well known for its pacifist position on war. Indeed, the 1660 Declaration to Charles II in which Quakers rejected "all outward wars and strife, and fightings with—outward weapons, for any end, or under any pretense whatsoever" is often presented as evidence of Quakers' commitment to peace from the earliest days of the sect.[1] In response to Friends' early twentieth-century peace work, the 1947 Nobel Peace Prize was awarded to the British Friends Service Council and the American Friends Service Committee for "300 years of Quaker efforts to heal rifts and oppose war . . . [particularly] the work done by the two recipient Quaker organizations during and after the two world wars to feed starving children and help Europe rebuild itself."[2] This recognition, alongside the post-WWII efforts of the Quaker United Nations Office (QUNO) at the United Nations "representing Friends' concerns for global peace and justice to the international community," suggests that the 1660 commitment to peace has been both enduring and unchanging.[3] Yet, as historians have demonstrated, except for a handful of individual conscientious objectors including George Fox, Quakers had no

---

1. "A Declaration from the harmless and innocent people of God, called Quakers."
2. American Friends Service Committee Nobel Peace Prize.
3. Quaker United Nations Office.

collective peace testimony before 1660.[4] And, just as the 1660 Declaration had been shaped in war, ongoing Quaker views on pacifism have had a complex and complicated history often formed and reformed in response to the circumstances of specific wars.

Through the eighteenth-century imperial wars in which privateering and arming ships "in a warlike manner" had become a practice for some Quakers, the Society clarified its corporate commitment to an anti-war testimony, eventually advising quarterly and monthly meetings "to testify against" or disown offenders.[5] Nineteenth-century conflicts like the American Civil War proved particularly troublesome. Faced with what many Friends perceived to be an "antislavery war," American Quakers were forced to weigh their antislavery and antiwar testimonies against one another. Some Quakers enlisted; some meetings turned a blind eye to that choice.[6] World War I elicited a similarly divided position. While accurate and reliable statistics on Quaker enlistment in WWI are not readily available, it is generally accepted that thirty per cent of eligible British Quakers and fifty per cent of eligible American Quakers enlisted for active military service.[7] Some studies suggest even higher rates of participation.[8] Even so, throughout the First World War the official position of all Yearly Meetings in Canada, the United States, and the United Kingdom remained pacifist.

What of Canadian Quakers and the South African War? Despite claims that the three branches of Canadian Friends (Orthodox, Hicksite, and Conservative) were outspoken against the war, an examination of the records of the Religious Society of Friends in Canada suggests otherwise. While Canadian Friends were active in the growing global peace and arbitration movement, both within the Society itself and in ecumenical settings, the South African war received scant direct attention. In those cases where it was mentioned specifically, Canadian Quakers seem to have been divided, some deploring the conflict and others adopting the same

---

4. Maclear, "Quakerism," 240–70; Brock, *Pacifism in Europe*, 255–303; Barbour, "The Lamb's War," 145–58; Valentine, "Quakers," 363–76.

5. 1744 Advice in London Yearly Meeting, *Extracts from the Minutes and Advices of the Yearly Meeting of Friends Held in London, from Its First Institution*, 254.

6. Hamm, et al., "Decline," 48.

7. Hirst, *Quakers*, 538; Valentine, "Quakers," 372.

8. Hamm, et al., "Decline," 54.

imperialist "silver lining" conviction championed by the largest Canadian Protestant churches.⁹

Arthur Garratt Dorland, a Quaker himself and "the historian of the Religious Society of Friends in Canada,"¹⁰ provided the first commentary on Canadian Quakers' response to the South African War. In his formative history of Canadian Quakers, he remarked:

> The outbreak of the Boer War in 1899 found the Society of Friends in Canada, as elsewhere, very sensitive to the currents of opinion in the country, and deeply concerned at the passions which the war aroused on all sides. Both branches of the Society passed strong resolutions condemning the war spirit in Canada, which were given as much publicity as possible. This expression of opinion was far from popular. There were few groups or individuals who desired to run counter to the strong tide of Imperialism at this time, or who cared openly to criticize or to oppose that spirit of wilful domination and aggressive pride which for a period seemed to possess the whole British people.¹¹

Unfortunately, while other events in Dorland's book include specific reference to primary sources of various types, there is no citation for this statement on the Boer War. Dorland's assertions have been repeated, and altered to a small, but important, extent. In 1974, Carman Miller repeated Dorland's claim: "Apart from the Society of Friends, whose two Canadian branches passed and published strong anti-war resolutions, the only other Protestant body which opposed the war was the Women's Christian Temperance Union."¹² Again, there is no citation or quotation from the body of the resolutions issued by Friends. And the Canadian Yearly Meeting Archives includes an overview article by Lise Hansen, "Friends and Peace: Quaker Pacifist Influence in Ontario to the early Twentieth Century," in which one reads, "In 1899, when the British government became embroiled in the Boer War the Quakers passed and published strong anti-war resolutions, while the only other protestant body in Ontario to express opposition was the Women's Christian Temperance Union (whose membership included many Quaker women). Presbyterian and Methodist church newspapers ac-

---

9. Heath, *A War*, xx.

10. "A History of Canadian Yearly Meeting," abridged from the "Canadian Yearly Meeting Discipline."

11. Dorland, *The Quakers*, 327. Emphasis added.

12. Miller, "English-Canadian Opposition," 434.

tually endorsed the war."[13] Hansen does cite Miller as her source. In both Miller's and Hansen's articles, Dorland's "strong resolutions condemning the war *spirit* in Canada" became resolutions against the war itself. I have also repeated Dorland's assertion that, in response to the outbreak of the Boer War, "Canadian Friends passed stern resolutions condemning the bellicose spirit in Canada."[14]

The minutes of the three Yearly Meetings suggest something else entirely. And it is in the minutes that any resolution passed by any branch of the Society would be recorded. The Canada Yearly Meeting (Orthodox), the largest group of Canadian Quakers, recorded in 1897 that the Peace Committee made no report. In 1898 there was only a verbal report, "an appropriation of seventy-five dollars [was] made," and the Peace Committee was directed to raise an equivalent sum from the preparative meetings.[15] These funds were to cover the cost of printing and distributing peace materials that Orthodox Friends received from London Yearly Meeting or the American Peace Society.[16] In 1899, the year that the Boer War began, the Committee on Peace included no mention of the war; it reported briefly on its fundraising activities and concluded, "We regret that there is not more interest on the part of our members generally in this important subject."[17] In 1900 the Peace Committee did report that London Yearly Meeting had circulated an address, *Christianity and War*, a six-page pamphlet issued by London Yearly Meeting itself.[18] Canada Yearly Meeting directed "that 1000 copies be printed and placed in the hands of the Peace Committee for distribution."[19] Given that about 2,000 Canadians identified themselves as Quakers in the 1901 Census of Canada,[20] this was a significant number of copies, although it pales in comparison to the 181,000 copies printed

13. Hansen, "Friends and Peace."

14. Healey, "Quakers and Mennonites," 221.

15. Canada Yearly Meeting of Friends (Orthodox), 1886–1907, June 1897, 411; and June 1898, 444.

16. This included periodicals like *The Messenger of Peace*, and American publication of Orthodox Friends. It was not until 1905 that Canadian Orthodox Friends had their own publication, *The Canadian Friend*.

17. Canada Yearly Meeting of Friends (Orthodox), July 1899, 472.

18. *Christianity and War*.

19. Canada Yearly Meeting of Friends (Orthodox), July 1900, 526.

20. 1901 Census of Canada, http://www.bac-lac.gc.ca/eng/census/1901/Pages/1901.aspx (accessed 1 December 2016). It is important to remember that those identifying as Quaker would have included those faithful to all three branches of Friends.

by the Peace Committee of the London Yearly Meeting for distribution to Friends and other religious organizations.[21] London Yearly Meeting even filled a request for 2,000 copies in Welsh.[22] Regardless, the commitment to print 1,000 copies does demonstrate the Yearly Meeting's commitment to circulating ideas about the inconsistency of war with Friends' interpretation of their faith.

Canadian Hicksite Friends, members of the cross-border Genesee Yearly Meeting, seem to have had a more active Peace and Arbitration Committee that dedicated itself to general concerns about peace. In 1897, a delegation comprised of Isaac Wilson and William G. Brown, chair of the Peace and Arbitration Committee, visited Prime Minister Laurier to present the government with Friends' views on "The Responsibilities of Public Men; Militarism; Temperance, Judicial Oaths, and Capital Punishment." [23] The minutes suggest that, within this longer list, the death penalty was of considerable concern to Friends at this 1897 meeting. Brown's report paints a picture of a successful meeting. It is also full of imperialistic rhetoric. After assuring the Yearly Meeting that Laurier "spoke very kindly of Friends, both in England and America, as having been foremost in the advocacy of reforms, and of Friends everywhere as the best type of citizens," Brown described the events of that day:

> It was something of a coincidence that upon the very day the Petition was presented, asking that legislation keep in view the unity of the British Empire and an Anglo-Saxon Confederacy, the strength of whose moral force the world will not be able to withstand, the Finance Minister announced a trade policy which, by reason of England's situation, given her preferential trade with Canada, and which did more in 24 hours towards the unification of Empire than anything which has occurred for years. An exultant Canadian-Imperial sentiment is the result of this contribution to the Jubilee Year on the one side, and admiration and appreciation on the other.[24]

There is no doubt that in the 1890s Quakers had a growing commitment to peace and arbitration. This is evident in their leadership and participation in the annual Lake Mohonk Conference on International

21. Glover, "Aspects of Publishing by the Peace Committee," 41.
22. Ibid., 41–42.
23. Genesee Yearly Meeting, 1856–1927, June 1897, 13.
24. Ibid., 13–14.

Arbitration, founded in 1895,[25] and the Peace Association of Friends in America, founded in 1867 and incorporated in 1894.[26] Is it possible that those important peace efforts were compromised, or at least complicated, by imperialist sentiment, both British and American?

Consider the 1898 Genesee Yearly Meeting minutes. They express concern for "the war cloud now hanging over our nation," but recognized that "while as a Society we may not have exerted our greatest influence in averting it, yet great care is still necessary that as individuals we may not fail to maintain our profession of peace."[27] This Yearly Meeting, held in the midst of the Spanish-American War, noted "[b]y the written and verbal reports we learn that but little organized work has been accomplished in some localities, yet none were without those who are individually laboring to prevent or suppress the many evils of the age."[28] In 1899, the year the South African War began, the Genesee Yearly Meeting engaged earnestly in the subjects of Peace and Arbitration, and the minutes noted "anxious anticipation" about the results of The Hague Peace Conference underway at the time. But the minutes contain no comment or statement about the situation in South Africa.[29]

The following year the minutes of the Genesee Yearly Meeting did "deplore, no matter the cause, the war in connection with our own great Empire."[30] Even so, as far as work on Peace and Arbitration went, the committee reported, "No organized effort by the Society during the past year is there to report. Doubtless, individual influence was in harmony with the best traditions of our Society. This past year, or three years in fact [when Hicksite Friends had met with Laurier], have been exceptional in

---

25. Albert K. Smiley, an Orthodox American Friend, hosted the Annual Conference on International Arbitration at his Lake Mohonk estate in New York State. These conferences, attended by Orthodox and Hicksite Friends, shaped opinion favoring arbitration as a way of settling international disputes. Attendance at these conferences was not exclusive to Quakers; non-Quakers also attended. See Socknat, *Witness Against War*, 28–30.

26. Despite the lack of interest in "this important subject" that the Peace Committee of the Canadian Yearly Meeting (Orthodox) noted in 1899, the meeting did record that the Peace Association of Friends in America had expressed concern with mounting international aggression, and had invited Canadian Friends to appoint two members to their Advisory Board. Canada Yearly Meeting of Friends (Orthodox), July 1899, 472.

27. Genesee Yearly Meeting, June 1898, 18.

28. Ibid., 18–19.

29. Genesee Yearly Meeting, June 1899, 14–15.

30. Genesee Yearly Meeting, June 1900, 15.

opportunities to test the peace spirit among Friends."[31] Because the Genesee Yearly Meeting encompassed Hicksite Friends from both Canada and the United States, one might expect comments on either the South African War or the Spanish-American War. But the remarks of the Peace and Arbitration Committee suggest that the response to the wars in which either country were involved was anything but resolute, as Dorland suggested. William G. Brown, chairperson of the committee, was explicit:

> Friends after the declaration and commencement of war have raised here and there a *feeble* voice as a Society, and *when of the least possible avail*. We heard little of it in the times of difficulty leading up to hostilities. Out of all misfortune and trouble, however, good may arise. *Our own neglect* we may not wish to repeat. These wars themselves in Christian nations are convincing arguments and of telling influence for permanent peace. Sacrifices, deplorable though they may be, produce sympathy and unity.[32]

Brown, a Canadian, expressed faith in "our own great Empire," certain that "Great Britain and Saxon unity will be brought to bear on the affairs of the world in such a manner eventually as shall maintain justice and liberty with peace."[33] Even so, it is clear that the cost of this justice had become problematic. Despite his faith in the "indomitable and grand qualities of the Anglo-Saxon, making him an irresistible force in the fields of commerce and industrial pursuits," Brown bemoaned the fact that those very qualities had come to be associated with "the glitter and glamor of war and human butchery." He beseeched Friends to "call mankind to a sense of the horrors and immortality of war and its false glory" and to combat growing militarism in the world: "The Society of Friends is needed at this moment in connection with an educational campaign against the dangerous growth and power of the military spirit. Happily this need is felt by more than Friends. Both the religious and secular press of Canada is largely available. Neither the Genesee Yearly Meeting nor its Literature Committee lacks for something to do."[34]

Even that emotional call to action, and the apparent need for peace work, seemed to have resulted in little corporate activity. Brown's report to

---

31. Ibid., 14.
32. Genesee Yearly Meeting, June 1900, 15. Emphasis added.
33. Ibid.
34. Ibid., 16.

Yearly Meeting in 1902, the year the war ended, most clearly summarizes and assesses Hicksite Quakers' relatively feeble response to the war:

> It is a pleasure to report that the long chapter in the active stage of national carnage and crime in South Africa is closed, though the ruin, the blight, and the immorality will long survive. The heartache, even in victory, hangs as a cloud over gratitude and its effects sweep with devastating influence up on future life. Substance and life have been sacrificed to the demon of selfishness, pride and possession leaving behind as well the penalty for future life, character and citizenship, to pay. Friends in Canada have done little, except in an individual capacity, but it is to be hoped that such leaven will work until our professed Christian country shall resort to war no more. There is now a great need to watch carefully that militarism, in a measure triumphant, does not settle upon the people like a scourge, and that feeling of British Unity is not taken advantage of, to impose considerations and a system upon the plain, toiling people of Canada, inconsistent with true freedom and progress.[35]

Like their Orthodox brethren, Hicksite Friends considered war inconsistent with their interpretation of their faith.

The minutes of the Conservative Friends in Canada, the smallest group of Quakers, are also noticeably silent. At the 1899 meeting held in Pickering, Ontario, those in attendance heard from the Representative Meeting that "[t]he Committee appointed to have the oversight of our Government in relation to the interests of our Society report attention has been given to the appointment, and nothing has transpired to cause any action on our part."[36] Obviously, Canada's entrance into the South African War seemed to require neither action nor comment. The following year the same committee reported that "nothing came under its notice requiring attention."[37] In both years, however, the answer to the seventh query stipulated that "Friends are clear of complying with military requisitions and of paying any fine or tax instead thereof."[38] The 1901 meeting received no comment on interactions with the government, but in this case the seventh query stipulated that "Friends appear to be clear of complying with military requisitions or paying any fine or tax instead thereof."[39] By

35. Genesee Yearly Meeting, June 1902, 16–17.
36. Yearly Meetings (Conservative), 1881–1910, June 1899, 193.
37. Yearly Meetings (Conservative), June 1900, 203.
38. Ibid., 195, 205.
39. Yearly Meetings (Conservative), June 1901, 213.

1902, the "Committee appointed to have an oversight of [the] Government," reported again that "nothing has come under their notice requiring our attention at this time."[40] The answer to the seventh query that year was back to "clear of complying."[41]

What are we to make of Canadian Quakers' responses to the South African War in light of their clear commitment to arbitration and opposition to militarism? As has been shown, Friends themselves expressed disappointment in their collective response to this particular war. The context of the war itself and theological difference among Friends complicated any straightforward response. The South African War occurred within a period of intense imperial pride.[42] As Lonnie Valentine asserts, along with the Spanish American War, "British and American society had cause to celebrate their colonial power as well as inklings of what warfare could become."[43] Certainly Friends worked publicly to deny any connection between their faith and warfare. British Quakers' 1900 publication and widespread global distribution of almost 200,000 copies of *Christianity and War* is indicative of the pacifist position for which Friends are well-known. The publication makes no particular mention of the ongoing war in South Africa, stating only that London Quakers did "believe it right, at the present time to give fresh expression to our testimony to the peaceable nature of Christ's Kingdom, and the lawfulness of war to the Christian."[44] Friends assured Britons that England would not suffer if "she abandoned her reliance on armed force." Rather, "the energy, the self-sacrifice, and heroism which now sport their God-given strength in the service of death" would be harnessed to the "moral forces of righteousness and goodwill" which had "given our country her moral influence in the world, and are the true foundation on which her empire now rests."[45] True Christians, Friends concluded, would "shrink with horror from the wholesale slaughter of the battlefield," and would turn themselves instead to a "higher service ... the 'blessed ministry of reconciliation.'"[46] Not evident in this official statement in which Quakers clearly distanced themselves from war are the extensive

40. Yearly Meetings (Conservative), June 1902, 221.
41. Ibid., 220.
42. Heath, *A War*, 3–20.
43. Valentine, "Quakers," 372.
44. *Christianity and War*, 3.
45. Ibid., 9.
46. Ibid., 12.

public theological quarrels that had preceded its publication. These theological divisions, and disagreements on whether Friends should address the government, manifested themselves in a deeply divided Peace Session at the 1900 London Yearly Meeting where the South African War was the major topic of discussion.[47]

Canadian Friends who shared a deep connection to the London Yearly Meeting clearly agreed with the sentiments expressed by their British brethren, choosing to dedicate funds to the printing and distribution of the message. Canadian Friends also shared a deep connection to their American brethren, especially those with whom they shared theological convictions. Each of the three branches of Canadian Quakers—Orthodox, Hicksite, and Conservative—maintained close contact with their American counterparts through visitation and epistolary correspondence. And Canadian Hicksite Friends were part of a transnational Yearly Meeting. Importantly, in 1901 North American Quakers set their theological differences aside to gather representatives in Philadelphia at the American Friends Peace Conference. The conference was the idea of Benjamin F. Trueblood, the Secretary of the American Peace Society.[48] Trueblood had convinced those attending the Seventh Annual Conference on International Arbitration at Lake Mohonk of the importance of inviting "members of all the religious bodies in America calling themselves Friends" to gather in the cause of peace.[49] In advertising the conference, the organizing committee called on Friends to overlook their differences: "Do we not owe it to ourselves, to our history, to our profession before the church and the world, to the American public and to mankind everywhere, to declare ourselves anew today—and in a united way, as we have never done before—on the great and pressing question of the peace of the world, of the rescue of mankind from the awful iniquities and crushing burdens of modern militarism?"[50] Two branches of Canadian Quakers were represented on the forty-nine-member planning committee: William G. Brown and Samuel P. Zavitz represented Hicksite Friends; Sarah Ann Dale and Elias H. Rogers represented Orthodox Friends.[51] Brown was chair of Genesee Yearly Meeting's Peace and Arbitration Committee, and Dale and Rogers were both long-term members of the Canada Yearly

47. Hewison, *Hedge of Wild Almonds*, 127–43.
48. *The American Friends' Peace Conference*, 12–13, 229–30.
49. Ibid., 3.
50. Ibid., 4.
51. Ibid., 5–6.

Meeting's Peace Committee, which Rogers chaired. Isaac Wilson, another Canadian Hicksite Friend active in peace work, also attended.[52]

The Peace Conference was a significant opportunity for Friends to renew and clarify their commitment to peace and their opposition to war. Over the course of three twelve-hour days, they heard and discussed carefully-prepared papers on topics ranging from the theological bases for peace, to Friends' historical position on war and peace, and to future possibilities for peace. The papers, along with the transcribed discussions that followed them, were published and circulated by the conference. The South African War, ongoing at the time of the conference, was mentioned only three times throughout the conference, twice within the context of a paper, and once in a comment during the discussion period.[53] Nevertheless, it is notable that in that discussion, the commenter expressed "surprise ... that there are many Friends who lean strongly toward that sentiment [that "the war with the Boers was a necessity"] and who, if they do not openly express it, apologize for the war. So there is necessity even among the Friends of teaching the principles of peace anew."[54] The sentiment that Friends had been lax in upholding their own commitment to peace was echoed in Isaac Sharpless's closing comments: "Friends have not been very active propagandists. The very feeling of their own complete rightness has made many of them slow to take the stump and proclaim the arguments for the good cause. But this is changing."[55]

Canadian Quakers did become more active advocates for peace after the South African War. The minutes of the Yearly Meetings reveal more focussed attention to the topic, although progress within the meeting as a

---

52. Ibid., 14, 164.

53. In both cases where the South African War was mentioned in a paper, the authors were critical of English involvement in the war. In his paper, "Early Friends' View of Peace Sustained by Scripture, by Reason and by Higher Civilization," William Hubbard of Lansing Michigan suggested that after the Boers "offered to arbitrate ... every man killed was a man murdered" (42). Edmund Stanley, President of Friends' University in Kansas, asked why England would not "entrust the case with the International Court" if "England's claim is just and the demands of the Boers unjust" ("Principal Influences Making for Peace and How they may be Strengthened," 89). The Spanish-American War was given much greater attention, with eight mentions during the conference. This is to be expected given the conference's location in the United States. All papers are included in *The American Friends' Peace Conference*.

54. Discussion on Mary Jane Weaver's paper, "Woman's Responsibility and Opportunities for Promoting Peace Principles," *The American Friends' Peace Conference*, 107.

55. Ibid., 232.

whole remained slow. For instance, in 1903 Orthodox Friends requested that the Peace Committee try to arrange for an address on peace at the following yearly meeting, signaling what appears to be of greater interest.[56] That address did not happen, and in 1905 the yearly meeting was "encourage[ing] all our members to greater earnestness in this cause."[57] Despite the efforts of individual members of the Peace Committee, the collective attention of the meeting was pointed more towards temperance and prohibition than to peace. Nonetheless, Canadian Orthodox Friends did what they could, directing funds to the "Peace Association of Friends in America."[58] And in 1906 Benjamin Trueblood, Secretary of the American Peace Society, was warmly welcomed when he attended Canada Yearly Meeting.[59]

The Peace and Arbitration Committee of Hicksite Friends also continued its work pressing for an end to the growing global militarism. In 1903, they ordered one hundred copies of the proceedings of the 1901 American Friends' Peace Conference, providing the means to connect local meetings to broader peace discussions.[60] And, by 1904, they had formed a group known as the Friends' Association of Toronto; this association became increasingly active in peace work on behalf of Hicksite Friends. It investigated and combatted the "military spirit ... which had found its way into churches and schools under the form of Boys' Brigades and Military Drill."[61] And, through its interdenominational work, 1905 became a year that William Brown proudly reported that "Friends have during the year aided in the direction of peace and arbitration beyond all previous efforts."[62] The fruits of these efforts were realized in the endorsement of the principles of the 1906 Lake Mohonk Peace Conference by "the principal trade organizations of Canada," the Boards of Trade of Toronto, Montreal, Ottawa, Hamilton, Winnipeg, and the Canadian Manufacturers Association.[63]

---

56. Canada Yearly Meeting of Friends (Orthodox), June 1903, 652.

57. Canada Yearly Meeting of Friends (Orthodox), June 1905, 697.

58. Canada Yearly Meeting of Friends (Orthodox), June 1904, 690; June 1905, 697–98; June 1906, 764.

59. Canada Yearly Meeting of Friends (Orthodox), June 1906, 748.

60. Genesee Yearly Meeting, June 1903, 20.

61. Genesee Yearly Meeting, June 1904, 17–18.

62. Genesee Yearly Meeting, June 1905, 17.

63. Canada Yearly Meeting of Friends (Orthodox), June 1906, 764.

The South African War provided Canadian Quakers with an opportunity to revisit their position on war and peace, and to consider ways they could actively go beyond an anti-war position to promote peaceful relations between nations. But the evidence suggests that Quakers in Canada were not as resolute in their opposition to this war as they wish they had been when they reflected back on it as Dorland did. The century that followed the Boer War provided Quakers with many more opportunities to put their opposition to war into practice by engaging with the larger world. And it was in the twentieth century that the anti-war testimony came to be known as the Peace Testimony; this testimony is more focussed on proactive means of creating just societies and preventing war. But even in that context Friends have not been unified.[64] As Valentine has concluded, "the tension between maintaining a peace testimony and engaging in the larger world created problems for the Society of Friends . . . [A]s pacifism spread beyond the Religious Society of Friends, Quakers themselves were less cohesive about their own Peace Testimony."[65] Alongside their commitment to equality and simplicity, pacifism is a principle for which Quakers are most well-known. Its centrality to the Religious Society of Friends should not obscure its complex and complicated history.

BIBLIOGRAPHY

Primary Sources

The American Friends' Peace Conference Held at Philadelphia, Twelfth Month 12th, 13th and 14th 1901. Philadelphia: Published by the Conference, 1902.

Canada, Quaker Meeting Records, 1786–1988, Canada Yearly Meeting of Friends (Orthodox), 1886–1907. Online: http://www.ancestry.ca.

Canada, Quaker Meeting Records, 1786–1988, Yearly Meetings (Conservative), 1881–1910. Online: http://www.ancestry.ca.

Canada, Quaker Meeting Records, 1786–1988, Genesee Yearly Meeting, 1856–1927. Online: http://www.ancestry.ca.

The Canadian Friend

1901 Census of Canada. Online: http://www.bac-lac.gc.ca/eng/census/1901/Pages/1901.aspx (accessed 1 December 2016).

Christianity and War: An Address by the Religious Society of Friends. London: West, Newman and Company, 1900.

"A Declaration from the harmless and innocent people of God, called Quakers." Online: http://www.qhpress.org/quakerpages/qwhp/dec1660.htm (accessed 20 October 2015).

---

64. Hamm, et al., "Decline"; Healey, "Quakers."
65. Valentine, "Quakers," 375–76.

London Yearly Meeting, *Extracts from the Minutes and Advices of the Yearly Meeting of Friends Held in London, from Its first Institution.* London: James Phillips, 1783.
The Messenger of Peace

Other Sources

American Friends Service Committee Nobel Peace Prize. Online: https://www.afsc.org/nobel-peace-prize.
"A History of Canadian Yearly Meeting." Abridged from the "Canadian Yearly Meeting Discipline." Online: http://quaker.ca/archives/document/a-history-of-canadian-yearly-meeting.
Quaker United Nations Office. Online: http://www.quno.org.

Secondary Sources

Barbour, Hugh. "The Lamb's War and the Origins of the Quaker Peace Testimony." In *The Pacifist Impulse in Historical Perspective,* edited by Harvey L. Dyck and Peter Brock, 145–58. Toronto: University of Toronto Press, 1996.
Barbour, Hugh, et al. *Quaker Crosscurrents: Three Hundred Years of Friends in the New York Yearly Meetings.* Syracuse, NY: Syracuse University Press, 1995.
Brock, Peter. *Pacifism in Europe.* Princeton: Princeton University Press, 1972.
Dorland, Arthur G. *The Quakers in Canada: A History.* 1927. Reprint, Toronto: Ryerson, 1968.
Glover, Margaret McKechnie. "Aspects of Publishing by the Peace Committee of the Religious Society of Friends (London Yearly Meeting), 1888–1905." *Quaker Studies* 3.1 (1998) 27–51.
Hamm, Thomas D., et al. "The Decline of Quaker Pacifism in the Twentieth Century: Indiana Yearly Meeting of Friends as a Case Study." *Indiana Magazine of History* 96.3 (2000) 45–71.
Hansen, Lise. "Friends and Peace: Quaker Pacifist Influence in Ontario to the early Twentieth Century." Online: http://quaker.ca/archives/document/friends-and-peace-quaker-pacifist-influence-in-ontario-to-the-early-twentieth-century.
Heath, Gordon L. *A War with a Silver Lining: Canadian Protestant Churches and the South African War, 1899–1902.* Montreal: McGill-Queen's University Press, 2009.
Healey, Robynne Rogers. "Quakers and World War One: Negotiating Individual Conscience and the Peace Testimony." In *American Churches and the First World War,* edited by Gordon L. Heath, 107–28. Eugene, OR: Pickwick, 2016.
———. "Quakers and Mennonites and the Great War." In *Canadian Churches and the First World War,* edited by Gordon L. Heath, 218–40. Eugene, OR: Pickwick, 2014.
Hewison, Hope Hay. *Hedge of Wild Almonds: South Africa, the "Pro-Boers" & the Quaker Conscience, 1890–1910.* Portsmouth, NH: Heinemann, 1989.
Hirst, Margaret E. *Quakers in Peace and War: An Account of Their Peace Principles and Practice.* London: Swarthmore, 1923.
Maclear, James F. "Quakerism and the End of the Interregnum." *Church History* 19.4 (1950) 240–70.
Miller, Carman. "English-Canadian Opposition to the South African War as Seen through the Press." *The Canadian Historical Review* 55.4 (1974) 422–38.

Socknat, Thomas P. *Witness Against War: Pacifism in Canada, 1900–1945*. Toronto: University of Toronto Press, 1987.

Valentine, Lonnie. "Quakers, War, and Peacemaking." In *The Oxford Handbook of Quaker Studies*, edited by Stephen W. Angell and Pink Dandelion, 363–76. Oxford: Oxford University Press, 2013.

8

Canada's First Nations in the Anglo-Boer War

EVAN J. HABKIRK

IN 1899, THE DEPARTMENT of Indian Affairs began creating what would become a sixty-three page file entitled: "Correspondence regarding the Desire of Numerous Indian Bands across Canada to go to South Africa along with a Possible Contingent from the Six Nations Indians, Reports of Rumors Circulating in the North West that Indians Wish to Join the Boer Force in Transvaal and Donations to the Patriotic Fund by other Bands."[1] In the main, the correspondence within this file was written by non-First Nations people trying to understand the effect the Anglo-Boer War was having on First Nations communities: First Nations voices are almost completely absent. Although this file does report that some First Nations communities supported the British war effort in South Africa, it does little to inform its current readers why or how these responses were tied into First Nations holistic spirituality and ways of life.

This chapter has three objectives. First, it will demonstrate that, due to the holistic way Canada's First Nations people viewed the world, the treaties they signed with the British were regarded as sacred agreements between the First Nations, the British Crown, and the Creator. Second, that First Nations willingness to participate in the Anglo-Boer War was an outward expression of how seriously they took these sacred agreements. Finally, this chapter will take a close look at the sixty-three page Department of Indian

---

1. LAC, RG10, vol. 2991, file 215,977.

Affairs file and contextualize it within a broader First Nations spiritual understanding of treaties.

THE MEANING OF TREATIES

For many non-First Nations people, First Nations treaties were mere conveyances to allow non-First Nations people to trade, create alliances in times of warfare, create peace after war, and/or formalize land cessions for non-First Nations settlement. This secular interpretation and disconnect from the spiritual nature of the treaties has become harder for the wider contemporary Canadian society to empathize with as Canadians themselves have drifted away from their own religious understandings throughout the late twentieth and early twenty-first centuries.[2] The treaties made between non-First Nations people and the many First Nations communities throughout Canada were negotiated as non-First Nations people moved and settled across Canada, with the earliest treaties being on the east coast, Quebec, and Ontario, and moving into the Prairies in the early 1800s for trade purposes, and ending in the 1890s with the Numbered Treaties. Although viewed as a conveyance for non-First Nations, the rituals preformed with First Nations people brought non-First Nations people into the holistic world of the First Nations.

For First Nations people, the spirit and physical world were inextricably connected. Unlike the European nations with whom they established treaties, there was no separation of church and state, and rituals and ceremonies performed during the treaty process reflected this. The rituals would have varied, depending on the First Nations involved, but common threads can be found linking the agreement between both parties and the Creator including ceremonies like the pipe stem ceremony, or the use of words like the Thanksgiving Address which is spoken at the beginning and end of every formal gathering of Six Nations people. Those ceremonies were a part of First Nations culture, and were performed centuries before the arrival of Europeans, bringing all First Nations treaty relationships into the sacred realm.[3] As Jim Miller has pointed out, when Europeans arrived in the New World, they had to conform their ideas to the customs of the First Nations people, including how they made treaties. That utilization of First Nations treaty procedure brought Europeans into the sacred realm

---

2. Friesen, "Magnificent Gifts," 42; Williams and Nelson, "Kaswentha."
3. Miller, *Compact, Contract, Covenant*, 34; Friesen, "Magnificent Gifts," 41.

of the First Nations people.⁴ According to Miller, First Nations people wanted to bring Europeans into their systems. It was up to the government officials and fur traders, however, to learn those customs, language, and ideas to accurately communicate with First Nations people.⁵ First Nations protocols and ceremonies were well in place and mutually understood in the 1900s, binding First Nations and non-First Nations people into a shared sacred living arrangement.

Another way non-First Nations people were brought into the holistic life cycles of First Nations people was by making them a member of extended family units. In many cases, the non-First Nations individual whom the treaty was being made with was brought into some sort of familial relationship with the First Nation they were negotiating. This formalized a relationship based on trust, since it was understood by First Nations communities that one would never act against one's family. Without establishing this relationship, no treaty could be negotiated.⁶ The terms used to reference the people in the treaty negotiations had imbedded ideas of the role, relationship, and responsibilities both parties were to have with each other. Although details of the social obligations of these familiar titles varied from First Nation to First Nation, their general meanings remained consistent.

Those roles were understood by many of the government agents and members of the Royal family from the 1600s and into the mid 1800s, and were repeated by government officials while negotiating treaties in the 1900s. In early treaties of the 1700s and 1800s, if Europeans wanted a treaty with a First Nation, they would literally have to marry into the community. In a Six Nations context, their family connection to the management of their treaties with the British Crown was held by the Johnson family beginning with Sir William Johnson. After the death of Sir William Johnson, who married Molly Brant, the sister of Joseph Brant, the management of the Six Nations Affairs was handed down to Johnson's nephew, Guy Johnson, and after his death, the affairs of the Six Nations were handed down to his son, John Johnson. Due to their family relationship, the Six Nations trusted the Johnson's with their affairs from 1775 to the 1830s.⁷ Even into the 1920s, the Six Nations continued to trust the children of Europeans that married into the Six Nations. When Chief Deskaheh, Levi General, went

4. Miller, *Compact, Contract, Covenant*, 15, 32, 286.
5. Ibid., 284–85.
6. Ibid., 8; Friesen, "Magnificent Gifts," 44.
7. Miller, "Great White Mother," 219; Williams and Nelson, "Kaswentha."

to Britain to seek redress for the RCMP establishing a post on the Grand River Territory, he set out to meet with Winston Churchill, not because Churchill was the Secretary of the Colonies and could overrule the actions of the Canadian government, but because it was rumored that Churchill's mother, Jenny Jerome, had a grandmother who was part Mohawk.[8] In fur trading treaties, men of the Hudson's Bay and other companies also adhered to treaty customs of First Nations people including performing the ceremonies, gift giving, feeding, and marrying into the communities with which they were trading.[9]

By the mid 1800s, the literal marrying into First Nations families was replaced with the giving of symbolic family titles to non-First Nations people. Those symbolic roles still hold social obligations that were understood by both the parties being given the title and the First Nation. With most First Nations groups, there was a difference between male and female designations. Although the titles of Brother and Sister were usually used to note a relationship of equals,[10] terms such as younger/older or little/big could be added to note the respect and level of guidance that marked the relationship, with the older sibling guiding the younger into their newly designated roles.

One of the most misunderstood family roles by Europeans was the role of Children. For Europeans, the term Children was used to note a group of people who could not take care of themselves and needed to be controlled, therefore subordinating themselves to the "Adults" in the family relationship. For First Nations people, this moniker noted that support was needed by the "Adults" in the relationship, but Children in First Nations culture were not to be controlled or placed in a subordinate position. Children were free to learn and develop as they saw fit, with the support and encouragement of their parents.[11] This misunderstanding, however, guided British and Canadian policy towards First Nations since the 1820s, and is currently enshrined in the Indian Act, marking all First Nations people in Canada as wards of the Crown.

The most revered titles were those referring to Mother or Father; the meanings and obligations associated with terms were known and had

8. Williams and Nelson, "Kaswentha."
9. Miller, *Compact, Contract, Covenant*, 15, 18.
10. Williams and Nelson, "Kaswentha."
11. Miller, "Introduction," viii; Miller, *Shingwauk's Vision*, 18; Haig-Brown, *Resistance and Renewal*, 47.

been used by First Nations people in their treaty relationships with each other before European contact. The importance of those titles, however, depended on whether or not the individual First Nation followed matrilineal or patrilineal descent. While it is agreed that the use of Grand Mother or Grand Father referred to respected elders within First Nations cultures, the terms Mother and Father could have a different interpretation. For the Six Nations, who followed a matrilineal society, the title of Mother was held in a higher regard than that of Father, as fathers usually had little authority over the day-to-day lives of his children, making the care of children entirely within the Mother's domain.[12] This positioning, however, may not have been shared by other First Nations. What is agreed upon is that parental terms like Mother and Father noted high respect and a responsibility to care for their people. In fur trading treaties, for example, the term Father was used to refer to the traders who then had a duty to provide and aid the community with which they entered into treaty.

In the time period of the Anglo-Boer War, the title of Mother was used by all First Nations to describe Queen Victoria. As pointed out in many historical documents as well as interviews with contemporary Elders, the Queen's title of Mother was used not as a placeholder of power, but as someone with reciprocal responsibilities who would genuinely take care of the people. In an interview, Elder Lazarus Roah recalled a story of the negotiations during Treaty 6: "A very old man stood up and said, '*Ahow Okeymow* (chief), I do not believe what you are saying. Does the Queen feel her breasts are big enough to care for us all? There are many of our people' . . . The official replied to him immediately, 'yes, she has a large breast, enough so there will never be a shortage.'"[13] This image of a nurturing mother was repeated by other elders. Treaty 6 Elder Alma Kytwyhat believed, "It was the [queen] who offered to be our mother and to love us in the way we want to live." This sentiment is echoed by Treaty 4 Elder Danny Musqua stated in an interview, "The Queen adopted [First Nations] as children . . . a joint relationship will come out of that. And so we have a joint relationship with the Crown because the Queen is now our mother."[14] Not only was the Queen considered their Mother, but the treatment she was supposed to endow on her new First Nations children was to be the same as her natural children. According to Peigan Chief John Yellowhorn: "The

---

12. Williams and Nelson, "Kaswentha."
13. Lazarus Roah quoted in Price, *The Spirit*, 116.
14. Alma Kytwyhat and Danny Musqua quoted in Asch, *On Being Here*, 78, 90.

Queen has made the Indian people her children. I do not fully understand what it means when the Queen makes us her children. I have been asking around, and to this day I still do not know. If I take someone as my child, and I already have lots of children, should my own children get better treatment then the one I have adopted? No."[15]

Although the meanings of these relationships were better understood by the fur traders living with First Nations families, these family terms, ceremonies, and the customs of feeding and gift giving were also employed by treaty negotiators hired by Crown by the mid to late 1800s. The best documented source of these exchanges can be found in Alexander Morris' 1880 account of his, and other commissioners', treaty negations along the Prairies during the Numbered Treaties. Throughout his text, Morris quotes many instances in which he and other treaty commissioners reference the Queen as the "mother" to First Nations people, refers to the First Nations people as "brothers," and even goes as far to note that the commissioners and First Nations all shared the same Creator.[16] Other scholars have pointed to the similarities in Morris's and early fur traders' approach and terminology when negotiating treaties. As pointed out by Jean Friesen, "The similarity of ceremonial forms [to that of trade ceremonies] of western treaties was not coincidental, but rather served a broadly based and well-understood Indian purpose."[17] Michael Asch illustrates that the words used by Morris fall in line with First Nations spirituality, making the treaty not only one based in kinship, but a spiritual agreement. In Morris' own words, the earth, trees, grass, and stones were created by the Great Spirit for all his children to use. Through this logic, Morris concluded that "The lands are the Queen's under the Great Spirit."[18] Morris, in negotiating Treaty 4, went on to say, "The Queen cares for you and your children and she cares for the children that are yet to be born," making this a family relationship, and like in other First Nations kinship treaties, a continuing relationship.[19] Those terms and ideas were continued by other treaty commissioners after Morris left the Indian service. In his negotiations of Treaty 7 in 1877, according to Elder Pat Weaselhead, Commissioner David Laird told the First Nations people gathered that, "our great Queen Victoria is the person who

15. Chief John Yellowhorn as quoted in Price, *The Spirit*, 141.
16. Morris, *The Treaties of Canada*.
17. Friesen, "Magnificent Gifts," 44.
18. Morris quoted in Asch, *On Being Here*, 92.
19. Morris quoted in ibid., 95.

speaks; I am not the one telling you what I am saying, it is the Queen who says it. The reason the Queen sent me, or the reason for the treaty, is so that we can all be related as brothers and sisters, as one family." According to the Elders of various communities involved with the making of Treaty 7, that family and sacred relationship continues today.[20]

Morris and other treaty commissioners were also connected to the sacred realm of First Nations peoples by participating in the pipe stem ceremony. For some First Nations, treaty negotiations could not begin without the pipe stem ceremony, or, in some cases, finalized in good faith, since after the ceremony is performed only the truth can be told in the pipe's presence.[21] Although Miller and John Leonard Taylor make the argument that Morris and others may not have fully understood the significance of the ceremony and other First Nations protocols they were participating in,[22] the ceremony was used in the confirming of Treaties 3–8, binding First Nations and non-First Nations people, and their agreement, to the Creator.[23] For First Nations people, the presence of missionaries and other Christian clergy at the negotiations of the Numbered Treaties would have also given them the sense that the non-First Nations participants held the treaty negotiations in the same sacred manner.

For most First Nations in Canada, treaties with other First Nations and Europeans alike were added into their sacred holistic perspective of living. Like family relationships, those mutual obligations were to continue forever. Six Nations scholar Susan M. Hill compares the Six Nations treaty relationship with the British to being similar to a marriage: "the treaty relationship did not end because of violations by either party; instead, the subsequent treaty addressed the wrongdoings and created a means to rectify the wrongs."[24] Treaty historian Jean Friesen points out that in all cases, treaties were based on reciprocal relations in which both parties needed to meet continually to ensure peace and friendship, and in which their mutual obligations to each other were being met. The promises of annual gifts and annuity payments outlined in the Numbered Treaties not only mirrored that of annual meetings between First Nations people and fur traders that

---

20. Hildebrandt, et al., *The True Spirit*.
21. Ibid., 272; Taylor, "Two Views," 18; Hickey, et al., "T. A. R. R. Interview," 111.
22. Miller, "Great White Mother," 219; Taylor, "Two Views," 18.
23. Asch, *On Being Here*, 139; and Taylor, "Two Views," 18.
24. Hill. "The Clay," 189.

pre-dated the Numbered Treaties,[25] but those meetings also ensured that First Nations people and government officials would meet annually to discuss the treaties, keeping their agreements and family relationship alive.[26]

Royal visits also continued the familiar relationship in the minds of First Nations people and also acted as a place where the agreements reached in the treaties could be discussed. With Queen Victoria and First Nations people both using the title of Mother to describe her familial role, the family of the Queen also used related kinship titles when visiting First Nations communities in Canada. When the Marquis of Lorne visited First Nations communities in the Prairies in the 1880s, he referred to himself as their Brother-in-law, since he was married to the Queen's daughter.[27] By introducing himself in this way, the Marquis was also noting his position of equality with the First Nations people he was addressing. Other Royal family members have a similar history with First Nations communities. When Queen Victoria's son, Prince Arthur (later the Duke of Connaught and Governor General of Canada), visited the Six Nations of the Grand River Territory in 1869, an honorary Chieftainship was conferred on him by the Chiefs of the Six Nations, marking him their Brother. The Duke later visited the Six Nations in 1913, where he, in a gesture of equality, sat in Council with his Brother Chiefs.[28] Furthering his familial commitments to the Six Nations, at the request of the Chiefs, the Duke visited the ailing Six Nations Poetess E. Pauline Johnson in Vancouver in 1912. This visit was an important symbol of the continuing family relationship the Duke had entered into with the Six Nations, since it was Johnson's father who had guided the Duke through the ceremony conferring his Chieftainship.[29] As expressions of these relationships, Royal visits also became opportunities for First Nations people to renew and remind the Royal family of their alliances and treaties and openly air any political concerns that threatened their family relationship. In this way, and through petitioning, the political grievances of Canada's First Nations population were always addressed

---

25. Miller, *Compact, Contract, Covenant*, 137, 295.

26. Miller, "Great White Mother," 260; Asch, *On Being Here*, 95; Friesen, "Magnificent Gifts," 41, 43, 48.

27. Friesen, "Magnificent Gifts," 47.

28. Reville, *History of the County*, 203–4; *The Brantford Expositor*, 15 February 1913.

29. Six Nations Council Minute, LAC, RG10, vol. 3166, file 388,623, Six Nations Agency—Correspondence regarding Pauline Johnson during Her Illness.

directly to the Crown, as the concerns were family matters and did not concern the Canadian government.[30]

THE ANGLO-BOER WAR: VIEWED FROM THE PRAIRIES

Within the sixty-three-page Department of Indian Affairs file are the responses of thirteen First Nations communities to the Anglo-Boer War, representing four in Ontario and nine in the Prairies.[31] Although not a large study sample, all of the responses would have been predicated on the community's individual historical treaty relationship with the British Crown. With Treaties 1–8 being negotiated from 1870–1899, the people of the nine First Nations from Assiniboine, Saskatchewan, and Alberta would have a clearer understanding of their relationship between the Crown at the time of the Anglo-Boer War. Due to alarming reports of an unknown person "influencing the Indians in the North by telling them that Britain is trying to take from the Boers their rights as original settlers of the land and describing conditions as similar to causes our rebellion eighteen eighty-five," circulars were sent to all Indian Agents in the Prairies to "take prompt action to contradict and offset any such disturbing representations."[32] The responses from the nine Indian Agents to this circular show that, in the main, the First Nations communities under their supervision did not harbor any negative feelings towards the British war in South Africa, and some actively supported the war effort. As shown by Blair Stonechild and Bill Waiser, First Nations people who signed the Numbered Treaties bound themselves to the ideals espoused by them, as they were sacred agreements signed between them, the British Crown, and the Creator.[33] Two of the communities, Duck Lake and Moosomin Agency, even volunteered men to help fight.[34] Although some government officials saw those offers in opposition to agreements reached through the treaties,[35] Morris' accounts of the

30. Miller, "Queen's Hand," 244; Henry, "Great White Mother," 90, 99–100; Williams and Nelson, "Kaswentha."

31. LAC, RG10, vol. 2991, file 215,977.

32. Telegram from Clifford Sifton to be forwarded to various Indian agencies in Alberta, Saskatchewan, and Assiniboia, 12 January 1900, LAC, RG10, Vol. 2991, File 215,977.

33. Stonechild and Waiser, *Loyal till Death*, vii, viii.

34. Letter from the Duck Lake Agency to the Secretary of the Department of Indian Affairs, 13 January 1900 and Letter from the Moosemin Agency to the Secretary of the Department of Indian Affairs, 22 January 1900, LAC, RG10, Vol. 2991, File 215,977.

35. Winegard, *For King and Kanata*, 96.

treaty discussions about military service only concerned the ability of the Queen's government to force First Nations people to participate in war.[36] It did not outlaw the right of First Nations people to volunteer military services to aid their Mother's family. This concern was also noted in the file, with members of the Assiniboine and Muscowpetung Agency being concerned that they and others may be forced into service, especially the First Nations men who were acting as scouts of the RCMP.[37] Other First Nations communities were very much interested in the war. The Indian agent of the Sarcee Agency reported that after he had explained the causes of the war to the members of his agency many had "made inquiries several times since, [to see] how the war is going on and several expressions the hope that the 'Great White Mother' would be successful."[38] Although records have not been located confirming whether or not any First Nations men from this geographic region served in the Anglo-Boer War, L. James Dempsey accurately demonstrates that these feelings of loyalty to the British Crown and their treaties was one of the many reasons First Nations peoples from the Prairies would again volunteer their services in the First World War.[39]

THE ANGLO-BOER WAR: VIEWED FROM BRITISH COLUMBIA

Although Governor James Douglas began the process for making treaties with the First Nations people of British Columbia in 1850s, little progress in this regard was ever made. This situation continued to go unresolved even after British Columbia entered Confederation in 1871. Throughout the 1880s and through to the 1900s, the Federal government funded a reservation commission to negotiate and survey First Nations reserves, which did not include a treaty process similar to that witnessed in Eastern and Western Canada.[40] In 1899, the need to remove First Nations people from lands became more urgent with the discovery of gold within British

---

36. Daniel, "The Spirit," 86; Morris, *The Treaties of Canada*, 28, 50, 69, 215, 218, 234.

37. Letter from the Assiniboine Agency to Clifford Sifton, 16 January 1900; and Letter from the Muskowpetungs Indian Agency to the Secretary of the Department of Indian Affairs, 22 January 1900, LAC, RG10, vol. 2991, file 215,977.

38. Letter from the Sarcee Agency to the Superintendent General of the Department of Indian Affairs, 19 January 1900, LAC, RG10, vol. 2991, file 215,977.

39. Dempsey, *Warriors of the King*.

40. House of Commons Debates, Various Volumes from February 1880 to May 1900.

Columbia.⁴¹ While some of this land was included within Treaty 8, much of British Columbia remains unceded First Nations land. Although not mentioned in the Department of Indian Affairs file, and without the promises given to other First Nations groups through treaties, First Nations man George McLean would enlist as a Private in the 2nd Canadian Mounted Rifles, serve overseas, return home, and re-enlist in the First World War.⁴²

THE ANGLO-BOER WAR: VIEWED FROM ONTARIO

Four of the First Nations communities noted in the Department of Indian Affairs file came from Ontario. Many of the First Nations groups in this region had a treaty relationship with the British Crown dating back to at least the 1700s. Viewing the British as a treaty partner, ally, and extended family member, and realizing their ally was in distress, Six Nations of the Grand River Territory and the Chippewa of Saugeen offered the Imperial authorities their men as soldiers.⁴³ With both offers rejected, the Chippewa offered $36.00 to the Canadian Patriotic fund.⁴⁴ This indirect way of helping their ally was also followed by the Chippewa at Nawash (Cape Crooker) First Nations, who offered the Canadian Patriotic fund $35.00.⁴⁵ Private Walter White, a First Nations man from the Anderdon Reservation and former color sergeant of the 21st Battalion, Essex Fusiliers, enlisted in the 2nd Canadian Mounted Rifles and served overseas, only to be killed in action at the battle of Paardeberg 18 February 1900.⁴⁶ Although Privates White and McLean found official ways to enter the war as soldiers, other First Nations men, in their bid to aid their relatives, the British Crown, found other ways to get into the war as can be seen with the Six Nations of the Grand River Territory.

---

41. House of Commons Debates, 4th Session, 8th Parliament, 62–63, Victoria, 16 March–17 May 1899, 5703.

42. Winegard, *For King and Kanata*, 38.

43. Letter from W.H.S. Scott to the Earl of Minto, November 1899; and Letter from the Six Nations Council to Queen Victoria, 10 November 1899, LAC, RG10, vol. 2991, file 215,977.

44. Letter from John Scoffield to the Secretary of the Department of Indian Affairs, 19 March 1900, LAC, RG10, vol. 2991, file 215,977.

45. Letter from John McIver to the Secretary of the Department of Indian Affairs, 2 April 1900, LAC, RG10, vol. 2991, file 215,977.

46. Winguard, *For King and Kanata*, 38; Lackenbauer, et al., "A Commemorative History," 60; Moses, et al., *A Sketch*, 60.

On 16 November 1899, the Chiefs of the Six Nations of the Grand River Territory wrote to Queen Victoria "offering Your Majesty a contingent of Chiefs and warriors, offered by Indians or those in connection with them to serve Your Majesty in the Transvaal if required in conformity with the customs and usages of their forefathers and in accordance with existing Treaties with the British Crown."[47] Although the letter went through the proper administrative channels set up by the Department of Indian Affairs in Canadian Canada, the letter was forwarded to the Lord Minto, the Governor General, and to British authorities on 21 November. With rumors circulating that the Canadian government would be raising a second contingent of mounted troops for the war effort, Visiting Superintendent of the Six Nations E. D. Cameron wrote to the Secretary of the Department of Indian Affairs reminding him of "the Six Nations desire to assist in the defense of the British Empire, and having offered an Indian Contingent ... The Six Nations are good horsemen, good marksmen and have proved first class soldiers."[48] Unlike their previous offer of troops, this was directed to the Canadian Department of Militia and not the imperial authorities. On 13 February 1900, the Six Nations were notified through the Governor General, that, although Her Majesty gave her "sincere thanks for the loyal and sympathetic assurances contained in their Resolutions," she was "unable to avail herself of their patriotic offer."[49] Gestures such as these were oftentimes dismissed by imperial authorities due to a fear of a revival of First Nations militarism. In academic literature about First Nations people participating in the First World War, this vein continues, with many scholars agreeing that First Nations enlistment had more to do with a continuing "warrior ethic."[50] While this warrior ethic is never clearly defined by academics or colonial administrators, instances where it is used infer a First Nations need to participate in warfare, rarely mentioning the ceremonial need for, or peaceful side of, the First Nations warrior. By analyzing Six Nations traditional knowledge and anthropological reports, it can be seen that at the time of the Anglo-Boer War, a "warrior ethic," in the sense promoted

47. Letter from the Six Nations Council to Queen Victoria, 10 November 1899, LAC, RG10, vol. 2991, file 215,977.

48. Letter from E. D. Cameron to the Secretary of the Department of Indian Affairs, 21 December 1899, LAC, RG10, vol. 2991, file 215,977.

49. Letter from J. Chamberlain to Governor General Lord Minto, 13 February 1900, LAC, RG10, vol. 2991, file 215,977.

50. Winegard, *For King and Kanata*, 3; Lackenbauer, et al., "A Commemorative History," 2, 3, 66; Dempsey, *Warriors of the King*, vii.

by the imperial authorities and academic scholars, was not apparent within the Six Nations spiritual and holistic way of life, therefore making their offer of troops for the Anglo-Boer War a statement about the sacredness in which they held their treaty obligations to the British.

In traditional Six Nations languages, the term warrior, as used by the non-First Nations population, has no direct translation. As noted by Paul Williams, the closet translation to this term in Mohawk is "one who maintains peace."[51] Even with the formation of the Five Nations (later Six with the addition of the Tuscarora in 1722), the Peacemaker told the people of Six Nations that "the Great spirit never planned for humans to hurt one another or to slaughter one another."[52] Even with those ingrained ideas of peace, Six Nations history is riddled with stories of war and conflict, especially in the post contact period. Military conflict in the post contact era, however, was based in a Six Nations treaty relationship with Europeans. The Six Nations entered into a treaty relationship, based on the Two Row Wampum Belt and Covenant Chain of Friendship with the Dutch of New Netherlands in the early 1600s. That relationship was extended to the English in 1664, based on the allegory that, although the Two Row Wampum stated that they were separate nations and would not interfere with each other's internal and external affairs. The Covenant Chain that connected them, originally made of rope, would later on be said to be made of iron, making the chain and agreement stronger. In 1677, this allegorical chain was said to be made of silver, ensuring that the British and Six Nations would meet periodically to ensure their relationship did not tarnish and would stay bright and strong.[53] Like the ceremonies and allegories found with the negotiations of the Number Treaties, the allegory of the Covenant Chain relationship was found in First Nations treaties with each other before the arrival of Europeans, making its interpretation well known to First Nations communities.[54] With their treaty relationship beginning two hundred years earlier than the Numbered Treaties, it should be noted that the Six Nations/British treaty relationship developed over time with other treaty agreements being added onto the original treaty framework.[55] With every treaty council, however, the same rituals were followed making the

51. Williams and Nelson, "Kaswentha."
52. Ibid.
53. Muller, "Two 'Mystery Belts,'" 132.
54. Miller, "'Queen's Hand,'" 243.
55. Williams and Nelson, "Kaswentha."

Six Nations treaties agreements between the British, the Six Nations, and the Creator.

Before the Six Nations would make a treaty with anyone, two conditions needed to be met: (1) giving wampum and (2) saying the Thanksgiving Address. Wampum, whether in strands or in belt form, had to be given or else the messenger and his message was not taken seriously.[56] For Six Nations, wampum was sacred. The message contained within the wampum, not the paper treaty written by the British that accompanied it, was binding.[57] Adding to the sacredness of the wampum was the Thanksgiving Address. Before any meeting of the Six Nations began and ended, the Thanksgiving Address was recited. The address itself aligned and connected the Creator to all things the Creator had created, including humans, highlighting that the decisions made during the meeting had consequences for all creation. Humans were not above nature, but a part of it. The Thanksgiving address was also believed to bring together the minds of the people taking part in the negotiations.[58] As with the Convenient Chain relationship, both of those elements were well understood and practiced when the Six Nations established treaties with either First Nations or non-First Nations people.[59] For every treaty negotiated between with the Six Nations and the British Crown, both elements were present, making their treaty agreements a sacred part of how the Six Nations viewed their place in the world. The relationship noted by the Two Row Wampum belt and the Covenant Chain relationship, sealed in the sacredness of the Thanksgiving Address and wampum, continued to guide the Six Nations and their relationship with the British Crown.[60] It was this sacred obligation that led to the Six Nations offering their men to the British during the Anglo-Boer War.

After the American Revolution, a reforming voice was also changing the way the Six Nations viewed their place in the world. After suffering from illness, Handsome Lake awoke from a near death coma with a series of prophecies about how the Creator wanted the Six Nations to live their lives in the new colonial world they found themselves. In his visions, Handsome Lake was guided by messengers showing him lessons of what would happen if the Six Nations did not follow the way the Creator

56. Miller, *Compact, Contract, Covenant*, 39, 42.
57. Williams and Nelson, "Kaswentha."
58. Williams and Nelson, "Kaswentha."
59. Ibid. Miller, "Great White Mother," 218.
60. Williams and Nelson, "Kaswentha."

wanted them to live. Those prophecies did much to reorient the Six Nations, both in the United States and Canada, back to the peace-driven society they had been before their participation in European conflicts. Ingrained in his teachings was the fact that Six Nations people were not to participate in White Men's wars. In his telling of the Code of Handsome Lake, Chief Jake Thomas states:

> The messenger said, "Look and watch closely in that direction, about the middle of the sky. So again he did look. He saw a white man pacing back and forth. He seemed to be angry about something. He was prodding the ground with a bayonet and wearing a red jacket or coat. The messengers said to him, "What do you see?" He replied, I saw a man and it seems he is angry about something. He is holding a bayonet or fork, and he is prodding the ground with it." Then the messengers said, "It is true what you saw. We think and feel that there will be many people who will die if he does not settle down. We are hoping he will change his mind. He is thinking of war. If war does start, tell your relations not to get involved in this conflict. We understand that there are two white brothers arguing, and the only way this will be settled is by war." The messengers continued, "Do not let your relations take sides. If they do, they will suffer and lose their homelands. So tell your chiefs not to let this happen to your people." This is how the messengers and Handsome Lake told it.[61]

The central message of Chief Thomas's telling of the Code of Handsome Lake was also recorded by Anthropologist and Six Nations member A. C. Parker during his field work in 1913,[62] making this teaching common knowledge among the Six Nations at the time of the Anglo-Boer War.

The Code of Handsome Lake also affected the ceremonial life of the Six Nations, changing some ceremonies that were linked to war to peaceful, and sometimes, healing, ceremonies. In his field work, Parker noted two dances that were traditional linked to war: (1) the Sun Dance and (2) the Wasaze, the Thunder Dance that honors the spirit Hi'no. The Sun Dance "begins promptly at high noon, when three showers of arrows or volleys from muskets are shot heavenward to notify the sun of the intention to address him. After each of the volleys the populace shout their war cries, 'for the sun loves war.'"[63] While performing the Wasaze (Thunder Dance),

---

61. Thomas, *Teachings*, 93–94.
62. Parker, *The Code*, 65–66.
63. Ibid., 103 n. 1; Parker, "Iroquois Sun Myths," 473.

participants were supposed to sing their war songs as "Hi'no is supposed to delight in war songs and these are sung to please him."[64] During his fieldwork in 1912–1915, Anthropologist Fred Waugh also noted a Wasaze, although he noted it as no longer a war dance, but a rain-making ceremony.[65] He wrote:

> When the speaker gets through, the people go into the longhouse, with the exception of the warriors and the women with the water. As soon as the people have all got inside, the warriors give three cheers... Then the woman with the pail scatters water towards the warriors at the fire, using her hands for the purpose. The warriors now begin to dance, moving slowly towards the longhouse. The dancers sometimes whoop and shout very loudly, "like thunder," until they get into the longhouse.[66]

Waugh later notes that, although this is called a war dance, due to Handsome Lake's influence, it was now a Thunder Dance.[67] According to fellow Anthropologist David Boyle, the ceremony to "turn thunderstorms" was still practiced at Six Nations Grand River in 1902, and is still practiced today.[68]

In his 1949 study of Six Nations ceremonies, Frank Speck also noted changes in ceremonies that, due to the message of Handsome Lake, had been repurposed. In reference to the Sun Dance, Speck noted that the ceremony had changed to a "rite of prayer and thanksgiving," where "The personal chants were tinged with the warrior' spirit."[69] Another ceremonial dance, the Skin Dance, was affected by the message of Handsome Lake. Before his message to the people of Six Nations, "the Skin Dance was to afford an opportunity for the war chiefs and warriors to recount their war records and to discuss raids and cruelties inflicted upon other tribes. Handsome Lake condemned this type of performance and told the people they must give up the mention of their exploits and the evil deeds of the past and speak only of the wonders of creation."[70] According to Speck, a War Dance (Wasaze) of any kind was only called for "to make ceremonial

64. Parker, *The Code*, 104.
65. Waugh, *Iroquois Food*, 23.
66. Ibid., 26.
67. Ibid., 26 n. 1.
68. Boyle, *Ontario Archaeology Report*, 1902, 184 as cited in ibid., 28.
69. Speck, *The Midwinter Rites*, 136.
70. Ibid., 138.

friendship for a child who is sick when the medicine man prescribes 'need for a friend' to give relief."[71] In his analysis, other ceremonies used for war, like the Eagle Dance, traditionally used for protection in war hunting or from witch craft, was now "performed as a curative rite when requested by an individual or as a social dance,"[72] the Clasping of Hands Dance, noted by Speck and Boyle during their field work, was "danced by warriors to strengthen them against enemies and to serve as a medicine to shield the warriors before going to invade an enemy's country,"[73] and was used to link any two people for life especially to aid each other in times of distress, like when one of the two became sick.[74] Like treaties, however, changes in Six Nations ceremonial culture did not affect the core of Six Nations spirituality or how they viewed their military role within their own communities or within their treaty relationship with the British. As noted by Cornplanter in 1902, "The doctrines expounded by him [Handsome Lake] did not displace any of the old ceremonies so dear to the heart of the Iroquois. In fact, he urged the observance of all the religious dances, saying they were pleasing to the Creator."[75]

Therefore, when the Six Nations saw their treaty partner in trouble or in distress, like during the Anglo-Boer War, the Six Nations felt a responsibility to offer their services either *en masse* or as individuals. In total, two Six Nations men were able to find their way over to South Africa during the Anglo-Boer War. In April 1902, Joseph Hanaven enlisted in Toronto with the 6th Canadian Mounted Rifles for service in South Africa. His time there was brief, returning to and being discharged at Halifax, Nova Scotia in July 1902.[76] After trying to enlist in the Canadian Mounted Rifles, Six Nations band member John Brant-Sero, living in Hamilton Ontario, went to South Africa to enlist in one of the many British or South African Mounted troops there. When this was not possible, Brant-Sero found employment at the No. 4 Remount Depot in Queenstown where he brought fresh mounts to the front lines, and continued to apply to different mounted units in the

---

71. Ibid., 60.
72. Ibid., 118, 119.
73. Ibid., 152.
74. Ibid. Boyle, *Archaeological Report*, 182.
75. Canfield, *The Legends*, 180.
76. Letter from J. W. Martin, Commissioner, to A. F. MacKenzie, 29 October 1930, LAC, RG10, vol. 2991, file 215,977.

hope of becoming a mounted soldier.[77] Other members of the Six Nations found ways to volunteer their service to their British allies. Dr. W. A. H. Oronhyatekha, son of Grand River born and raised Dr. Oronhyatekha (Peter Martin), applied to be a surgeon for the South Africa Police Force in January 1901. Although his name was put forward to be considered, it is unknown if he ever made it overseas.[78]

CONCLUSION

With 617 different First Nations communities currently in Canada, it is impossible to create a single uniformed narrative of how those groups physically and spiritually connected themselves to the British Crown.[79] What can be understood, however, is that there were commonalities in the way they negotiated treaties within a cultural framework that fit their world view. By recognizing ceremonial and spiritual elements as part of the treaty making process, any and all agreements were considered binding among the First Nations, the British, and the Creator. When Great Britain found their troops being beaten back by the Boers in December of 1899, Canada's First Nations, remembering their sacred treaty agreements, volunteered to come to Britain's aid. No matter when the treaties were signed or whether one side ignored their obligations within the treaties, the sacred nature of how the treaties were made ensured that First Nations people, as they had in times past, came to the aid of their ally, the British Crown.

BIBLIOGRAPHY

Primary Sources

Newspapers

The Brantford Expositor
The Times

Archival Material

LAC, RG10: vol. 2991, file 215,977; vol. 3166, file 388,623 (Library Archives Canada) Department of Militia Files, vol. 36, no. 19907 (Library Archives Canada)

77. *The Times*, 2 January 1902.
78. Department of Militia Files, vol. 36, no. 19907, Dr. W. A. H. Oronhyatekha Application for the Position of Surgeon in the South Africa Police.
79. Indigenous and Northern Affairs Canada. "First Nations People in Canada." https://www.aadnc-aandc.gc.ca/eng/1303134042666/1303134337338.

House of Commons Debates, 4th Session, 8th Parliament, 62–63, Victoria, 16 March–17 May 1899, 5703.
House of Commons Debates, Various Volumes from February 1880 to May 1900.

Secondary Sources

Asch, Michael. *On Being Here to Stay: Treaties and Aboriginal Rights in Canada.* Toronto: University of Toronto Press, 2014.
Boyle, David. *Archaeological Report 1898: Being Part of Appendix to the Report of the Minister of Education Ontario.* Toronto: Warwick & Rutter, 1898.
Canfield, William W. *The Legends of the Iroquois told by "The Cornplanter."* 1902. Reprint, Port Washington, NY: Ira J. Frieman, 1971.
Daniel, Richard. "The Spirit and Terms of Treaty Eight." In *The Spirit of the Alberta Indian Treaties.* edited by Richard T. Price, 47–100. 3rd ed. Edmonton: University of Alberta Press, 1999.
Dempsey, L. James. *Warriors of the King: Prairie Indians in World War One.* Regina, SK: Canadian Plains Research Centre, 1999.
Friesen, Jean. "Magnificent Gifts: The Treaties of Canada with the Indians of the Northwest 1869–1876." *Transactions of the Royal Society of Canada* 1 (1986) 41–51.
Haig-Brown, Celia. *Resistance and Renewal: Surviving the Indian Residential School.* Vancouver: Arsenal Pulp, 1988.
Henry, Wade A. "Imagining the Great White Mother and the Great King: Aboriginal Tradition and Royal Representation at the "Great Pow-wow" of 1901." *Journal of the Canadian Historical Association* 11.1 (2000) 87–108.
Hickey, Lynn, et al. "T. A. R. R. Interview with Elders Program." In *The Spirit of the Alberta Indian Treaties*, edited by Richard T. Price, 103–60. 3rd ed. Edmonton: University of Alberta Press, 1999.
Hildebrandt, Walter, et al. *The True Spirit and Original Intent of Treaty 7.* Montreal: McGill-Queen's University Press, 1996.
Hill, Susan M. "The Clay We Are Made of: An Examination of the Haudenosaunee Land Tenure on the Grand River Territory." PhD diss., Trent University, 2006.
Indigenous and Northern Affairs Canada. "First Nations People in Canada." Online: https://www.aadnc-aandc.gc.ca/eng/1303134042666/1303134337338.
Lackenbauer, P. Whitney, et al. "A Commemorative History of Aboriginal People in the Canadian Military." Online: http://www.cmp-cpm.forces.gc.ca/dhh-dhp/pub/boo-bro/abo-aut/index-eng.asp>.
Miller, J. R. *Compact, Contract, Covenant: Aboriginal Treaty-Making in Canada.* Toronto: University of Toronto Press, 2009.
———. "'I will accept the Queen's hand': First Nations Leaders and the Image of the Crown in the Prairie Treaties." In *Reflections on Native-Newcomer Relations: Selected Essays*, J. R. Miller, 242–66. Toronto: University of Toronto Press, 2004.
———. "Introduction." In *Sweet Promises: A Reader on Indian-White Relations*, edited by J. R. Miller, xii–xix. Toronto: University of Toronto Press, 1991.
———. "Petitioning the Great White Mother: First Nations' Organizations and Lobbying in London." In *Reflections on Native-Newcomer Relations: Selected Essays*, J. R. Miller, 217–41. Toronto: University of Toronto Press, 2004.
———. *Shingwauk's Vision: A History of Native Residential Schools.* Toronto: University of Toronto Press, 1996

Morris, Alexander. *The Treaties of Canada with the Indians of Manitoba and the North-West Territories*. 1880. Reprint, Toronto: Prespero, 2000.

Moses, John, et al. *A Sketch Account of Aboriginal Peoples in the Canadian Military*. Ottawa: Department of National Defence, 2004.

Muller, Kathryn V. "Two 'Mystery Belts' of Grand River: A Biography of the Two Row Wampum and the Friendship Belt." *American Indian Quarterly* 31.1 (2007) 129–64.

Parker, Arthur C. *The Code of Handsome Lake, The Seneca Prophet*. 1913. Reprint, Ohsweken, ON: Iroqrafts, 2000.

———. "Iroquois Sun Myths." *Journal of American Folk Lore* 23.90 (1910) 473–78.

Price, Richard T., ed. *The Spirit of the Alberta Indian Treaties*. 3rd ed. Edmonton: University of Alberta Press, 1999.

Reville, Douglas F. *History of the County of Brant*. Vol. 1. Brantford, ON: Hurley, 1920.

Speck, Frank G. *The Midwinter Rites of the Cayuga Longhouse*. 1949. Reprint, Ohsweken, ON: Iroqrafts, 1987.

Stonechild, Blair, and Bill Waiser. *Loyal till Death: Indians and the North-West Rebellion*. Markham, ON: Fifth House, 1997.

Taylor, John Leonard. "Two Views on the Meanings of Treaties Six and Seven." In *The Spirit of the Alberta Indian Treaties*. edited by Richard T. Price, 9–45. 3rd ed. Edmonton: University of Alberta Press, 1999.

Thomas, Jacob E., and Terry Boyle. *Teachings from the Longhouse*. Toronto: Stoddart, 1994.

Waugh, Fred W. *Iroquois Food and Food Preparation*. Ottawa: Government Printing Bureau, 1916.

Williams, Paul, and Curtis Nelson. "Kaswentha." *For Seven Generations an Information Legacy of the Royal Commission on Aboriginal Peoples*. CD-ROM, Ottawa: Royal Commission on Aboriginal People, 1997.

Winegard, Timothy C. *For King and Kanata: Canadian Indians and the First World War*. Winnipeg: University of Manitoba Press, 2012.

9

"The Boers standing in the way of progress in Africa must be swept aside"

Patriotism and Imperialism in the Canadian Jewish Times during the South African War

GORDON L. HEATH

BY THE END OF the nineteenth century Canadian Jews had maintained a small but vibrant community since the founding of their first synagogue in Montreal in 1768.¹ If anyone was concerned about their patriotism and loyalty to the empire when war broke out in October 1899, they only needed to read the following commentary in the *Jewish Times* to assuage their fears:

> The Boers standing in the way of progress in Africa must be swept aside. There is no intention to deprive them of any liberty save the liberty of depriving others of liberty, and it will be better for them in the long run, as it will be for the world at large when their corrupt, fanatical, fantastic rule shall be abolished and the way made clear through the heart of Africa for the march of civilization from Cape to Cairo.²

---

1. For a history of the development of Jews in Canada, see Abella, *A Coat of Many Colours*; Tulchinsky, *Canada's Jews*; Brym, et al., *The Jews in Canada*; Sack, *History of the Jews*.

2. "The War," *Jewish Times*, 27 October 1899, 377. For Canada's role in the war, see Miller, *Painting the Map Red*. For Canadian imperialism, see Berger, *The Sense of Power*; Page, *The Boer War*.

Those comments were not an outlier, for throughout the war years the pages of the *Jewish Times* were replete with statements of support for the British and Canadian imperial cause in South Africa. As B. G. Sack notes, "The outbreak of the Boer War in October, 1899 evoked new affirmations of loyalty to the Motherland from the Dominion and the Jews of Canada participated wholeheartedly in this sentiment."[3] In fact, their imperial zeal was quite similar to that of the ardent supporters of empire such as the culturally dominant Protestant denominations of Anglicans, Baptists, Methodists, and Presbyterians.[4] However, there were important differences due to the marginal standing of Jews. At the turn of the century, with a census count of only 16,000 (0.03% of the total population), a faith that was not Christian, and a background that was not Anglo-Saxon, Canadian Jews were in a precarious position: they demonstrate loyalty, or face—and even fuel—an anti-Semitic backlash. The imperialism expressed in the *Jewish Times* may have been a genuine conviction, but it served a pragmatic purpose as well—that of demonstrating their patriotism to avoid the dangers inherent with living on the margins.

The focus of this chapter is the *Jewish Times* and its coverage of the war.[5] The Canadian religious press at the end of the century was formidable in numbers and sway,[6] and the English-language *Jewish Times* was one of those papers that used its clout not only to build identity and community among its constituents, but also to express and shape political convictions. As a result, within its pages one can get a glimpse of ways in which the Jewish community responded to the war, as well as the nature of its discourse related to patriotism, war, and empire. Of course, the Jewish

---

3. Sack, *History of the Jews in Canada*, 259.

4. Heath, *A War with a Silver Lining*.

5. One of the oldest and most important Canadian Jewish newspapers, the *Jewish Times* was founded in 1897 in Montreal by Samuel W. Jacobs, a lawyer and a Member of Parliament, and Lyon Cohen. The first editor was Carrol Ryan, a sympathetic Christian who had significance experience with newspapers. For brief commentary on its origins, see Sack, *History of the Jews*, 234–35; Rhinewine, "The Jewish Press in Canada," 457. Daily Yiddish papers were established in the early 1900s in Montreal, Toronto, and Winnipeg. See Schnoor, "The Contours of Canadian Jewish Life," 181. A close reading of those Yiddish papers would provide a helpful and much needed sense of Jewish attitudes to national identity and imperialism in the years leading up to the First World War. The *Jewish Times* is located at the Ontario Jewish Archives, Blankenstein Family Heritage Centre, Toronto, ON. This research on the *Jewish Times* was made possible through the Dr. Stephen Speisman Bursary, Ontario Jewish Archives, Blankenstein Family Heritage Centre.

6. Heath, "'Forming Sound Public Opinion,'" 109–59.

community was heterogeneous in that there were many perspectives on all manner of issues. That being the case, the perspective on the war in the pages of the *Jewish Times* was remarkably homogeneous in its support for the imperial effort.

A number of Jews fought on the side of the British in the War of 1812 and the Papineau Rebellion (1837–1838), and also with the new Dominion of Canada during the Fenian Raids (1870).[7] That pattern of support continued into the South African War, and would be generally followed in the First World War. Studies on Canadian Jews and war are relatively undeveloped, and this chapter is the first sustained attention paid to Canadian Jews and the South African War. Not only will it provide the first analysis of their response to the conflict, it will also provide the necessary context for subsequent Jewish engagement in Canada's twentieth-century wars.[8]

The following examination of the *Jewish Times* is in two parts. The first section summarizes the nature and extent of coverage of the war. The second analyzes the discourse related to war, nation, and empire.

NATURE AND EXTENT OF WAR COVERAGE

There are copious examples of Jewish belief in the justice of the imperial cause in South Africa. An article summarizing a service at the Spanish and Portuguese synagogue in Montreal provides a snapshot of support for the empire, as well as the type of religious discourse used to describe the justice of the imperial cause.[9] The service was attended by the Jewish Lad's Brigade. The speaker reminded all those in attendance of their responsibility to be loyal to government, and extolled the virtues of Britain and its empire. Wherever the flag of Britain flew, he stated, "justice is administered without fear or favor, distinctions of race and creed are unknown, oppression is absolutely impossible." He went on to declare that the motto on the British

---

7. Rosenberg, *Canada's Jews*, 248. B. G. Sack notes how, while some Jews were sympathetic to Papineau, the majority supported the loyalists. See Sack, *History of the Jews in Canada*, ch. 11. See also, Hart, *The Jew in Canada*, 503 11.

8. For the precedent-setting nature of the war for Canada's churches, see Heath, "Canadian Churches," 15–33. For works on Canadian Jews and wars in the twentieth century, see Granatstein, "Ethnic and Religious Enlistment," 175–80; Kay, "A Note on the Formation," 171–77; Menkis, "'But You Can't See,'" 25–50; Tulchinsky, *Branching Out*, ch. 8; Rome, *Canadian Jews in WWII*; Pollins, "Jews In the Canadian Armed Forces," 44–58; Spier, "Israel Joseph Friedman," 117–22. For a general work on Jews and the military, see Penslar, *Jews and the Military*.

9. "The British Motto," *Jewish Times*, 10 November 1899, 396.

standard should be "Righteousness, Justice, Liberty," and that those who engaged in "hysterical denunciations" of Britain's war aims were profoundly missing the mark due to the fact that "England was fighting to secure equal rights for all men." The service ended with the singing of the National Anthem twice, once in Hebrew and once in English. In his prayer for the Queen, Rabbi De Sola "inserted a special petition for the triumphant and speedy termination of the war."

That idealistic discourse equating British rule with justice and liberty was expressed in other ways as well. The poem "The Briton" portrayed Britons as freedom loving people whose primary intention was the emancipation of the oppressed: "The liberties our fathers won / We'll grant to every nation, / Till peace and justice, like the sun, / Shall shine o'er all creation."[10] That sun, it was hoped, would soon be shining over South Africa. At the war's conclusion that dream had purportedly become a reality, and what had been prayed for had finally come to fruition: "Now that end has come, as we hoped and prayed it would, in a victory for the British . . . There is no desire to gloat over their downfall. All they have to do is sincerely, honorably accept the situation, and in a few years they will enjoy greater freedom and a better form of government under the British flag than could ever have been theirs under the corrupt system established by Kruger."[11]

While Britain and its empire were idealized, the Boers were often demonized.[12] The Jewish harsh rhetoric in many ways mirrored constructions of the "other" in the Protestant religious press. The "stupid, corrupt, tyrannical oligarchy which ruled the Transvaal" had, it was argued, unwisely led its people to destruction.[13] British rule and institutions were deemed to be "infinitely superior" to those of the "corrupt, fanatical Dutch."[14] As for the Boers themselves, their "indolent spirit and the antiquated methods" condemned generations to suffer hunger and poverty.[15] In regards to their religion, the Boers were considered entirely out-of-touch with modern sensibilities. Particularly vexing was the usurping of the Jewish claim to be God's chosen people. As one commentator wrote: "These foolish people are

---

10. "The Briton," *Jewish Times*, 22 December 1899, 29. For examples of this type of poetry in the Christian religious press, see Heath, "Passion for Empire," 127–47.
11. "Peace," *Jewish Times*, 6 June 1902, 216.
12. Heath, *A War with a Silver Lining*, 36–39.
13. "Peace," *Jewish Times*, 6 June 1902, 216.
14. "The War," *Jewish Times*, 5 January 1900, 40–41.
15. "South Africa," *Jewish Times*, 11 May 1900, 185.

fond of comparing themselves to the Israelites of old, but the resemblance is purely imaginary. Uneducated, stupid, narrow, cunning and cruel, their characteristics are all the reverse of those which distinguished the people who followed Moses out of Egypt."[16]

Other targets of attack were international and domestic critics of the war, of which there were many. Britain's European imperial competitors celebrated the bungling of the empire's armies, and hoped for a Boer victory to humiliate and weaken the British. The *Jewish Times* addressed such activities in a poem that targeted criticism emanating from France.[17] Critics in the United States were also identified and condemned.[18] One such critic was Rabbi Emil G. Hirsch, a prominent rabbi of Chicago Sinai Synagogue. However, even his lofty position did not make him unassailable, and an article detailed point by point his mistakes in declaring against the British.[19] Domestic critics were also of concern, and articles in the *Jewish Times* attacked those in Quebec who celebrated Boer victories: "Breathing the free air of Canada and enjoying the blessings of British institutions, contented, prosperous, happy, these refugees from countries cursed by the triple abominations of tyranny, fanaticism and ignorance, are struck with astonishment that anyone could be found in Canada so stupid and ungrateful as to rejoice in British reverses and exult in what they regard as signs of the decline and fall of the British empire."[20] Such bold statements could certainly endear the Jewish community to the English, but it was no way to make friends with the French-speaking majority in Quebec.

The paper provided readers with a number of updates on political developments and the course of the war. The unity of the empire and the sending of contingents to aid the "motherland" was praised.[21] Support was

---

16. "The War," *Jewish Times*, 27 October 1899, 377. For similar commentary, see "Boers and Jews," *Jewish Times*, 13 October 1899, 360; "Britons, Boers, and Bible Parallels," *Jewish Times*, 2 March 1900, 105–6. The issue of who was actually the modern-day "ten tribes of Israel" was potentially a point of controversy, for British Israelism (a movement among Britons) claimed that the British were descendants of the lost tribes. Surprisingly, one article was published in the *Jewish Times* that supported that notion. See "Are The British the Lost Ten Tribes?" *Jewish Times*, 24 May 1901, 196. For an article critical of contemporary theories, see "The Ten Tribes," *Jewish Times*, 8 December 1899, 5.

17. "The 'Absinthe'-Minded Beggar," *Jewish Times*, 16 March 1900, 123.

18. "Boerism," *Jewish Times*, 8 June 1900, 216–17; "Great Britain's Conquest," *Jewish Times*, 4 July 1902, 240–41.

19. "Britons, Boers, and Bible Parallels," *Jewish Times*, 2 March 1900, 105–6.

20. "Bigotry and Disloyalty," *Jewish Times*, 19 January 1900, 56–57.

21. "The War," *Jewish Times*, 27 October 1899, 377.

expressed for a triple Anglo-Saxon alliance comprised of Britain, America, and Germany.[22] Opening battles and British fortunes were outlined.[23] Canadian participation in the Battle of Paardeberg was praised, noting that while people rejoiced over the victory and "proudly exult[ed] in the heroism of her sons" the nation "mourn[ed] the loss of the brave lads who have cemented Imperial unity with their life-blood."[24] Subsequent British advances were identified, with cautious optimism over what looked like an impending British victory.[25] When the war eventually ended, commentary was marked by relief, along with a sense of pride in the Jewish involvement in the war effort: "Among no class of His Majesty's subjects was the news of the Boer surrender and the proclamation of peace received with more joy and satisfaction than among Jews . . . Jewish patriotism has shone conspicuously throughout the struggle, Jewish blood has flowed freely on the battle-field [sic], and they have earned the right to rejoice in the successful conclusion of the war."[26]

As noted in the peace announcement, there was pride that Jews had played their part in the war effort. In fact, it was argued that they had "given more soldiers of all ranks to the army in the field, in proportion to their numbers, than any other class."[27] In order to make that point even clearer to those who doubted or disparaged Jewish abilities and loyalty to their country of citizenship, the paper published a significant amount of articles identifying instances of Jewish patriotism and martial skill. With unconcealed satisfaction, the *Jewish Times* identified Jews who served in foreign armies, such as an officer in the Turkish army,[28] a knight of St. John,[29] or a war minister in Italy.[30] Accounts of Jews from England and the empire who served with distinction in the military were noted with pleasure,[31]

22. *Jewish Times*, 8 December 1899, 8.
23. "The War," *Jewish Times*, 27 October 1899, 377; "The War," *Jewish Times*, 5 January 1900, 40–41.
24. *Jewish Times*, 2 March 1900, 104.
25. *Jewish Times*, 27 April 1900, 172; "The War," *Jewish Times*, 25 May 1900, 201.
26. "Peace," *Jewish Times*, 6 June 1902, 216.
27. Ibid.
28. "General Dr. Jacques Nissim Pasha," *Jewish Times*, 5 July 1901, 241.
29. "A Jewish Knight of St. John of Jerusalem," *Jewish Times*, 16 August 1901, 289.
30. "General Ottolenghi," *Jewish Times*, 4 July 1902, 241.
31. "Colonel A. E. Goldsmid," *Jewish Times*, 29 September 1899, 337–38; *Jewish Times*, 27 October 1899, 376; "Colonel David Harris," *Jewish Times*, 10 November 1899, 385–86; *Jewish Times*, 10 November 1899, 393; "Dr. J. Alton L. Harris," *Jewish Times*, 24

as was Jewish funding of a hospital for troops at the front.³² The death of Lieutenant F. M. Raphael of the South Lancashire Regiment in the battle of Spion Kop was held up as an example of a noble and virtuous Jewish officer "particularly popular with his men."³³ Jews were portrayed as dying for the empire, and their loyalty beyond question: "British Jews fully concur with and share in these national sentiments and have proved their loyalty by not only giving freely of their material substance, but have also sealed their devotion with their blood. Jews are now serving in all ranks of the British army, and no battle has been fought in South Africa in which Jews have not been among the killed and wounded."³⁴ Lord Roberts's comments on the important role played by the Jews in fighting for the empire was provided as further evidence of Jewish ability and loyalty.³⁵ A description of a patriotic service at Central Synagogue, London, that included a "large assembly" of Jews who had served in South Africa, was just one more example of how Jews around the empire had fought faithfully for the empire.³⁶

As for Canadian Jews, the existence of Jewish cadet units such as Baron De Hirsch cadets,³⁷ and talk of forming a Zion Cadet Corps³⁸ or a "Jewish lads battalion" in Canada³⁹ were deemed proof positive of Jewish loyalty.⁴⁰ Other practical ways in which Canadian Jews supported the war effort were through the proposed formation of a women's group called the "The Daughters of the Empire,"⁴¹ or support for the Patriotic Fund established

---

November 1899, 414; "Children of Israel in the Indian Army," *Jewish Times*, 22 December 1899, 27; "Jews under Arms for England," *Jewish Times*, 1 March 1901, 101.

32. "Mr. Alfred Mosely," *Jewish Times*, 16 February 1900, 81–82; *Jewish Times*, 16 February 1900, 88.

33. "The Late Lieut. F. M. Raphael," *Jewish Times*, 2 March 1900, 97–98.

34. *Jewish Times*, 16 February 1900, 88. See also "The Jewish Situation in South Africa," *Jewish Times*, 6 June 1902, 220–21.

35. "The Jews as a Soldier," *Jewish Times*, 14 September 1900, 326–27; *Jewish Times*, 25 October 1901, 373.

36. "Jews in the British Service," *Jewish Times*, 3 January 1902, 36–37.

37. "The Baron De Hirsch Cadets," *Jewish Times*, 21 July 1899, 257; *Jewish Times*, 6 July 1900, 247.

38. "The Zion Cadet Corps," *Jewish Times*, 31 August 1900, 311.

39. "The Jewish Lads Battalion in Canada," *Jewish Times*, 14 February 1902, 89; "The Jews Lad's Brigade," *Jewish Times*, 14 February 1902, 89.

40. Those formations sound similar to what was occurring in church-based programs for children. See Heath, "'Prepared to do, prepared to die.'"

41. "For the Women and the Children of the Empire," *Jewish Times*, 8 June 1900, 212.

to provide support for soldiers and their families.[42] A number of Canadian Jews were fighting alongside Canadian troops in Africa. Hyman Lightstone from Montreal was identified as being the only Jew in the Second Contingent, and the *Jewish Times* wished him "God speed."[43] There was a didactic purpose portraying gallant Jewish soldiers winning accolades throughout the world for their martial skills. Those examples were simply to be followed. In one summary of a synagogue service it was declared: "Jewish soldiers had distinguished themselves in the South African campaign, and it behooved every Israelite who lived under the glorious flag of England to be similarly ready to serve the Empire that gave them a happy home."[44]

A further demonstration of Canadian Jewish patriotism was the response to events surrounding the death of Queen Victoria. The fact that Queen Victoria was dearly loved in her later years by the majority of her subjects seems to be beyond dispute, and the empire-wide mourning in response to her death on 22 January 1901 merely confirms that that was the case.[45] Philip Buckner has noted how in 1901 "loyalty to the institution of the monarchy was a [Canadian] national phenomenon" that transcended regional differences,[46] and the reaction by both English Protestant leaders and laity to her death provides evidence of such Canadian devotion.[47] The commentary in the *Jewish Times* demonstrates that that fidelity to the monarchy included religious minorities, and it provided details on the memorial service held at the Spanish and Portuguese synagogue in Montreal,[48] printed resolutions of loyalty made by Jewish organizations,[49] and included

---

42. "Winnipeg Jews and the Canadian Patriotic Fund," *Jewish Times*, 16 March 1900, 121. See also Sack, *History of the Jews*, 259. Many in the churches were also caught up in the enthusiasm surrounding the Patriotic Fund. See Heath, *A War with a Silver Lining*, 80–82.

43. "Off to the War," *Jewish Times*, 5 January 1900, 35.

44. *Jewish Times*, 21 June 1901, 228–29.

45. The books on Queen Victoria are too numerous to list here. For a cursory examination of works, see the following biographies: Longford, *Victoria R. I.*; Hibbert, *Queen Victoria*; and Erickson, *Her Little Majesty*. For a discussion of the Queen's popularity, as well as contemporary criticisms of the Queen, see Williams, *The Contentious Crown*. For reaction to her death, see Packard, *Farewell in Splendor*.

46. Buckner, "Casting Daylight upon Magic," 158.

47. For English-Protestant reactions to her death, see Heath, "'Were We in the Habit.'"

48. "Spanish and Portuguese Synagogue," *Jewish Times*, 15 February 1901, 90.

49. "Union of Orthodox Synagogues," *Jewish Times*, 15 February 1901, 91–92.

commentary on her illustrious reign and how Jews benefited from it.[50] The paper also featured expressions of loyalty to her son, King Edward VII,[51] as well as positive commentary on the visit of the Duke and Duchess of Cornwall and York later that year.[52]

Despite the majority of wartime commentary being supportive of the imperial and Canadian cause in South Africa, there were articles that opened Jews to accusations of being unassimilated and unpatriotic immigrants. For instance, in a number of places war was deemed a foolish waste of life, a curse, and the "greatest misfortune that could befall a nation."[53] The Boxer Rebellion (1899–1901) initiated in society a flurry of criticism of regarding western imperial abuses in China, and criticisms in the *Jewish Times* echoed a familiar refrain in the English-speaking world. For example, the conduct of European Christian empires in China were judged quite harshly for their brutal treatment of the Chinese, leading to comments on the alleged superiority of Christian civilization: "A man who is not infatuated with the idea that the present system of European Christian civilization is so perfectly good that its blessings should be forced on the Chinese and other races at any cost of blood and suffering, may well ask wherein the superiority of Christianity and western civilization consists?"[54] The militarism of Christian churches was also targeted: "Christian churches, in pandering to the lust of war, would apostatize not only from the principles of the New, but from those of the Old Testament."[55] At first glance those comments indicate confidence to criticize western imperialism, Christian civilization, and even churches. A closer look, however, reveals that, while

50. "Queen Victoria," *Jewish Times*, 1 February 1901, 72; "Jewish Progress in the Victorian Age," *Jewish Times*, 1 February 1901, 73–75.

51. "King Edward VII," *Jewish Times*, 1 February 1901, 72–73; "King Edward and the Jews of England," *Jewish Times*, 7 June 1901, 209–10; "The King's Illness," *Jewish Times*, 4 July 1902, 248.

52. "The Duke and Duchess of Cornwall and York," *Jewish Times*, 13 September 1901, 321–22.

53. "Peace," *Jewish Times*, 6 June 1902, 216. See also "The Jews and Peace," *Jewish Times*, 6 December 1901, 2; "Waste of Life in War," *Jewish Times*, 10 November 1899, 390.

54. "Christianity and Civilization," *Jewish Times*, 14 September 1900, 328–29. See also "War and the Preachers," *Jewish Times*, 4 January 1901, 41–42; "Atrocities in China," *Jewish Times*, 15 February 1901, 89; "China to the Nations," *Jewish Times*, 26 April 1901, 170; "The Powers and China," *Jewish Times*, 3 August 1900, 282; "Chinese Boxers and European Bigots," *Jewish Times*, 17 August 1900, 291–92; "The Folly of War," *Jewish Times*, 23 November 1900, 413.

55. "The Jews and Peace," *Jewish Times*, 6 December 1901, 2.

the response of the imperial powers in China was considered to be disturbing, the primary focus of criticisms was clearly not on the war in South Africa. The conduct of some Christian ministers caught up in a war fever may have been distasteful, and the impact of western civilization may not have been so benevolent as was often portrayed, but the case for the justice of the imperial cause against the Boers seemed to remain impeccable. It should also be noted that pointing out the folly of war, criticizing militarism, and identifying the shameful actions of European powers in China were standard fare even among Christian denominations supportive of the empire.[56] In fact, the same article that called war "a curse" expressed relief over the announcement of a British victory; a victory that had been "hoped and prayed" for.[57] Consequently, the uniqueness of the wartime criticisms in the *Jewish Times* lay primarily not in what was actually said, but, as will be expanded on below, in the decision to publish them in the face of possible misunderstandings of Jewish loyalty.

ANALYSIS OF DISCOURSE RELATED TO PATRIOTISM, WAR, AND EMPIRE

Jewish expressions of loyalty to the national and imperial cause in South Africa were rooted in a number of assumptions, conceptions, and experiences. Some of those assumptions and conceptions simply reflected a late-nineteenth century imperial *zeitgeist*, others were shaped by the experience of Jews living in and outside the empire. As for patriotic statements and actions, they served a number of practical purposes related to the experience of living on the margins. The following provides an analysis of these aspects of the responses to the war among Canadian Jews.

Ardent support for the imperial cause was rooted in the conviction that the British Empire was a force for righteousness and civilization in the world. In this regard, Canadian Jews were simply echoing a familiar nineteenth-century refrain regarding the advance of history through the spread of European empires, but especially with the British Empire in the vanguard: a "new era" was dawning with the rise of "Anglo-Saxonism" and the spread of its "free institutions to a commanding position on the earth."[58] Protestants linked the rise of the empire to God's providence and

---

56. Heath, "When Missionaries Were Hated"; Heath, *A War with a Silver Lining*, 126–28.

57. "Peace," *Jewish Times*, 6 June 1902, 216.

58. "The Coming Time," *Jewish Times*, 7 July 1899, 248–49.

blessing, and extolled its role in the spread of civilization and (Protestant) Christianity.[59] Jewish commentary balked when it came to mentioning the Christian missionary aspects of the empire, but fully embraced claims regarding the benefits of British rule. That focus on the positive good, however, was primarily related to the experience of Jews at home and abroad. More specifically, it was a relative good wherein Jews fared better under British rule than under any other. The contrast between Jews under Russian rule was a case in point:

> These two empires represent opposite, irreconcilable principles in civilization and government. Britain is democratic, Russia autocratic. The one stands for the freedom and equality of all men . . . the other recognizes no authority but that of the Czar backed by an infallible church . . . Given a choice between the two there is no doubt as to which a Jew would prefer. The conflict between these rival empires, which all men believe inevitable, is, therefore, of profound interest to the Jewish people all over the world.[60]

The relative good of the empire was also considered obvious when comparing British rule with the Boer's (or any other nation for that matter), and it was because of those conditions for Jews that support was so freely granted to the imperial cause:

> In common with all loyal subjects and knowing how infinitely superior British rule and British institutions are to those of the corrupt, fanatical Dutch of Africa, we earnestly hope and pray for the success of British arms and a speedy end to the war. Under the British flag everywhere Jews enjoy the same liberties and are protected by the same laws as all other citizens of the empire . . . Of the Jews under the sway of Great Britain it may be said with more accuracy than any other country that they can lay aside the haunting fear that has pursued them since the dispersion, or having at any moment to accept the edict of expulsion and submit to the horrors of martyrdom. Therefore let us rejoice in British victory and success in all parts of the earth and pray that the God of battles will lead their banners to final and complete triumph over all enemies.[61]

---

59. Brown, *Providence and Empire*.
60. "Britain and Russia," *Jewish Times*, 22 June 1900, 232–33.
61. "The War," *Jewish Times*, 5 January 1900, 40–41.

A number of Canadian Jews expressed appreciation for the "equal rights" shared with other British subjects in the empire,[62] praised Prime Minister Laurier's rule,[63] and were perplexed when people celebrated British reverses.[64] Rabbi Ashinsky, a Montreal rabbi speaking in Winnipeg, echoed those refrains.[65] He argued that Britain would rule the world with institutions of justice and equality. He went on to say that its "laws were worthy of the highest respect of Jewish citizens," all good Jews were to pray for the Queen and her family twice a week, and that the only hope for persecuted Jews around the world was British supremacy.

The concerns expressed for the condition of Jews were made in the context of the grim plight of Jews in Eastern Europe, or the antisemitism exhibited during the trial of Alfred Dreyfus in France. Commentary on the suffering of Jews was frequent in the *Jewish Times*.[66] Whether on the domestic or international front, the sentiment was that Jews faced either the threat or reality of hostile anti-Semitism. It was believed the only place where Jews had a reasonable chance of escaping such virulent attacks was the British Empire, not that all was well even in Canada—for prominent figures such as Goldwin Smith and Henri Bourassa made public their disdain for Jews, and incidents of anti-Semitism occurred across the Dominion, especially in Quebec[67]—but that many Jews considered themselves to be relatively safer in Canada than anywhere else.

It is with those concerns with antisemitism in mind that one begins to understand the very pragmatic element to public displays of support

---

62. "The War," *Jewish Times*, 27 October 1899, 377.

63. "Sir Wilfrid Laurier," *Jewish Times*, 2 November 1900, 395–96.

64. "Bigotry and Disloyalty," *Jewish Times*, 19 January 1900, 56–57.

65. "Rabbi Ashinsky on British Supremacy," *Jewish Times*, 17 August 1900, 290.

66. "Jacob Riis Defends the Jews," *Jewish Times*, 10 November 1899, 396; "The Anglo-Saxon and the Jew," *Jewish Times*, 27 October 1899, 372; *Jewish Times*, 20 July 1900, 264; *Jewish Times*, 28 September 1900, 344; "The Folly of War," *Jewish Times*, 23 November 1900, 413; "Anti-Semite Always Anti-British," *Jewish Times*, 17 January 1902, 57; "Jews and Jew-Baiters in Quebec," *Jewish Times*, 14 February 1902, 88; "Anti-Semitic Anglophobes," *Jewish Times*, 28 February 1902, 106; "Anti-Semitic and Anti-British Sentiments Being Published in Canada," *Jewish Times*, 14 March 1902, 116–17; "Alfred Dreyfus on an Amnesty," *Jewish Times*, 22 December 1899, 27; "Jews in the Transvaal," *Jewish Times*, 11 May 1900, 177–78; "The Jewish Situation in South Africa," *Jewish Times*, 6 June 1902, 220–21.

67. Abella, *A Coat of Many Colours*, 105–11; Tulchinsky, "The Contours of Canadian," 5–21. Sack argues that one needs to be careful neither to overplay nor underplay anti-Semitism in Canada at that time. See Sack, *History of the Jews*, 237.

for the imperial cause. Identifying Jews in the military, supporting the war effort, expressing fidelity to the monarchy, or extolling the virtues of the empire were deemed to be essential in order to provide a counter narrative to that of Jewish treachery and aloofness to nation affairs. The originators of that negative narrative were not always identified, but it is clear that the editor had certain "enemies" in mind. As the article "Warrior Jews" noted, "It is simply a proper use of facts to refute the falsehoods and slanders published by our enemies. In every army of Europe Jewish soldiers are serving with honour and distinction; some of them in the highest and most responsible positions. In the present war Jews have sealed their loyalty to Britain with their lifeblood; a grand fact which must stand forever to the honour of British Jews."[68] It was also hoped that such ardent displays of support would disarm opponents of non-British immigration who claimed that Jews did not assimilate and "become" Canadian. In this regard imperialism provided a means to move from the margins. Imperialism in late-Victorian Canada enveloped a wide and diverse range of sentiments, and it was that ambiguity that was a part of its strength and appeal.[69] Its fluidity meant that it could be embraced by Canada's Jews, with the positive consequence of identifying Jews with mainstream displays of national and imperial patriotic sentiment.

The need for public displays of Jewish support for the imperial cause was considered to be even more pressing than that for any other minority group. As the following comments indicate, it was believed that merely one instance of Jewish disloyalty could lead to widespread generalizations about all Jews:

> This matter is not put thus plainly because Jews more than any other class need to be reminded of their duty, for they do not, but because each individual Jew has the good name of all Jews in his keeping. If any man of any other race or nationality goes wrong, he only suffers, but when the Jew is in error he carries condemnation of all Jews along with him. Therefore he must avoid even the appearance of wrong doing, for as the moral sanctions of his religion are more exacting than those observed by men of other faiths, so are his responsibilities much greater and demand of him a clearer and more circumspect appreciation of the conditions by which he is surrounded.[70]

68. "Warrior Jews" *Jewish Times*, 16 February 1900, 89.
69. Miller, *Painting the Map Red*, 4.
70. "Anti-Semitism and Its Cure," *Jewish Times*, 25 April 1902, 168.

Other ethnic and religious minorities faced prejudice, but some Jews felt that their case was unique.[71] Due to fears of stoking the flames of prejudice, the pressure on every Jew to be the ideal patriot was palpable. The rise of antisemitism in Canada in the early twentieth century, and especially in the 1920s and 1930s, lends credence to their fears that they lived in what Arnold Ages calls an "uneasy calm."[72] Consequently, a unified and ardent patriotism was needed to avoid negative stereotyping of Jews and the harsh treatment that inevitably followed. In fact, the *Jewish Times* was created a few years earlier specifically to counter antisemitic narratives,[73] and that raison d'etre is one explanation why its pages constructed a uniform narrative of Jewish patriotism.

Another pragmatic reason for displays of imperial zeal relate to the late-nineteenth century rise of Zionism. Antisemitism during the Dreyfus Affair led to Zionism being perceived by some as a solution to the Jewish plight.[74] Zionism also protected and preserved Jewish identity, for it acted as a "powerful barrier against the strong assimilationist currents in their environment which often succeeded in uprooting them and isolating them completely from their cultural origins."[75] The rise of Zionism also led some to support the empire for quite pragmatic and tactical reasons.[76] As Rabbi Ashinsky stated, it would be "through the British that the Jews would ultimately be returned in full possession of the Holy Land."[77] To alleviate any fears that Zionist's loyalties were elsewhere, the concept of dual loyalties was invoked; in one synagogue sermon on the topic of Zionism listeners were reminded that one could love both the Motherland (England and empire) and Fatherland (Palestine) and at the same time be loyal to both.[78]

---

71. Jews also faced proselytism from Protestant missionaries, something dealt with in a number of articles. See "The Disgruntled Missionary Again," *Jewish Times*, 8 December 1899, 8; "A Missionary Taken to Task," *Jewish Times*, 22 December 1899, 25–26; "Some Questions Answered," *Jewish Times*, 7 December 1900, 3–4.

72. Ages, "Antisemitism," 383–95.

73. Sack, *History of the Jews*, 234–35.

74. Ibid., 236.

75. Ibid., 259.

76. Not all Canadian Jews supported Zionism. See Tulchinsky, "Contours," 13–16.

77. "Rabbi Ashinsky on British Supremacy," *Jewish Times*, 17 August 1900, 290.

78. "Zionism," *Jewish Times*, 27 April 1900, 164–66.

CONCLUSION

Evidence of Canadian Jewish support for the imperial war effort in South Africa is ubiquitous in the *Jewish Times*, and the imperial zeal and sentiments expressed and reported on were often quite similar to that of other ardent supporters of the empire. However, while such displays were not necessarily disingenuous, there was a pragmatic element to making their patriotism known. Jewish expressions of loyalty to the national and imperial cause in South Africa were rooted in a number of assumptions, conceptions, and experiences. Some of those assumptions and conceptions simply reflected a late-nineteenth century imperial *zeitgeist*, others were shaped by the experience of Jews living in and outside the empire. As for public patriotic statements and actions, they served a number of practical purposes related to the experience of living on the margins, one of which was to avoid any appearance of disloyalty that could provoke an antisemitic backlash feared lurking in the shadows.

BIBLIOGRAPHY

Primary Source

Jewish Times (Montreal)

Secondary Sources

Abella, Irving. *A Coat of Many Colours: Two Centuries of Jewish Life in Canada*. Toronto: Key Porter, 1999.

Ages, Arnold. "Antisemitism: The Uneasy Calm." In *The Canadian Jewish Mosaic*, edited by M. Weinfeld, et al., 383–95. Toronto: John Wiley & Sons, 1981.

Berger, Carl. *The Sense of Power: Studies in the Ideas of Canadian Imperialism, 1867–1914*. Toronto: University of Toronto Press, 1970.

Brown, Stewart J. *Providence and Empire, 1815–1914*. Harlow: Pearson, 2008.

Brym, Robert J., et al., eds. *The Jews in Canada*. Toronto: Oxford University Press, 1993.

Buckner, Phillip. "Casting Daylight upon Magic: Deconstructing the Royal Tour of 1901 to Canada." *The Journal of Imperial and Commonwealth History* 31.2 (2003) 158–89.

Erickson, Carolly. *Her Little Majesty: The Life of Queen Victoria*. New York: Simon and Shuster, 1997.

Granatstein, Jack L. "Ethnic and Religious Enlistment in Canada during the Second World War." *Canadian Jewish Studies* 21 (2013) 175–80.

Hart, Arthur Daniel, ed. *The Jew in Canada: A Complete Record of Canadian Jewry from the Days of the French Regime to the Present Time*. Toronto: Jewish Publications, 1926.

Heath, Gordon L. *A War with a Silver Lining: Canadian Protestant Churches and the South African War, 1899–1902*. Montreal: McGill-Queen's University Press, 2009.

———. "Canadian Churches and the South African War: Prelude to the Great War." In *Canadian Churches and the First World War*, edited by Gordon L. Heath, 15–33. Eugene, OR: Pickwick, 2014.

———. "'Forming Sound Public Opinion': The Late-Victorian Canadian Protestant Press and Nation-Building." *Journal of the Canadian Church Historical Society* 48 (2006): 109–59.

———. "Passion for Empire: War Poetry Published in the Canadian English Protestant Press during the South African War, 1899–1902." *Literature and Theology* 16 (June 2002) 127–47.

———. "'Prepared to Do, Prepared to Die': Evangelicals, Imperialism and Late-Victorian Canadian Children's Publications." *Perichoresis* 9.1 (2011) 3–27.

———. "'Were We in the Habit of Deifying Monarchs': Canadian English Protestants and the Death of Queen Victoria, 1901." *Canadian Evangelical Review* (Fall 2005–Spring 2006) 72–97.

———. "When Missionaries Were Hated: An Examination of the Canadian Baptist Defense of Imperialism and Missions during the Boxer Rebellion, 1900." In *Baptists and Mission*, edited by Ian M. Randall and Anthony R. Cross, 261–76. Milton Keynes: Paternoster, 2007.

Hibbert, Christopher. *Queen Victoria: A Personal History*. Cambridge, MA: Da Capo, 2001.

Kay, Zachariah. "A Note on the Formation of the Jewish Legion." *Jewish Social Studies* 29 (1967) 171–77.

Longford, Elizabeth. *Victoria R. I.* London: Weidenfeld and Nicolson, 1964.

Menkis, Richard. "'But You Can't See the Fear That People Lived Through': Canadian Jewish Chaplains and Canadian Encounters with Dutch Survivors, 1944–1945." *American Jewish Archives Journal* 60 (2008) 25–50.

Miller, Carman. *Painting the Map Red: Canada and the South African War, 1899–1902*. Montreal: McGill-Queen's University Press, 1998.

Packard, Jerrold M. *Farewell in Splendor: The Passing of Queen Victoria and Her Age*. New York: Dutton, 1995.

Page, Robert J. D. *The Boer War and Canadian Imperialism*. Ottawa: The Canadian Historical Association, 1987.

Penslar, Derek J. *Jews and the Military: A History*. Princeton: Princeton University Press, 2013.

Pollins, Harold. "Jews in the Canadian Armed Forces in the First World War: A Statistical Research Note." *Jewish Journal of Sociology* 46 (2004) 44–58.

Rhinewine, A. "The Jewish Press in Canada." In *The Jew in Canada: A Complete Record of Canadian Jewry from the Days of the French Regime to the Present Time*, edited by Arthur Daniel Hart, 457–59. Toronto: Jewish Publications, 1926.

Rome, David, ed., *Canadian Jews in WWII*. Montreal: Canadian Jewish Congress, 1947–1948.

Rosenberg, Louis. *Canada's Jews: A Social and Economic Study of Jews in Canada in the 1930s*. Canadian Jewish Congress, 1939. Reprint, Montreal: McGill-Queen's University Press, 1993.

Sack, B. G. *History of the Jews in Canada*. Montreal: Harvest House, 1965.

Schnoor, Randal F. "The Contours of Canadian Jewish Life." *Contemporary Jewry* 31 (2011) 179–97.

Spier, Joe. "Israel Joseph Friedman: A Fallen and Forgotten Soldier—Remembered." *Western States Jewish History* 42 (Fall 2010) 117–22.
Tulchinsky, Gerald J. J. *Branching Out: The Transformation of the Canadian Jewish Community*. Toronto: Stoddart, 1998.
———. *Canada's Jews: A People's Journey*. Toronto: University of Toronto Press, 2008.
———. "The Contours of Canadian Jewish History." In *The Jews in Canada*, edited by Robert J. Brym, et al., 5–21. Toronto: Oxford University Press, 1993.
Williams, Richard. *The Contentious Crown: Public Discussion of the British Monarchy in the Reign of Queen Victoria*. Aldershot: Ashgate, 1997.

Index of Subjects

Afrikaner, 18, 165
Alberta, 143
America, *see United States of America*
American Civil War, 121
American Peace Society, 123, 129, 131
American Revolution, 40, 148
Ancient Order of Hibernians, 47
Anglicanism, 3, 4, 17, 20, 26, 88, 156
Australia, 2, 46, 71, 78

Baptists, 3–5, 28, 70, 71, 156
Boer War
    Battles, 1, 2, 29–31, 45, 51, 73, 89, 90–92, 96, 145, 160, 161
    Black Week, 30, 31, 45, 51
    Casualties, 2, 73
    Guerrilla Warfare, 1, 30
    Pro-Boer Sympathy, 7, 8, 10, 29, 47, 74, 81, 133
Boxer Rebellion, 96, 16
Britain, *see England*
British Columbia, 29, 41, 56, 57, 103, 106, 107, 109, 142, 144, 145

Canada
    Conservative Politics (Liberal-Conservative Party of Canada), 26, 32, 44, 45, 49
    Department of Indian Affairs, 135, 143–46
    Dutch Communities, 10

First Nations, 4, 7, 40, 105, 135–52
Galician (Eastern European) Immigrants, 5, 6, 9
Government, 9, 10, 16, 25–30, 38, 42, 46, 48, 49, 58, 64, 72, 115, 116, 124, 127–29, 137, 138, 142–44, 146, 157, 158, 165
Liberal Politics, 22, 23, 26, 36, 45, 49
Military, 11, 16, 19–21, 25, 30–32, 36, 40, 42, 48–62, 70, 89–95, 117, 121, 126, 127, 144, 147, 151, 167
Militia, 46, 47, 56, 58, 60, 61, 73
Nationalism, 2, 9, 21, 26, 27, 29, 33, 36, 38, 64, 70, 81, 85, 105, 108, 110, 155, 156, 160–69
Canada Congregational Woman's Mission Board, 112, 115
Canadian Manufacturers Association, 131
Canadian Mounted Rifles, 31, 48, 54–56, 151
China, 78, 96, 163, 164
Colonial Missionary Society, 103, 117
Colonialism, 2, 101, 128, 146, 148
Congregational Union for Canada, 105
Congregationalism, 4, 28, 29, 100–119

Democracy, 17, 42, 165
Dutch, *see Netherlands*

Index of Subjects

England, 1, 3, 6, 17, 26, 27, 31–33, 36, 46, 49, 50, 51, 58, 71, 72, 75, 77–79, 86, 88, 92, 97, 100–102, 104, 106, 108, 109, 111, 116, 118, 124, 126, 128, 130, 138, 143, 152, 157–68
Europe, 3, 5, 6, 9, 10, 30, 37, 46, 69, 74–79, 87, 104, 120, 136–41, 147, 149, 159, 163–67

France, 70, 159, 166
Friends University, 130

Germany, 10, 41, 54, 56, 160
Grand Ligne Mission, 71
Great Britain, see England
Great War, see World War I

Hague Peace Conference, 27, 110, 125
Holland, see Netherlands

Imperial Federation League, 32, 44
India, 78, 96, 161
Indigenous Peoples of South Africa, 2, 135, 138, 142–50
Ireland, 6, 22, 23, 36–68, 83
Italy, 37, 39, 40, 160

Japan, 104
Jewish Peoples, 4, 22, 155–70
Jesuits, 40, 42

Kingdom of God, 20, 96, 101, 104, 111, 113, 116, 128
Knights of Columbus, 47, 55

Lake Mohonk Peace Conference, 124, 125, 129, 131
Laval University, 73
Lutheranism, 4, 7, 8, 10

Manitoba, 4, 41, 43, 57
McGill University, 26, 32, 73
Mennonite/Anabaptism, 4, 8–10, 22, 33, 123
Methodism, 3, 4, 20, 27, 28, 71, 86, 88, 104, 118, 122, 156

Missionary Work (Christian), 3, 17, 18, 20, 21, 25, 30, 32, 40, 54, 69, 71, 72, 75, 86, 101–18, 141, 164, 165, 168,
Monarchy, 3, 17, 115, 116, 162, 167

Netherlands, 10, 17, 18, 20, 36, 95, 147, 158, 165
Newfoundland, 86, 103
New Brunswick, 38, 40, 44, 48, 54, 57, 103, 115, 118
New Netherlands, 147
New Zealand, 2, 6, 71
Northwest Mounted Police, 54, 60
Nova Scotia, 7, 22, 38, 44, 46, 48, 49, 54, 57, 58, 62, 103, 115, 151

Ontario, 4, 9, 24, 27–29, 37–44, 47, 48, 54–57, 61, 63, 70, 100, 102, 103, 109, 115, 122, 127, 143, 145, 150–53, 156
Orange Free State, 49, 55, 94
Orangemen, 71

Pacifism, 8, 11, 18, 29, 33, 101, 106, 107, 110, 120–22, 128, 132
Papineau Rebellion, 157
Poland, 9, 37
Portugal, 88, 110, 113, 157, 162
Presbyterianism, 3, 4, 27, 28, 71, 73, 88, 118, 122, 156
Prince Edward Island, 23, 38–40, 44, 46, 54
Protestant Protective Association, 71
Protestantism, 3–5, 7, 10, 12, 17, 21–23, 27, 38–42, 53, 69–83, 100, 102, 107, 115, 122, 156, 158, 162, 164, 168
    Canadian French-speaking, 69–82

Quakerism, 8, 22, 33, 120–32
Quebec, 3, 4, 12, 17, 20, 26, 27, 32, 36–39, 41, 43, 45, 52, 57, 62, 69–82, 95, 100, 102, 103, 109, 110, 115, 136, 159, 166
Queen's University, 24

Index of Subjects

Reformed Churches, 10, 18
Religious Society of Friends, *see* Quakerism
Renfrew and Lanark Highlanders, 55
Roman Catholicism, 3, 4, 6, 12, 17, 23, 26, 36–72, 77–82
    Canadian English-speaking, 40, 42, 52, 53, 63
    Canadian French-speaking, 39, 48, 53, 69–72, 82, 109
    Canadian Irish-Catholics, 23, 38–42, 46–62
Royal Canadian Mounted Police, 138, 144
Russia, 85, 165

Salvation Army, 4, 6, 85–98
Saskatchewan, 48, 143
Scotland, 37, 39–41, 45, 47, 49, 53–56, 60–64
Scottish Highlanders of Cape Breton, 39

South African Constabulary, 33, 33, 63
Spanish-American War, 126

Transvaal, 5, 28, 49, 77, 79, 80, 85, 88, 90, 92, 101, 115, 118, 135, 146, 158, 166,
Treaty of Vereeniging, 2

United Kingdom, 75, 88, 121
United States of America, 7, 8, 10, 21, 25, 31, 32, 39–41, 63, 76, 77, 79, 100, 104, 109, 120, 121, 123–31, 148, 160

War of 1812, 158
Women's Christian Temperance Union (WCTU), 10, 11, 33, 107, 122
World War I, 5, 8–10, 20, 62, 72, 93, 120, 121, 144–46, 156, 157
World War II, 120

Index of Persons

Almond, John M., 17
Arthur, Prince, 142
Ashinsky, Rabbi, 166, 168

Bainton, J. Herbert, 29, 106, 108
Bainton, Roland, 104, 106–8
Booth, William, 86, 93, 94
Bourassa, Henri, 22, 23, 45, 49, 72, 109, 166
Butler, Martin, 23,

Chamberlain, Joseph, 14, 23, 48–50
Charles II, King, 120
Chiniquy, Charles, 71, 72
Churchill, Winston, 138
Courtice, Andrew Cory, 27

Deskaheh, Chief, 137
Diaz, Bartholomew, 88
Dickey, M., 29
Donovan, Michael, 23, 49, 50
Donovan, William, 62
Dorland, Arthur Garratt, 122, 123, 126, 132
Douglas, James, 144
Dreyfus, Alfred, 166, 168

Edward VII, King, 97, 115, 163

Fox, George, 120

Fitzpatrick, Charles, 36, 37, 42, 44–46, 48, 49, 63, 64

Grant, George Munroe, 24

Herd, J. C., 28
Hirsch, Emil G., 159
Howard, Major, 97
Hughes, Sam, 37
Hutton, Sir Edward Thomas Henry, 46

Johnson, Sir William, 137, 142

Kilbey, George A., 85, 88–90
Kipling, Rudyard, 32, 62
Kitchener, Herbert, 21, 95, 96
Kruger, Paul, 18, 21, 23, 49, 50, 79, 158

Laurier, Wilfrid, 26, 31, 32, 36, 43–46, 49, 52, 72, 73, 77, 124, 125, 166

MacDonald, John A., 108
Macdonell, Alexander, 40, 43, 68
Macdonell, Archibald C., 63
Macdonell, Archibald H., 52, 62
McClung, Nellie, 33
McInnis, John Kenneth, 23
McLeod, J. D., 27
Moore, Cecil, 97
Murray, W. L., 55

Index of Persons

O'Brien, Cornelius, 43, 44, 58
O'Leary, Peter, 17, 52, 62, 63
Otter, William D., 17, 95

Pelletier, Oscar, 17
Power, Lawrence Geoffrey, 46
Puttee, Arthur, 24

Redpath, Amy, 27
Reid, W. D., 27
Rhodes, Cecil, 28, 42, 50, 87
Ridsdel, William, 87, 88
Riel, Louis, 45, 48
Roberts, Lord Frederick, 21, 95, 161

Scott, Frederick G., 17, 18, 20, 40
Scott, Sir Richard, 46, 48
Smith, Goldwin, 22, 23, 25, 29, 72, 76, 166

Speer, J. C., 28
Steyn, Matinus Theunis, 94

Thompson, Thomas Phillips, 23
Tarte, Joseph-Israel, 45
Thomas, Chief Jake, 149
Tupper, Charles, 32

Victoria, Queen, 5, 18, 52, 61, 97, 112, 117, 139–46, 157, 162, 163, 166

Washington, George, 76
Wilkenson, Corporal, 97
Wood, Morgan, 28
Woodsworth, J. S., 9, 33
Wrigley, George Weston, 22

Yellowhorn, Chief John, 139, 140

www.ingramcontent.com/pod-product-compliance
Lightning Source LLC
Chambersburg PA
CBHW062045220426
43662CB00010B/1658